ASIAN STUDIES ASSOCIATION OF AUSTRALIA

Southeast Asia Publications Series

DEVELOPMENT PROFESSIONALS IN NORTHERN THAILAND

Hope, Politics and Practice

DEVELOPMENT PROFESSIONALS IN NORTHERN THAILAND

Hope, Politics and Practice

Katharine McKinnon

ASIAN STUDIES ASSOCIATION OF AUSTRALIA

in association with

NUS PRESS and NIAS PRESS

First published by:

NUS Press
National University of Singapore
AS3-01-02, 3 Arts Link
Singapore 117569

Fax: (65) 6774-0652
E-mail: nusbooks@nus.edu.sg
Website: http://www.nus.edu.sg/nuspress

ISBN: 978-9971-69-522-4 (Paper)

Published in Europe by:

NIAS Press
NIAS – Nordic Institute of Asian Studies
Leifsgade 33, DK–2300 Copenhagen S, Denmark
tel: (+45) 3532 9501 • fax: (+45) 3532 9549
E–mail: books@nias.ku.dk • Website: www.niaspress.dk

The Nordic Institute of Asian Studies (NIAS) is a research and service institute located at the University of Copenhagen and collaborating closely with the wider Nordic Asian Studies community. NIAS works to encourage and support Asian Studies in the Nordic countries as well as actively participating in the international scholarly community in its own right. In so doing, NIAS has published books since 1969 and in 2002 launched NIAS Press as an independent, not-for-profit publisher aiming at a premium reputation among authors and readers for relevant and focused, quality publishing in the field of Asian Studies.

British Library Cataloguing in Publication Data
A catalogue record for this book is available from the British Library.

ISBN: 978-87-7694-084-3

Cover: Terry Grandstaff chatting with Karen via interpreters at Doi Inthanon, c. 1975 (courtesy of John McKinnon).

Typeset by: Scientifik Graphics
Printed by: Mainland Press Pte Ltd

For Jean and John

Contents

List of Maps

List of Plates

Glossary and Abbreviations

AAA	American Anthropological Association
Amphoe	District — a level of local government administration below the Province
BPP	Border Patrol Police (Thailand)
CGIAR	Consultative Groups on International Agricultural Research
CMU	Chiang Mai University
DFG	Deutsche Forschungsgemeinschaft
DPW	Department of Public Welfare (Thailand)
DTEC	Thai Department of Technical and Economic Cooperation
Farang	Foreigner in Thai
HASD	(Thai-Australia) Highland Agricultural and Social Development Project
ICRAF	World Agroforestry Centre
INGO	International Non-Government Organisation
KIP	Knowledge and Innovation Partnerships
KKU	Khon Kaen University
Nai Amphoe	District Chief Officer
NESDB	National Economic and Social Development Board of Thailand
NGO	Non-Government Organisation
NRCT	National Research Council of Thailand
PAR	Participatory Action Research
PLA	Participatory Learning and Action
PRA	Participatory Rural Appraisal
RFD	Royal Forest Department
SEATO	Southeast Asia Treaty Organisation
SEED	Supporting Entrepreneurship for Sustainable Development
SWAT	Special Weapons and Tactics — a paramilitary unit within United States police forces
TAHAP	Thai-Australia Highland Agronomy Project

TAHASD	Thai-Australia Highland Agricultural and Social Development Project
Tambon	A level of local government administration below the District (Amphoe)
TGHDP	Thai-German Highland Development Program
TRC	Tribal Research Centre
TRI	Tribal Research Institute
UNDCP	United Nations Drug Control Program
UNICEF	United Nations Children's Fund
USAID	United States Agency for International Development
Yaa baa	Methamphetamines, literally 'crazy medicine'.
YMCA	Young Men's Christian Association

A Note on Referencing

In Thailand it is normal practice to use individuals' first names in the same way surnames are used in English. I have kept with this convention for all Thai names mentioned in this book and all Thai authors cited throughout the text are listed in the bibliography by their first name rather than their surname, except where the authors themselves do not follow this convention.

Preface

At the age of 24 I found myself living in a village in the highlands of northern Thailand. I had spent much of my childhood there but after more than a decade living with my family in New Zealand, this was my first time back as an adult. I had returned to work as a volunteer for a local NGO and came armed with a recent training in development studies and the optimistic idea that I could be part of a grassroots effort to make a difference in the lives of the women we were working with. Instead I discovered that I had joined the ranks of countless outsiders who for decades had been venturing into highland villages with the intention of helping to make a better life for local people, only to leave without having achieved their goals.

Development is a loaded word. It had promised to deliver improved livelihoods, stable incomes, even social justice and emancipation. But for the Akha communities I came to know, life seemed to be harder and less fulfilling than ever before. Village farmland was being claimed by the state, rates of drug addiction were phenomenal, stories of police brutality and harassment abounded. There were stark contrasts between rich and poor villagers to a degree unknown in the past and traditional knowledge was on the wane as few young people stepped forward to train as priests or healers. Everyone seemed to be struggling in different ways. This community had been the target of development interventions for decades but I could see few of the benefits that development had promised and strived for.

What had gone wrong? Why had development failed this community? The people I met and worked with blamed the racism of the Thai state or the lack of adequate respect for highland communities. Others argued that highlanders themselves had failed to take advantage of their opportunities or had been so harmed by their confrontation with modernity that they were no longer able to heal their communities and move forward. I was dissatisfied with these explanations and realised that to find better answers, I would have to learn more about how development interventions themselves had shaped life in the hills. When my one-year contract was complete I left for Australia to investigate these issues as a PhD student. In 1999 I enrolled as a PhD candidate at the Australian National University and the following year returned to the highlands to research the role that development had played in the exclusion and exploitation of highlanders in contemporary Thailand.

I chose not to undertake a 'village study', nor to focus on highlanders and highland communities. Plenty of researchers were already conducting ethnographies of different highland groups and I had no desire to add to the numbers. While I recognise and appreciate such work, I have never been able to reconcile myself to the role of the outsider seeking to understand and explain the indigenous other, to speak on behalf of or represent highlanders to the world at large. In my experience this is a responsibility that is best borne by highlanders themselves. Besides, what I really wanted to know about was what was happening at the other end of the development 'machine'. If something was going wrong with development, could the answers be found by investigating not the faults of delivery mechanisms, shortcomings of implementation or planning, or cultural 'barriers' within local communities, but instead that seldom-examined group of people, the professionals who do development work? Were the attitudes and approaches of these people in some measure to blame for the appalling situation in the hills? My aim as a doctoral student was therefore to delve into the workings of a community that was my own, the world of foreign researchers and development professionals. Who were these people who travelled so far to work in the mountains? What were they doing there? How had their presence become necessary? In other words, how had the highlands come to be seen as needing development? And how had the presence of the developers created a place of such apparent misery and hardship?

Behind my desire to return to the highlands and investigate development professionals lay a largely unacknowledged romanticism about the highlands as a place that would probably have been better off had it been left alone. Like many who spend time in mountain communities, I had fallen in love with the place. My efforts to be a critical academic contradict the abiding romanticism that re-emerges whenever the feeling of being in those mountains is evoked. Near my flat in Sydney is a park where, if I stand in just the right spot and the breeze is moving in the right direction, I catch a smell reminiscent of those mountains. Immediately I think of ridge-top roads in the morning mist, when each side of the hill drops away into nothingness. The smoky hearth in the kitchen of the Akha house where I always used to stay. Bamboo slat floors. The extraordinarily slippery sticky red mud that makes mountain pathways impossible in the rainy season. Mountain rice eaten balled up in the fingers of one hand. Scandalous gossip when all the grandmothers gather in the kitchen in the evenings. Rice whisky with breakfast on ceremony days. The sense I used to have in the mountains of being always on the edge of understanding, and on the edge of being safe. And through the relationships I made in those communities, gaining an inkling of what it might be to live without the right papers, without the apparent order and ostensible ease of a Western middle-class existence, without the security of belonging that I enjoyed as a white, middle-class woman in a society dominated by white middle classes. Such romanticism stands alongside the knowledge that life in the mountains is hard, almost always coloured by uncertainty, moments of brutality and times of poverty. Yet people live ordinary lives through all of this — experiencing friendship, misunderstandings and mistakes, falling in and out of love, sharing silly jokes and gossip, caring for families, and negotiating with troublesome in-laws, disobedient teenagers and wilful toddlers.

In contrast to such romantic and nostalgic notions of the highlands, the development industry was counterpoised in my imagining as a cynical business of well-paid foreign consultants who made their living by pretending to be experts and interfering whether invited to or not. My perspectives were shaped by both upbringing and training. Growing up in northern Thailand I often heard my father, a geographer and sometime development consultant who was among the first generation of researchers in the highlands, lament the failures of development with his colleagues in Thailand and at 'home' in New Zealand. During my training in development studies at Victoria University in Wellington my suspicions of development were deepened and honed through exposure to critical analyses of development from the likes of Wolfgang Sachs, Gustavo Esteva, Arturo Escobar and Uma Khotari. Using the latest acronyms and armed with the empty rhetoric of 'working for a world free of poverty', 'capacity building', 'participation' and 'gender equality', the development industry seemed an insidious machine, often deployed to serve geopolitical interests over the interests of the local people. Worse still in my mind were the researchers who befriended the local people and then made their careers on the reappropriation of highland cultures and representation of highlanders to the world. Such contrasts helped to fire up a driving sense of injustice and motivated a young scholar on her first forays. Yet by the time I had spent a year working with my developer 'subjects', I could no longer tell such a simple story.

While searching for 'culprits', I found instead a community of dedicated and struggling development professionals who could not easily be described as agents of unjust development. The professionals I fell in with were well aware of the political complexities of their work and sensitive to the ways in which their efforts could be co-opted by the aims of state powers. Nevertheless, they still held true to the overall ideals that guided them: altruism, emancipation, advocacy and working for the local people. They faced an existential problem experienced by professionals worldwide: they continued to work knowing that their interventions were often tied (intended or not) to geopolitical concerns rather than the moral values and emancipatory visions that motivated them. Answers to the question 'What had gone wrong?' still seemed to lie with the insidious politics of the development machine, but what became more interesting and more relevant was the question of how to understand these professionals who remained so optimistic and persistent in the face of an industry that seemed to operate in contradiction of its stated aims.

As a result, I had to contemplate an unexpected paradox: how is it possible to acknowledge and honour the hope and the good intentions that drive these professionals while recognising the corruptions and limitations of the industry they work within? As well as asking who the professionals were and how they came to be involved in the highlands, I now began to ask how a development enterprise that is always tangled up with politics and complicated by geopolitical agendas can still be called upon by development professionals as something which may indeed make the world a better place for the people it is supposed to help. How might such a 'development' be thought of? What kinds of professional identities would be tied to it? In short, behind the many stories of failed development programs and the hardship visible in many highland communities, are the everyday efforts and struggles of those who 'do' development — the consultants, researchers, government officials, NGO workers and village partners — pointing towards new ways of thinking and doing development that might genuinely enable and empower highlanders.

This book is the result of my delving into this list of weighty questions. It is an enquiry that has taken place in conversations and exchanges I have had with development professionals in Chiang Mai over several years. Needless to say, the professionals I worked with do

not represent the totality of those engaged with highland development over the years. The examples discussed in the following pages
tell stories of an even smaller subset of those whom I came to know
in Chiang Mai. It was difficult to choose which stories to tell and
the result is inevitably a partial exploration of just some of the key
issues and problems that revolve around the practice of being a
development professional in northern Thailand. In most cases, the
stories exemplify issues or concerns that seemed to be foremost in
the minds of my research partners. What I offer here is my exploration of them and the lessons that I learned in the process about what
it means to 'do' development and how this enterprise might still be
valid and valuable in this turgid world of post-colonial politics.

Acknowledgements

The writing of this book has taken many years since it began as a doctoral dissertation. Turning it into a book has spanned moves to new houses, jobs, countries, my marriage and attempts to keep my brain working through two pregnancies and the births of my two wonderful daughters. I would not have been able to complete the project were it not for the support and enthusiasm of a great many people. The boundless support and constant critical engagement of Katherine Gibson has carried me through from the beginning of my PhD to the completion of the book. I am indebted to the contributions of colleagues and friends in Thailand who allowed me to step into their lives, gave me the opportunity to participate and learn, and proffered their support and encouragement for this project. Of my colleagues in Chiang Mai, a few stand out: the determined and inspiring staff at the organisation I have named the Highland NGO; Ken Kampe for his heartfelt dedication beneath a veneer of cynicism to the cause; Ronald Renard for his incredible generosity with his time and precious library; Peter Hoare, who was so welcoming and who gave so freely of his time and energy; Andreas Neef who took so much time to give me his honest and critical feedback on earlier drafts of the manuscript; David Thomas, whose wonderful response to this study gave me the idea to include a series of postscripts to the book; and all of the above for their willingness to meet and discuss my findings as this text transformed from doctoral research into the book it is now. I would also like to express my enormous gratitude to Leo Alting von Guseau, Deuleu, Asue and John 'Helicopter' for welcoming me into their family and inspiring many of the questions explored in this book. In addition, the comments and enthusiasm of John Paul Jones III and Leif Jonsson were a great encouragement to transform my original PhD research into a book. The boost given by the Australian National University's Crawford Prize and the Asian Studies Association of Australia Presidents Prize with the enthusiasm and patient editing of Howard Dick as Editor of the ASAA Southeast Asia Series have made the transformation possible, while Richard Lever gave tremendous editorial assistance in the later stages. Jonathan Rigg and Philip Hirsch reviewed an earlier version of the manuscript and their comments provided valuable direction on how to strengthen and clarify the text. Finally there was the support provided by colleagues in Development Studies at Massey University and geographers at Macquarie University and Queen Mary, University of London who gave me space and time to rework the manuscript.

Many others have contributed to the development of my thinking and writing over the years, including colleagues and friends too numerous to name and whose friendship and intellectual nourishment over the years have been wonderful. In particular I wish to thank Linda Malam, Nick Purdie, Vincent del Casino, Ben Dierikx, Catherine Mills, Donna Housten and Greg Martin. I am deeply grateful to my whole family, new branches and old, for their ever present support, encouragement, understanding and love. To my father John I owe an especial debt of gratitude for bringing us to Thailand to begin with and for encouraging my forays into a world he knows so well. And finally, there is Lucia, Rafaella and Marco, who kept everything in perspective.

Sydney, June 2010

Plate 1 The author in Chiang Mai, 1979

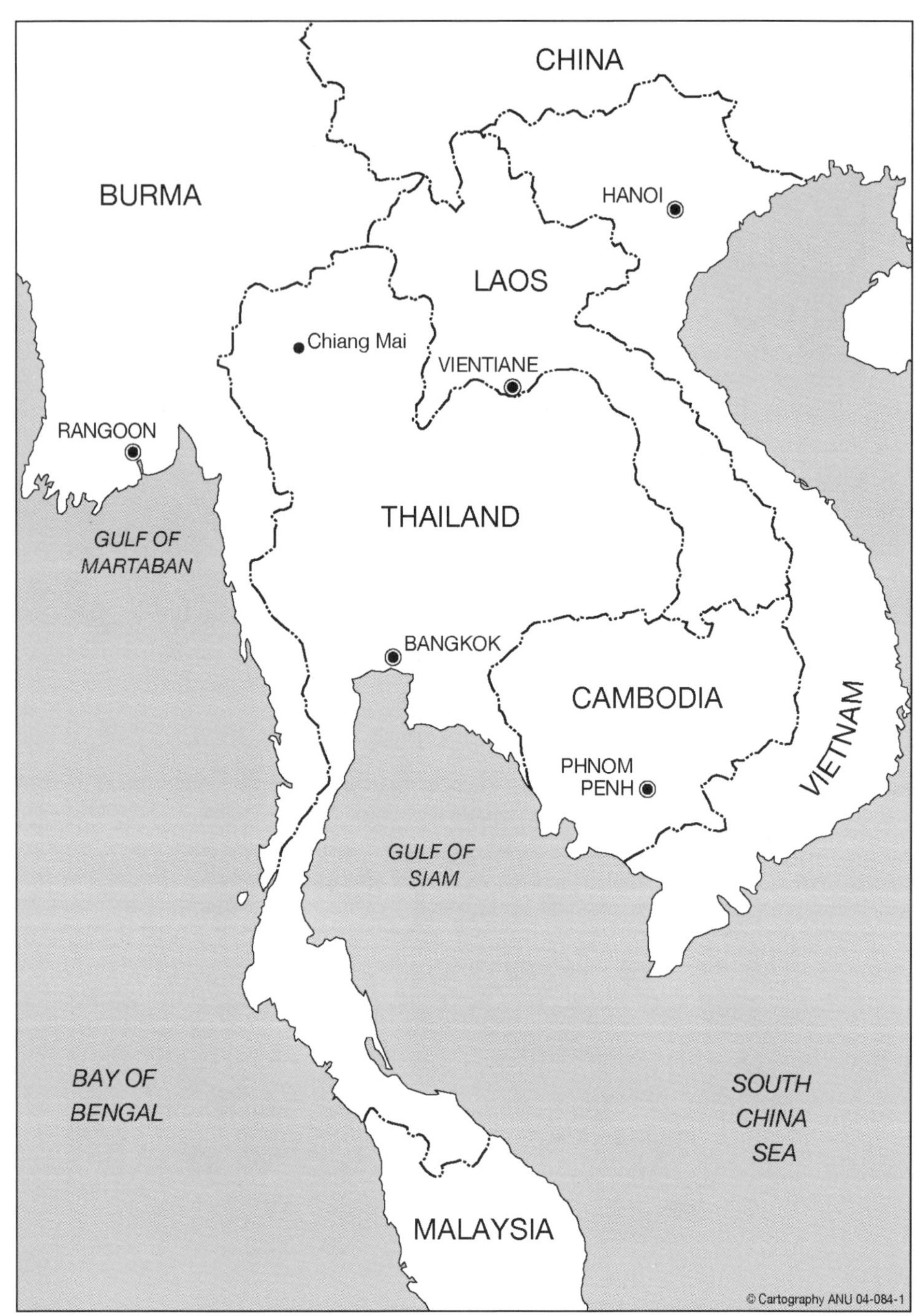

Map 1 Map of mainland Southeast Asia

Map 2   Map of Thailand

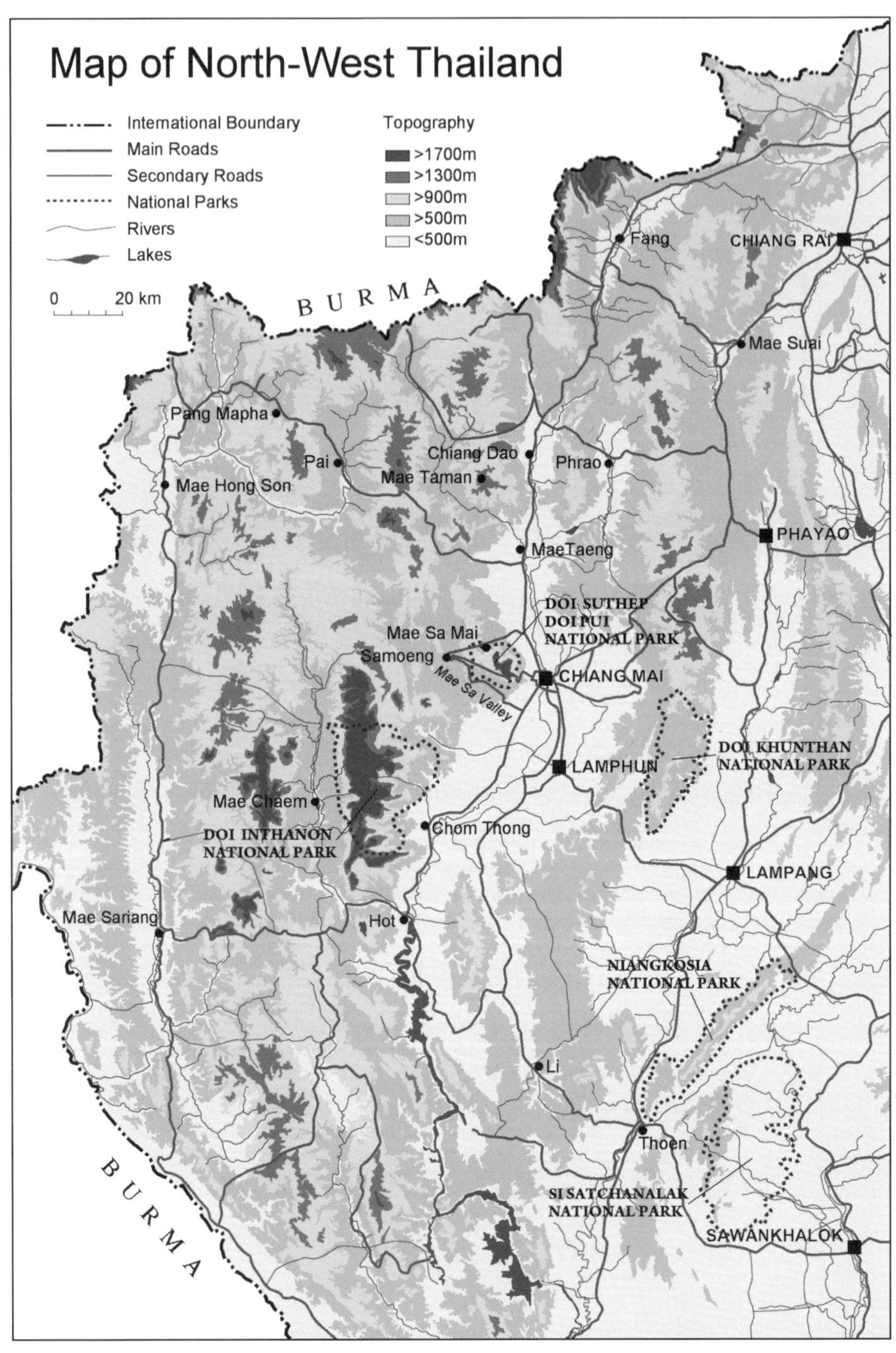

Map 3   Map of north-west Thailand

1

Development Professionals and the Post-development Project

Leave the villagers alone.
Four simple words. Let's try it again.

Leave
The
Villagers
Alone.

So easy to say.
So difficult to do.
When you're charged with
Their development
And so full of yourself.

(Somsak, 2005: v)

The president of the ironically titled Office of Retired Developers in Chiang Mai is a man whose 30 years of experience in development work have culminated in one simple piece of advice: leave the villagers alone. The president is a self-declared cynic who is fond of speaking about how little the development 'industry' contributes to the lives of the people it is supposed to help. He attributes the ongoing failures of the industry to the interference of self-important bureaucrats, the bumbling consultants who enjoy their excellent pay and international lifestyle too much to want to put themselves out of a job, and the hypocrisy of state agencies reluctant to place any decision-making power in the hands of the people. To listen to the president speak one might assume that he had long since thrown up his hands in disgust and walked away from such a corrupt business. On the contrary, and despite his claims to being 'retired', the president is still an active and determined development consultant. He is determined to address the worst foibles of the industry, to persuade reluctant bureaucrats and officials that control over development programs should be placed in the hands of the people they are supposed to help, and making sure that the voices of local people are listened to and respected. Although he would deny it, he is working very hard to do himself out of a job.

The president's persistent hope and optimism sit alongside his equally persistent sense of pessimism. This pessimism emerges from the seemingly inevitable failure of development to achieve what it is meant to, that is, making life better for the poor and dispossessed. The development industry as a whole was predicated upon the belief that the right interventions would lift underdeveloped regions up to the standards of the industrialised economies of the West, thereby bringing to an end the stark differences between the levels of health and well-being enjoyed in the so-called First World and the poverty endured in the Third World. Yet, as the president notes, development has seldom brought these benefits. A great many critics have analysed the failures of development. Wolfgang Sachs (1992: 1), for example, argues that "delusion and disappointment, failures and crime have been the steady companions of development and they tell a common story: it did not work". Arturo Escobar (1995a: 4) in turn speaks of how the dream of development "progressively turned into a nightmare"; instead of prosperity and abundance "the discourse and strategy of development produced its opposite: massive underdevelopment and impoverishment, untold exploitation and oppression".

Escobar's seminal work *Encountering Development* (1995a) has been particularly influential in spearheading what has become known as 'post-development': a body of critical work that draws on post-colonial and post-structural theory in its analysis. Post-development is distinguished from other critical analyses which argue that develop-ment simply needs to be done better, using more appropriate tools and approaches. It is also distinct from the anti-development position which argues that the whole project should be abandoned because development perpetuates the exploitations and oppressions of the colonial era while disguising them behind a language of altruism. Post-development theory, like the president himself, treads a precarious line between these two positions. For post-development critics, devel-opment has always been closely intertwined with international and domestic politics, so that the naive aim of 'making things better' is always being pursued in the midst of larger power plays. The dynamics of domination and control at the heart of the development enterprise are impossible to ignore. Nevertheless, post-development scholars still search for ways to address global inequities. Although it is seldom acknowledged, at the heart of their critiques is the belief that development really *should* have made the world a better place, and that it should still be able to do so. Yet while a handful of actors are pursuing a variety of post-development practices, no-one quite knows how to propose a new way of undertaking development that is substantially different, which can acknowledge the pervasive politics of development and find ways to create change in spite of it.

Among development professionals I have encountered, the aid workers, consultants, NGO staff who 'do' development for a living, post-development is not popular. Yet many accept the fundamentals of the post-development critique and recognise that development is not about improvement or assistance but about domination and control; not about the people it is supposed to help but the geopolitical agendas of the day. Nevertheless, these professionals continue to devote their working lives to the project of development. They continue despite cynicism and disappointment and despite being well aware of the neo-colonial overtones of development in general. Who are these people? Why do they persist in their work? What is it that drives them? Most importantly, what role do they play in this enterprise that has been so strongly critiqued as a technology of power and control? It is easy to assume that development professionals persevere in a corrupt industry because of naive idealism, cynical enjoyment of the exotic lifestyle, or a simple acclimatisation to the avarices of development, rather like miners who no longer notice the oppression of the darkness and the coal dust. Yet the cynical awareness of many professionals suggests that there is a more complex explanation of why and how these professionals engage with both the development industry and the communities with whom they work.

Little research has been done on the role of development professionals themselves and none that seeks to analyse their presence in the Third World in light of the very serious accusations levelled against development by post-development critics like Sachs and Escobar cited above. Post-development provides the tools to examine how development in the northern Thai highlands took shape through an intimate relationship with local and global geopolitics and international development discourses. Post-development is also the starting point for looking critically at professional conduct, intermingled as it is with these interrelationships between development, politics and power. A post-development perspective does not lead to any easy solutions to the professional dilemmas — and that precisely is why the perspective is so useful. Rather than looking for the 'right' solutions to the ills of development, post-development has tended to focus on a critical rethinking of what development is or should be. Such rethinking acknowledges a history of paternalism and imperialism but remains hopeful. It is appropriate to use this approach in an examination of development professionals because it is they who struggle daily with the contradictions between an imperialist past and a hopeful present.

The ways in which professionals are already dealing with this contradiction may help in the search for radical post-development practices. In their daily work, many professionals are already engaged in an ongoing rapprochement between the development they seek and the failures they regularly encounter. How might these everyday negotiations generate the reconceptualisations to take development thinking and practice in new directions? This book begins to open up an understanding of who development professionals are and what drives them. Using post-development critiques as a starting point, it examines how professionals see the failures of development and where they find the hope that continues to drive even the most cynical and pessimistic amongst them.

In the highlands of northern Thailand, development professionals have been working in development programs since the late 1950s. This is a very good setting to examine questions around professional practice, both because of the longevity of programs and the way they have been so enmeshed in questions of power and politics. When these programs got underway, they were tied explicitly to the geopolitical priorities of the day, primarily the need to secure Thailand's borders against the threat of communist incursion. The politics have changed significantly over the intervening decades. Yet, whatever the politics, development programs continue to be pursued under the stated aim of improving the lives of ethnic minority peoples who live in the northern highlands. As with many other locations that have been the focus of the development industry, it is not at all clear that five decades of development have done much to improve life in the hills. What is clear is that a great many development professionals have spent their working lives engaged in pursuing this aim. How are we to understand their working lives and their efforts? Have these professionals been duped by a rhetoric of altruism? Consciously or not, are they the agents who facilitate the oppressions and exploitations wrought by development? Are they all critically aware but struggling cynics like the president? How, if at all, do they articulate the promise of development? How do they tread the line between pessimism and hope, between the failures and corruptions of the development industry and the promise that it really can help the people it is supposed to?

In this book I argue that the answers to these questions lie in better understanding how professionals are entangled with the politics and power plays that shape the places in which they work, the myths and ideologies of development that inform their professional identities, and the driving vision of a better world that they hope to help bring into being. Despite widespread acceptance that development is inescapably political, we have barely begun to think of development professionals as political actors. This book argues that only by making this shift and reconceptualising development practice as first and foremost a political practice can we begin to see how development might be done differently and what kinds of professionals may yet have a role to play in realising newly reconfigured hopes of what change development can bring. This book explores the interrelationships of these three dynamics: the geopolitical machinations that have shaped the highlands, the myths and ideologies that shape professional identities, and the persistent sense of hope evident in the pursuit of development. This chapter briefly introduces each of these, beginning with the place upon which I will focus: the highlands of northern Thailand.

The Place

The highlands of northern Thailand have long been infamous as one of the three points of the Golden Triangle, the border zone between Thailand, Burma and Laos that was the source of most of the world's heroin before it was surpassed by Afghanistan following the fall of the Taliban. In the 1960s, 1970s and 1980s the Golden Triangle was known for its isolated hill tribes, inaccessible and heavily forested mountains, and its unpatrolled borders, across which the opium warlords moved their goods and communist rebels sought refuge. These days the Golden Triangle is much tamer, at least on the Thai side of the border. The warlords are gone, opium production is a fraction of what it once was, and the communist rebels have long since taken up offers of amnesty and moved back to the cities. On the back of millions of dollars of development aid money, the Thai state has gradually extended formal rule to the most inaccessible of mountain villages.

Since the late 1950s development professionals have been in action, helping to 'tame' and transform the highlands. Between the late 1960s and the year 2000, highland villages were the focus of activities for at least 20 internationally funded bilateral development projects with a shared budget of approximately US$185 million; at least 158 registered non-governmental organisations (NGOs) if not more; and an indeterminate number of researchers — including at least 101 foreign researchers who registered with the Tribal Research Institute between 1968 and 1992 (Renard, 2001: 70–1; Kampe, unpublished data 1995; Tribal Research Institute, 1992).

The focus of all this attention was the highland peoples of the border regions. These were distinct groups whose languages, cultures and traditions set them apart from lowland Thais. Numbering less than one million, highland peoples have been the subject of extensive community development and research work for decades. Reliable figures are difficult to obtain and the accuracy of census data on the highlands is questionable. The highland population was estimated to be only about 770,000 in 1997 by the Hill Tribe Welfare Division of the Department of Public Welfare (cited by Satawat and Nipatvej, 2001) while unofficial estimates put the number much higher. These figures are for the combined population of groups classified by the Ministry for the Interior as 'hill tribes', who constitute a very small minority of the total population in Thailand of approximately 67 million.

Although lumped together under the terms 'hill tribes' or 'highlanders', highland peoples are in fact too diverse and varied for such singular identification. The list of officially recognised 'hill tribe' groups (Karen, Hmong, Mien, Akha, Lisu, Lahu, H'tin, Lu and Khamu) gives some sense of this diversity. Each of these groups speaks its own language and maintains distinct cultural and spiritual traditions, though none make claim to a territory or a homeland of their own. There are shared characteristics: their lack of a territorial 'homeland', traditional use of swidden or 'slash-and-burn' farming methods, animist belief systems, and the state of transition highlanders are experiencing as they adapt to modern Thai life. Life in the hills was hard and villages subsisted on what food could be grown on the poor mountain soils or gathered from the forest. Homes were built of simple materials — mud, bamboo slats or split timber for walls and floors, and thatched roofs — and the whole structure lashed together without the use of a single nail. Each tribal group wore distinct costumes, made from cloth they wove themselves and often elaborately decorated with embroidery, beads or silver. Historically these are border peoples whose villages were scattered throughout the mountains that span the borders of Thailand, Laos and Burma and stretch through southern China to the foothills of the Himalayas.

It is extremely problematic to generalise about highland people, whether describing individual tribes or highlanders in general. The complexity and diversity of highland cultures are well recognised by many anthropologists who have studied these communities. While some scholars persist in describing essential features of tribal culture, others recognise that such descriptions almost always obscure important diversities within groups (Conrad, 1989; Hinton, 1967, 1979, 1983; Jonsson, 2000a, 2000b, 2005; Kammerer, 1989, 1990; Kustadter, 1979; McKinnon, 1983, 1989; McKinnon and Michaud, 2000; Tapp, 1989, 2003). While many colourful monographs on highland cultures continue to describe highlanders as if they were isolated and primitive tribes, many scholars recognise the degree of integration with modern Thailand, as well as recounting some of the costs of that for highland people (Deuleu and Næss, 1997; Kunstadter, 2000; Toyota, 1998, 2003; Geusau, 1992). The things that used to identify highlanders as distinct, such as their costume, language and spiritual practices, have changed much in recent decades and it is now rare to find a community still living as all highlanders might have lived 30 or 40 years ago. The changes of the last 40 years reflect the long history of trade, exchange and cultural interaction that have characterised relationships between highland and lowland communities. Even though their communities were difficult to access from the lowlands, highland communities have never been isolated.

Nevertheless, ethnographers and policy makers have emphasised a history of separateness and difference. As an object of ethnographic study, highlanders have been exoticised as examples of a primitive way of life, romanticised as conflict-free and egalitarian communities, categorised according to language, culture, religion, farming practices and even the altitude at which their villages could be found. The desire of scholars to differentiate and describe highlanders has contributed to a longstanding tendency among researchers and state officials alike to impose labels that disguise the complexities of highland cultures.

The term 'hill tribes' has been a convenient label for state administration but it sets up a false dichotomy between highlanders and Thais, concealing the deep and intricate interrelationships between the two. In contemporary Thailand, many highlanders live and work in lowland towns and cities. Moreover, a significant proportion, if not the majority, of those living in highland areas are in fact 'lowland' Thais (Hinton, 1969; McKinnon and Wanat, 1983). In addition, the term is linked to several negative stereotypes, including the one of highlanders as outsiders and aliens who have invaded Thai land and continue to dwell illegally in the Kingdom's precious forests when, in fact, they had built their villages in the mountains and upland valleys and cleared pockets of forest to cultivate their crops of rice, vegetables and opium well before the modern borders were drawn between Thailand, Burma and Laos.

In the middle of the twentieth century, when Thailand was still emerging as a modern nation-state and at the same time under threat from the apparent spread of communism in the region, difference was recast as danger. Despite their communities being within the boundaries of the Thai state, highlanders were not accepted as Thai citizens and their cultures were not recognised as being a legitimate part of the Thai national identity predicated on a common language, religion and history. As outsiders, highlanders came to be seen as a potentially damaging and dangerous presence in the borderlands. Their lack of 'national loyalty' was equated with the potential to be seduced by communist ideologies and ambitions of rebellion; their use of forestland was suspected of damaging national forest reserves; and their production of opium was assumed to supply a booming business of illicit heroin exports.

The image of highlanders as opium producers and potential communists mapped easily onto international concerns of the day. In the 1960s there was heightened interest in the Southeast Asian border zone following the emergence of the Cold War and related conflicts in Vietnam, Laos and Cambodia, as well as growing concern about heroin trafficking. With these items on the international agenda, the highlands of northern Thailand began to attract programs designed to address issues of opium production and border security, environmental management and improved livelihoods for highland people. Funding was provided by international donors such as the United States and its Cold War allies. With the noble aim of developing the highlands, teams of professionals arrived comprising of 'expert' researchers, agronomists, extension officers, transport specialists, foresters, educators, foreign consultants and Thai civil servants. The introduction of development to the highlands was thus defined not by development needs of highland communities but the geopolitical concerns of the day and negative stereotypes of highlanders.

In the decades since the 1960s, and despite marked reduction in security concerns, the negative stereotyping of highlanders remains powerful and highlanders are still positioned as outsiders to the Thai mainstream. Concerns around opium production and border security have since waned as opium production shifted to new locations and the Cold War declined. However, issues around environmental management and highland livelihoods have not abated (Forsyth and Walker, 2008).

Despite the claims of development programs to improve living conditions in the mountains, five decades of development intervention have not brought an end to poverty and disadvantage among highland minorities. Although they have been the target of many aid programs, highlanders have become one of the groups that Rigg (2003) describes as being excluded from regional and national development. Few are able to benefit freely from the modern infrastructure, better education and health care, or increased prosperity that has transformed life for the urban middle classes and elites of Thailand over the last few decades. Sturgeon's work with the Akha (2005) has shown how efforts to transform traditional land use practices, ostensibly to protect the environment and to provide better incomes, have in fact severely reduced the ability of communities to either maintain the forests or produce a sustainable livelihood.

Nevertheless, the picture is not entirely gloomy. In the face of their ongoing marginalisation and exclusion from mainstream Thai society, highlanders have begun to step outside their assigned role as recipients of development assistance and to organise and engage with the development industry on their own terms. With the support of Thai and international scholars and development professionals, a number of NGOs and networks based in the highlands have emerged since the 1990s. As the political situation in Thailand has become more democratic, these groups have gained strength. Highland NGOs now participate actively in domestic policy debates and have become partners in internationally funded development programs with their own community-based actions to help highland peoples survive and prosper in the contemporary Thai state.

With these shifts the highlands has been shaped as a complex and contested space of development. The failures and successes of development programs and professional practices must be understood in relation to this setting and the historic tensions through which it was produced. Highland communities, Thai and international development actors and policy makers, and highland activists and NGOs act within the parameters of existing national and international geo-political interests. It is important to highlight this point because so often development and the aims of development programs are discussed as if they were politically neutral, meeting the needs of poor communities without being influenced by petty politics or local power structures. What is very clear in the north of Thailand is that political struggles, whether they are local struggles over highlanders' rights and interests or international struggles around Cold War ideologies, have had a big role in shaping highland development since the beginning.

The Professionals

While highland development has been shaped by larger political forces, on-the-ground implementation of development programs has also been affected by the individuals involved and the visions and ideals they have brought to their work. This book therefore focuses on the development professionals and one particular community of professionals based in the northern Thai city of Chiang Mai. I spent many years of my childhood in Chiang Mai where my father worked at the Tribal Research Institute. I returned to the north as an adult to enter the development industry as a volunteer for a local NGO. With that experience of volunteering arose many of the questions this book seeks to answer. Building on relationships established during that time, as well as relationships that were not mine but my father's, I returned again to Chiang Mai as a postgraduate researcher to speak with development professionals about their work. This book reflects on these conversations and interviews, on what I saw and learned during this later period of research.

Few scholars have focused critical consideration and scholarship on development professionals themselves. Georgia Kaufmann is one exception. In her paper "Watching the Developers", she "turns the lens on the developers" to examine what kind of people become developers (Kaufmann, 1997: 108). Other work examining development practices has argued that new managerialism and neo-liberal modes of development practice and governance have become dominant. The development industry is portrayed as facilitating the imposition of Western knowledge systems and modes of practice that tend to devalue non-Western knowledge and approaches (Nightingale, 2005; Townsend, Porter and Mawdsley, 2002, 2003, 2004). David Mosse (2005), on the other hand, presents an exceptionally deep ethno-graphic analysis of development practice that reveals the chaotic and haphazard relationship between policy and practice. My research has much in common with Mosse, whose focus is on professionals them-selves as a focus of ethnographic enquiry.

The professionals I discuss work for development in many dif-ferent ways but I have grouped them together under the generic title of 'development professionals'. By 'professionals' I mean people who are trained to do the work that they do, whether that training is formal through tertiary institutions or informal on-the-job training, and who are paid to undertake this work as consultants, project staff or NGO staff. But even this broad definition is too restrictive. It implies a divide between the professionals who do the work — the 'developers' — and the local people with (or on) whom they work. In northern Thailand this distinction is not always so clear. Many of the professionals whom I interviewed are also members of highland communities and not all the work that is done is strictly develop-ment work. The examples I bring together in this book also include development-related research that does not seek any immediate impact, and work that is more activism than development, but which is undertaken by organisations that supposedly focus on community development. What these professionals whom I describe have in common is that they work to enact some kind of positive trans-formation in highland communities, be this transformation imme-diate or in the future. It is this desire to make a difference that defines these professionals.

Nevertheless, my focus is not just development professionals but more specifically, professional *subjects*. When I speak about the professional subject, I am referring to an identity, an ideal, a role that is used, created by and materialised in the individuals who count themselves as development professionals. My use of the term 'subjects' draws on the work of Judith Butler (1990, 1993a, 1993b, 1997, 2000) and Ernesto Laclau (Butler *et al.*, 2000; Laclau, 1991, 1996; Laclau and Mouffe, 1985) who place identity and the process of subject formation at the heart of contemporary politics. The subject is seen here as a core component of contemporary modes of power, and a unit both formed by and productive of systems of social order. Subjectivity, discourse and relationships of power are understood as interconnected and mutually constitutive. In these theories of the subject, there is the opportunity to analyse the ways in which subjects are formed through relationships of power, and furthermore, to explore in new ways the possibilities for political and social change.

My decision to think about professionals in terms of subjects was arrived at for three reasons. The first is that by looking at professionals as subjects, the focus of this enquiry shifts from the individuals themselves in all their human complexities to a more precise investigation of their professional identities and, in particular, on how these identities are constituted through language and representation. Secondly, concepts of the subject highlight the very tangible and material connections between language and representation and the actualities of social and political life. Theories of the subject are unlike theories of identity, which often invoke the problematic idea that there is an underlying *essence* to our own sense as individuals (Pratt, 2000). Even when used in conjunction with disclaimers regarding the fluid and situational nature of identities, the idea that one has an identity, or moves between several identities, implies that there are discrete and stable essences based in structured social relations describing some foundational truth about who we are (Butler, 1990). In place of such essentialism, the concept of subject formation envisions a process of identification not in underlying social structures. Instead, it is seen as the product of a process of identifying *with* often conflicted and always fluid ideas of who we are, such as man, woman, mother, Australian and so on. Rather than appealing to any underlying truth, the idea of the subject is a way of seeing how we form our senses of self in relation to shifting ideas and ideals about what the world is and where our place is within it. Through such processes of identification, we bring ourselves into being as certain kinds of subjects with certain kinds of practices and perspectives. It is in ourselves as subjects, in the identifications that we make and the selves we thereby bring into being, that particular ideas and understandings — particular discourses — are brought into very real and material existence.

Thirdly, as we bring subjects into being, we encounter the inevitable disjunctures between our ideas about who we are and the concrete realities of being. These disjunctures are not unexpected, nor are they unusual, but they are important. Throughout my exchanges with development professionals, the stories they told me, the conversations we shared and my reading of documents found, I learned that if professional identities were defined by anything, it was by a shared sense of the complex tensions and contradictions between the ideals and intentions that drove development work and the perceived shortcomings and failures of development in practice. Here was a disjuncture between the identities professionals aspired to and the roles they felt they actually played; their ideas of what they ought to be doing and the description of the work they actually had to do. When they spoke about these tensions, they were identifying how their hopes and aspirations met the messy imperfections of daily life. It is here that the clash between the ideals of development and the complex particularities of implementation became visible.

How such points of failure are seen and understood, and how they are negotiated and overcome, are my core concerns in this book. It is how professionals negotiate these moments, how they shape their professional lives around them or in spite of them, how they manage these tensions and contradictions that is so interesting. At these points of disjuncture, professionals also articulate their means of persistence and hope. By examining their stories of failure and of hope we may come to a better understanding of how professional subjects shape development and perhaps, find ways to begin to think about how development may yet lead to a better world.

The Hope of Post-development

Hope is rarely prominent in debates around development, yet the hope that development can produce positive change in the world underlies even the most disparaging critiques. Post-development in particular has been accused of offering little more than a critique. In post-development thinking there is a clear acknowledgement and analysis of the failings of development. Post-development critics argue that development is a politically embedded and politically motivated practice, tainted by an imperialistic attitude left over from the colonial era. Some argue that development is part of a neo-imperialist agenda through which Western powers maintain their position of political and economic strength (Cowen and Shenton, 1995, Escobar, 1995a, Esteva, 1992, Sachs, 1992). Other, more ethnographic, analyses point to the ways development programs are caught up in the vagaries of local power plays, creating unintentional outcomes that 'happen' to favour regional powers (Ferguson, 1994). Alongside such negative critiques, however, is an emerging focus on finding new post-development approaches through which to realise that hope. As a result, post-development offers a useful perspective from which to analyse the conduct of development professionals who tread the line between cynicism about the inevitable politics of development and the hope that they may be able to do some good in the world.

Post-development is not a cohesive movement and post-development writing varies widely in scope, aim and intellectual and ideological position. Rather than referring to post-development as a movement or a school of thought, it is better to refer to it as set of debates. Nevertheless, these debates share an intellectual heritage and some core concerns. As with other theories that carry the 'post' prefix (post-modernism, post-structuralism, post-colonialism), post-development is grounded in a particular way of thinking about the nature of truth and knowledge. The challenge of post-modernism to the certainty and accuracy of our knowledge of the world has greatly influenced the humanities and social sciences. This has in turn shaped a post-development perspective that is imbued with much suspicion of claims to objectively describe reality or prescribe any fixed program for change.

Since the post-modern shift to focusing on the nature of knowledge itself, it can no longer be assumed that knowledge about human societies can be assessed on the basis of its truth or accuracy. Instead, scholars have started to analyse how certain knowledge and certain ways of knowing are tied to relationships of power.[1] In current scholarship, much knowledge that was previously accepted as truth

---

[1] See Barrett and Philips, 1992; Dixon and Jones, 1996; Gibson-Graham, 1996, 2000.

(such as the idea that Western societies are more 'advanced' than the 'Third World') has become framed as 'discourse' and examined for its links with dominant power structures and the ways in which it can actually shape or create the phenomenon that it is supposed to describe.

The discourse of development is a prime example of the links between knowledge and power. In post-development thought there has been a shift to seeing both the concept and the practice of development not as the description of a real state of progress or interventions to improve standards of living but as discourse. Conventionally, the term 'development' is often used to describe a state of being, developed or underdeveloped, that applies to regions or nations and indicates a level of economic advancement and wealth: the 'developed' countries are in Western Europe, North America, Australia and New Zealand and enjoy a level of health and prosperity to which 'underdeveloped' countries aspire. The term also refers to the practice of making development happen by intervening to make underdeveloped countries more like developed countries. As President Truman put it in 1949, development is about the West "making the benefits of our scientific advances and industrial progress for the improvement and growth of underdeveloped areas" (Truman, 1949). At face value this would seem a noble aim.

Post-development scholars, however, do not look at development as a description of a state of being or a process that countries go through to improve their standards of living. For post-development scholars, development is a discourse that originated in uneven power relations between the First World and the Third World and has served to perpetuate these uneven relations of power. The discursive approach sees ideas of development as culturally and historically situated. Thus the practice of development is less about delivering the poor from a state of oppression than about imposing Western economic rationalities and cultural and political forms in ways that continue to support the dominance of the West and the poverty of the 'rest'.[2] In short, these critiques accuse development of being the very opposite to what it is supposed to be.

---

[2] See Cowen and Shenton, 1996; Escobar, 1995a; Esteva and Prakesh, 1998; Ferguson, 1994; Li, 1999; Sachs, 1992; Yapa, 2002.

Although the post-development critique seems to leave little room for hope, post-development thinkers have begun to explore ways to move on from these critiques to thinking about how to do development in new ways (Escobar, 2004, 2007). The current question for post-development thinkers is how developers, scholars and activists can face up to the criticisms of development and engage productively and positively with "the dirty worlds...which lend it a reason for being" (Escobar, 2007: 202). More recent work focuses on the challenge of how to move forward — how to continue a project of assistance and positive transformation — while being aware of the political complexities of development.[3]

No cohesive set of principles has emerged from this new literature. In fact, post-development thinkers are more likely to reject any attempt to codify or prescribe specific approaches. Nevertheless, some shared priorities are emerging. First, there is a commitment to pro-local, community-focused development. Second, there is an argument that development must not attempt to follow rigid guidelines but begin by embracing the fact that development efforts are part of an ongoing and constantly adaptive and shifting process that is highly dependent on changing political, social and economic circumstances. Third, there is an awareness that all development is tied to power relations and ideological struggles. Any intervention or program should therefore identify its own ideological position and act with an awareness of how it connects to both formal and informal political processes and power struggles.

Post-development debates have thus proved to be both a source of radical critique and a hopeful starting point for thinking about ways to do development differently. They are the basis for the analysis in this book, lending a set of analytical tools and perspectives that help us to think critically and hopefully about development professionals and the highlands. Consequently, my central purpose is not to describe a pattern of domination, whether of the centre over the periphery or of the First World over the Third (Gillogly, 2004). The intention is, instead, to search for *both* the patterns of oppression *and* the possibilities for hope that the development industry might yet be a place where positive change can occur.

---

[3] See Cahill, 2008; Corbridge, 2007; Curnow, 2008; de Sousa Santos, 2004; Gibson-Graham, 2005, 2006.

Techniques and Approaches

The approach I took in the research for this book was broadly ethnographic and based on a vision of social research as a conversation with respondents aimed at building shared understandings (Gudeman and Rivera, 1995). My 'data' were based on records of formal interviews, informal conversations, meetings, workshops and seminars, stories told by professionals of themselves and their work, and the written records that they have produced over the years, including project reports, published and unpublished papers and manuscripts. Learning from the debates of the 'cultural turn', I have tried as much as possible to be true to what I learned from the people I spoke with and the documents I read (di Leonardo, 1991; Duncan and David, 1993; Marcus and Fisher, 1986). Nevertheless, what I present here is also, inevitably, a subjective understanding, an account of what I came to know about highland development and the professional subject through conversations and exchanges with my 'informants'.

From all my interviews and field notes I have chosen just a few stories that exemplify issues and themes that I take to be central. They do not comprise empirical evidence in the way a rigorous scientific study would demand. The stories do, however, capture trends and tendencies that are profoundly important in the northern Thai context.

Besides these stories, I refer to historical texts, newspapers and project reports for an understanding of the geopolitical processes and discursive shifts that have shaped subjects and spaces of development in the north. For this aspect of the research, I chose to focus, for the most part, on English-language sources. This decision was because my interest lay primarily in the intersections between international discourses of development and research, domestic processes of intervention, and international involvement. The texts with which I was most concerned were therefore those produced by and for an international audience, made up of the Thais and foreigners who worked together in the highlands. These texts were usually written in English.

My research partners included those from educated, urban, European backgrounds, as well as 'hill tribe' villagers who had become part of the indigenous NGO movement in Thailand. This broad cross-section of professionals deliberately spans the binaries of developed/underdeveloped, Third World/First World, and 'problem'/ 'non-problem' regions by including professionals who could be seen to come from either side of these divides (Yapa, 2002). Yet it is also a very small community of actors who are all based in one town (Chiang Mai) and who know each other and regularly attend the same meetings and conferences, sometimes working for the same organisations or on the same projects.

During my fieldwork, I contacted a wide range of organisations working in the highlands. From my base in Chiang Mai, I sought out researchers, developers and activists to take part in the research. I made contact with development practitioners in government agencies, or those who used to work for the bilateral highland development projects that ran from the 1970s through to the 1990s. From these I ended up focusing most closely on the partnerships between the Thai and Australian governments, programs that ran from 1972 until 1993. I also contacted researchers, including social and physical scientists, well-established scholars and those who were undertaking their first-ever fieldwork. Of this broad group, I focused my attentions upon a recently established cooperative research program between Thai and German institutions: the Uplands Program. Finally, I visited most of the Chiang Mai-based NGOs working in the highlands but chose to work most closely with an organisation that was actually run by highlanders, which I refer to as the Highland NGO.[4] As to deciding with whom to work most closely, the decision was largely a function of who was willing and interested to take part. To an extent this was based on the degree of personal rapport I shared with respondents, and this in turn was influenced by the existence of prior personal and professional relationships.

As explained in the Preface, this book explores a history of development and of a professional community that is closely intertwined with my personal history and that of my own family. While some connections with the professionals I worked with came from introductions by others such as my supervisors, the majority of my initial contacts with participants were possible because of my father's work in northern Thailand. John McKinnon was employed as an advisor to the Tribal Research Centre in Chiang Mai in the mid-1970s. Trained as a geographer, he went on to be an active

---

[4] Because the work of the Highland NGO involves ongoing interventions into the sometimes volatile sphere of Thai politics, I have used pseudonyms in place of the name of the organisation and its staff.

member of the community of development workers and researchers working in the highlands through the 1970s and 1980s. Although we came and went from Chiang Mai as a family, I always felt a strong personal connection to the region and an emotional commitment to the highlands as a result of the childhood years we spent there. This emotional bond drew me back to the north as an adult, when I was able to find work as a volunteer and begin to establish my own connections with the community of professionals to which my father had belonged. When I returned again as a researcher, I built on my father's connections as much as my own. The family connection opened doors but also shaped what people expected of me and, I am sure, the tone of the stories they told me.

As I discovered, my father's opposition to many aspects of government policy in the highlands and his strong advocacy of placing control over development interventions in the hands of highlanders themselves, earned him a certain respect that then translated into a generosity towards me and definite preconceptions about the kind of research I would be doing. I remember, for instance, being asked how on earth I was going to compete with his legacy. My answer is that it is exactly this idea — of a legacy and the influence of individual development professionals — I wish to examine. As it turns out, my father is only briefly drawn into this examination in terms of the cohort of critical voices that I discuss in Chapter Four. Nevertheless, the personal connections flowing from the fact that I was John McKinnon's daughter certainly influenced the shape of the study. It was through these connections that I gained many of the initial introductions that enabled me to work with professionals who had been part of early bilateral development programs discussed in Chapter Four, as well as professionals involved in the indigenous NGO discussed in Chapter Seven.

Of course, much had changed since my father's last stint in Thailand and many new organisations and new professionals had arrived to work in Chiang Mai. I established relationships with professionals who had neither met nor heard of my father. Yet here too the lines between research participant and colleague, interviewee and friend were very thin. As with most forms of ethnographic research, I became a member of the community that I was investigating, although in this case my personal connection to the community encompassed not only me but my family. Because of these personal connections, both those that developed through fieldwork and those that remained from the years during which I lived with my family in Chiang Mai, this study is very much one of a community of which I was a part — both as a researcher and as a resident through my childhood and my time spent in the north as a volunteer.

Structure

This book is structured as a chronological journey from the beginnings of the development era in northern Thailand to the issues and dynamics that shape contemporary development. Chronology helps to establish the origins of a development era in the highlands and to examine the preconditions required before development programs could commence. As discussed in Chapters Two and Three, the highlands and highlanders had to be identified as problematic and requiring the intervention of development professionals, who were expected to solve these problems and transform these communities. Once these preconditions were met, the first development professionals began to arrive in the highlands. They stepped into a space already shaped by political forces beyond their control and already populated by the problematised 'hill tribes'. Their experiences were coloured by their own ideals and expectations of what they would achieve and their stories about the early days of highland development reveal how quickly they faced a sense of disillusionment and disjuncture as they sought to put their ideals into practice.

While the chronological structure of the book may imply that things have progressed since then, my account of contemporary development work in Chapters Five, Six and Seven reveal that disillusionment and disjuncture have been the steady companions of development professionals. Stories of the failures of development remain favourite topics of conversation in the professional community. What have changed are the geopolitical context and the nature of the ideals that shape professional identities. The ideal of a 'pro-local' professional has come to the fore alongside increasing democratisation in Thailand and the increasing political power of highland actors (Chapter Five). This has provided new standards against which professional practice is measured and new ways in which the constant desire to do good and transform communities may be seen to fail. My analysis of the stories of failure recounted about the first year of operation of the Uplands Program point to the impossibility of living up to the pro-local ideal and highlight how, even after so many years of failure, the desire to bring the ideal into being and the expectation that it is possible to do so persists.

Through the last two chapters, I argue that a different kind of engagement with development and the role of the professional is possible. While the same hopes and disillusionments linger, the politically aware approaches evident in the work of the Highland NGO allow a more pragmatic engagement with development ideals and norms of professional conduct (Chapter Seven). At a fundamental level the professional practices of Highland NGO staff demonstrate an awareness of how the interventions of development professionals are always, inescapably, embedded in broad geopolitical processes, local politics and institutional politics. I believe their approach points to a way forward for development professionals who struggle to reconcile their ideals of what development should be with the knowledge that, despite their best efforts, those ideals are impossible to achieve. The Highland NGO's politically aware approach to development constitutes an alternative to the stories of failure that professionals tell about themselves.

The ideals of doing good and making a difference are still as much an imperative for professional engagement and the 'pro-local' ethic that has emerged, not just in Thailand but globally, as an important corrective to the imperialistic tendencies of the development industry. Nevertheless, these ideals do not serve professionals well without a more politically astute and strategic imagining of what development is and who development professionals should be. The aim of this book is to explore the idealism and disappointment, the hope and the politics with which professional identities are entangled. In the journey, perhaps the stories of failure of which the Chiang Mai professionals are so fond will be able to reveal some new possibilities for a different approach to development practice.

2

An Imperative for Doing Good

The starting point for most professionals embarking on a career in the development industry is a desire to do something worthwhile. They may seek to address the poverty and suffering of communities they have seen while travelling or learned about at university, or perhaps the suffering of their own communities in 'underdeveloped' regions in the world. My own start in development began at the family dinner table. I grew up in a household where dinner-table conversations often turned to the frustrations my parents faced in their work as development consultants and researchers in Southeast Asia and the Pacific. As a result I like to think that I never naively assumed that I could just walk into a community and bring about change. When I entered university to study development, I was exposed to a broader range of views about what development professionals are, how they should conduct themselves and what it takes for them to be success-ful. Implicit in the literature, and likewise in the dinner-table con-versations, was an assumption that development professionals could and should improve the lives of those they worked with. The proviso was always that tangible improvement could come only through the right professional practices and approaches.

These debates shaped my expectations about what I could do as a development worker long before I took my first forays into the field as a volunteer. As I later discovered in my conversations and inter-views with development professionals in Chiang Mai, I was not the only one who had entered 'the field' with such expectations. All these professionals had a sense of what their role would be, informed to varying degrees by longstanding discourses of development and implicit assumptions about what development actors contribute.

The professional subject imagined throughout these discourses of development is one who is uniquely positioned to do good in the world. This is the case even when the debate turns to the ethical problems and systemic challenges of doing development well. The professional is seen as having a primary responsibility to the communities he or she works in and to improve the lives of the people there, while acting according to a code of moral and ethical conduct that overrides politics. Such a vision of professionalism sets the scene for most of the outsiders who have arrived to work in the mountains since the late 1960s. As we will see, however, these assumptions contrast starkly with the realities of development work and do not necessarily equip professionals well for their chosen careers.

Although more and more highlanders have joined the development industry in a professional capacity, the discourse of the professional as the aiding outsider still persists. In the 1960s and 1970s no local highland people were engaged in professional development work. Thais employed on development programs were often cast in the role of trainees, learning from their foreign counterparts who had been trained in agrarian transformation, infrastructure development, social development, education and health. By the 2000s the role of foreign professionals has diminished as Thais and highlanders have taken charge of development in the north. Yet, whatever their origins, professionals usually occupy a position of privilege compared to the local people with whom they work. The contrast is extreme when comparing a World Bank consultant who is paid US$1,000 a day with a villager who can barely scrape together a daily meal. Even in the case of villagers who work for local NGOs, their circumstances are often very different from the majority in their home communities. A paid job, an urban lifestyle, and opportunities for education, travel and networking are open to them in ways very rare for the average highlander.

It is the job of the professional to bridge the divide of power and privilege whose existence is the basic premise of the development project as a whole. In this chapter I explore the ways in which global discourses of development have portrayed the role of development professionals. I argue that professionals have consistently been constructed as subjects with particular emancipatory roles and responsibilities. This lays the foundation for the professional identities that developers would go on to construct in the northern Thai context:

as apolitical, pro-local actors who seek to improve the lives of highland peoples.

A Duty to Aid and Assist

The duty to lend assistance to the poor and marginalised lies at the very foundations of the professional identities in development, anthropology, geography and wider social research in the 'Third World'. Such professionals build on a much older set of ethical and moral responsibilities. Discourses of development and ethnography draw on Judeo-Christian concepts of charity and missionary work, along with a more secular tradition of Western ethics. The subject who intervenes in communities perceived to be poor, disadvantaged or somehow backward follows in the steps of Christ as an advocate of the poor, the sinner and the underdog. Missionary work institutionalises the religious duty of Christians to help the poor and provide an opportunity for redemption. While often philosophically opposed to missionary endeavours, development workers and ethnographic researchers share a similar vision of a mythical subject who can 'do good' in communities of the other — whether that 'other' is characterised as 'primitive', 'native', 'underdeveloped', 'Third World' or 'disadvantaged'.

The idea that professionals can do good in poor communities is of course rather problematic. After several centuries of colonialism and decades of development work, the practice of 'First World' professionals travelling to work in poor communities in Asia, Africa, Latin America or the Pacific has become a matter of much critical reflection. Across the development studies literature there have been concerns about: What right do outsiders have to intrude? Where do their primary responsibilities lie? What is the nature of their relationship with local communities?

These questions of professional ethics and professional responsibility first emerged in the field of anthropology. The moral responsibility of the early anthropologists was to undertake the work of recording vanishing cultures (Eriksen and Nielsen, 2001). It was seen as vital to preserve 'primitive' cultures and societies against an apparently inevitable decline in the face of modernity. In the very earliest anthropological texts, the work of preserving and recording was closely tied to a concern for an in-depth understanding of other cultures. The 'founding fathers' of professional ethnography (Franz Boas, Bronislaw Malinowski, Alfred Radcliffe-Brown, and Marcel Maus) sought a close and sympathetic understanding of those being researched and expressed concerns for their well-being. Malinowski, for example, argued that the duty of the anthropologist is to be "a fair and true interpreter of the Native" and to fulfil the "moral obligation" to assist those devastated by European colonial authority:

> In reality the historian of the future will have to register that Europeans in the past sometimes exterminated whole island peoples; that they expropriated most of the patrimony of savage races; that they introduced slavery in a specially cruel, and pernicious form… The Native still needs help. The anthropologist who is unable to perceive this, unable to register the tragic errors committed at times with the best intentions … remains an antiquarian covered with academic dust and in a fool's paradise (Malinowski, 1945: 4).

In helping the struggling 'native', the anthropologist had to be politically engaged. An ethic of providing help has remained at the core of the discipline from Malinowski to the present day and is also central to other social science disciplines involving ethnographic field studies.

In discourses of development, the role of the development professional is also based on a sense of duty towards the 'needy' communities of the Third World. This sense of duty is present in the earliest emergence of what Arturo Escobar terms a 'classic' development paradigm requiring that there be someone to *do* development. This someone is usually an outsider, someone who brings First World skills and knowledge to the Third World and who helps to advance underdeveloped and disadvantaged communities through research or on-the-ground interventions.

Such discourse traces back to the colonial era when European nations championed themselves as bringers of progress and civilisation to primitive natives (Cowen and Shenton, 1996). Colonial imperialism imagined an intervening subject from the West who would bring progress and preservation, transformation and improvement. In a classic development discourse, the colonial agents of such change were reconfigured as development professionals. Instead of taking colonial subjects from an uncivilised to a civilised state of being, the developer would oversee a process through which the underdeveloped subject became developed. The belief that development professionals are simply fulfilling a moral obligation to lend assistance to the poor and marginalised in the world is thus more problematic than it might at first appear. The aim of transforming local communities derives as much from an imperialist European past as from a sense of altruism.

Professionals Working for the People

Transformation remains a central aim of development work in the post-colonial era, but these days the language is very different. Aims are no longer expressed in terms of advancement or civilisation. They are much more likely to be expressed as participatory development, empowerment and an ethic of working for the people. This discourse also has a long lineage. The figure of the developer as someone working 'for the people' goes back to a time before the recognised beginnings of the development era. James Yen, whose work on mass education in China began in the 1920s, spoke about the importance of bottom-up processes of change and empowerment through education, long before this discourse became part of the mainstream in the 1970s (Buck, 1945). Yen was a Chinese national born in Sichuan. After his education at Hong Kong University and Yale, he joined the International YMCA in France. He returned to China in 1921 to direct national mass literacy campaigns through the Chinese National YMCA. He held to an ethic of self-sacrifice and grassroots experience, giving up the luxuries of urban institutions in order to live alongside village people. James Mayfield, who wrote about Yen's work in light of an emerging discourse of participatory development in the 1980s, placed Yen alongside Mahatma Gandhi and Paolo Freire as a charismatic leader who achieved great things for ordinary people through vision, dedication and a special understanding of the plight of the downtrodden. For Mayfield, these figures set an example for the wide range of professionals involved in rural development.

> Rural development facilitators ... [must] have a deep sense of mission, a vision of where they want to go, a profound sensitivity and awareness of the culture in which they work, an intuitive sense of the most deep-seated yearnings and concerns that press down on their society, and most of all a spiritual message of hope and optimism, which may be based on religion or ideology (Mayfield, 1985: 8).

For Mayfield, successful development requires professionals closely attuned to the needs of the poor rural people whom they are trying to help. While the work of prominent figures such as Paulo Freire has been closely linked with the emergence of participatory approaches within development discourse, Yen's role has not been so widely recognised (Mayfield, 1985; Triantafillou and Neilson, 2001). Both Freire and Yen put forward an idea of the professional subject as a professional working 'for the people' — a role that in Freire's lexicon became the 'revolutionary leader' who would empower the oppressed other.

The focus on empowerment in contemporary discourses of participation owes a great deal to the influence of a liberal Marxist tradition and the impact of works such as Freire's *Pedagogy of the Oppressed* (1970). Freire emphasised the importance of educating 'the oppressed' so that they can achieve their own liberation. He advocated the intervention of enlightened teachers or revolutionary leaders to make the oppressed conscious of the forms of their oppression so that they would want to break free. Freire's revolutionary dictum may now seem dated but the logic of intervening to help poor and disadvantaged communities find freedom remains part of the discourse of empowerment in community development.

Robert Chambers, a British academic whose name is synonymous with participatory approaches, also sees empowerment as the main purpose of participatory development. His call for development to start "putting the last first" has had a huge impact on community development methods (Chambers, 1983). Chambers argues that the causes of poverty are as much to do with disempowerment as low yields or declining soil fertility. Neither of these problems can be addressed unless development practitioners act as facilitators rather than experts, supporting local people in their efforts to create change. While he does not use Freire's language, Chambers is in effect arguing that development professionals have to act as revolutionary leaders, helping the poor and disenfranchised achieve their own liberation.

The Myth of an Immutable Moral Good

The participatory professionals imagined by Chambers, Freire and Yen, the anthropologist imagined by Malinowski, and the developer with his colonial antecedents discussed by Cowen and Shenton were all, in their time, seen to be in service of a moral good. By doing their work well they could improve things: the savage would be civilized, the needy would be developed, the oppressed would be empowered. In each of these cases it was taken as self-evident that the professional was in the service of a universal good. These days it is difficult to sympathise with the civilising aims of the colonial administrator but the idea of civilisation was no less compelling in its time than the idea of empowerment is today.

Whether in regard to civilization or empowerment, the professional is ideologically justified as the catalyst for change. The participatory development professional invoked by Chambers is supposed to act as a catalyst for improvement, a facilitator of empowerment. The role of the professional is thus shaped by ideas of progress, democracy and freedom. Such an ideology of emancipation is represented by Chambers and also by Freire and Yen as belonging to a universal moral good.

The professional envisioned by Chambers, Freire and Yen is, of course, an *ideal* professional subject that was closely connected to the ideal world they hoped to bring into being. They dreamed of a world free of oppression, poverty and ignorance. When the ideal professional materialised, so too could this universal good of freedom and empowerment. Both the idealised professional subject and the ideal world they are supposed to bring into being exist in the realm of myth. Nevertheless they inform very real aspirations and shape tangible action.

The myth has mutated over time but the ideal professional is always a knowing subject who is sympathetic to and understanding of the local. A people's professional must be close to the people with whom he or she works, the 'needy', 'oppressed', 'poorest of the poor'. The professional is a subject able to 'translate' one society to another, allowing the urban West (or the colonial administrator) to understand the others whom they are supposed to administer. The professional subject may also be the 'rescuer' of cultures and societies on the verge of being lost forever. The mythical subject is also a transforming agent whose knowledge may allow interventions to transform local life, either to 'civilise' it according to colonial precepts or to 'make life better' through literacy, education and empowerment. Finally, this mythical professional may be a revolutionary leader, whose interventions will bring emancipation and will, in Yen's terms, bring "release" from "illiteracy, poverty, disease and mis-government" (Yen, quoted in Buck, 1945: 84); or, in Freire's terms, to bring emancipation from oppression; or, in Chambers' terms, to bring empowerment and freedom.

Each of these mythical figures is imagined at a remove from the machinations of politics. As subjects they are posited as existing in the service of an immutable moral good — the good of improvement and emancipation. They work according to what Li (2007) terms a "will to improve". By doing their job well, however that is defined, the professional ought to be able to materialise such improvements in the communities in which they work. The improvements that they would bring are seen as part of a moral duty that is above politics.

Situating the Professional in Politics: The Thailand Controversy

The assumption that professionals should act according to moral duty remains pervasive, but over the years it has also been seriously questioned and destabilised. In the 1970s the professional's effective autonomy from daily political life began to be challenged by post-colonial and post-structural theories, as well as by new ethical debates around the involvement of Westerners in the Third World. One of the incidents that brought these debates to the fore happened to focus on the conduct of professionals in northern Thailand. The so-called Thailand Controversy greatly affected professionals working in the highlands and remains a touchstone for debates about the ethics of research in the Third World.

The ethics of ethnographic research were already under debate when the Thailand Controversy erupted in 1970, of which a catalyst was the United States government's Project Camelot, which from 1964 employed American anthropologists as part of counter-insurgency programs in Latin America (Horowitz, 1967; Patterson, 2001). When the connection between anthropologists and counter-insurgency programs became public there was widespread outrage. The ensuing debate raised questions about the ethics of ethnographic research and challenged the naive ideal of the ethnographer as someone closely connected with local villages and doing good in those communities. The Thailand Controversy erupted only a few years later and centred on the disturbing accusation that anthropologists working in the highlands were contributing to the counter-insurgency programs of the

Thai and the US governments — to the detriment of the mountain communities they were researching. Social scientists working in highland communities were accused of providing information that would assist military operations and potentially put the lives of their informants at risk. Both debates made it clear that researchers did not always conduct themselves in accordance with the ethical standards of the discipline. The Thailand Controversy put the practice of researchers in northern Thailand at the centre of debates in the United States and Australia about the ethics of ethnographic fieldwork. It also led the American Anthropological Association (AAA) to introduce its Principles of Professional Responsibility.

The Thailand Controversy began when two members of the Ethics Committee of the AAA, Eric R. Wolf and Joseph G. Jorgensen, were handed documents that seemed to implicate anthropologists in collusion with counter-insurgency agencies. According to Wolf and Jorgenson (1970: 30) the key to the scandal was that research organisations were becoming "involved in linking the '[social science] community' to the purposes of the government". The Tribal Research Centre (TRC, later Tribal Research Institute) was identified as being at the core of this sinister cooperation:

> … anthropologists have known for some time of the operations of a Tribal Research Center at Chiang Mai, Thailand, which underwrites a large convocation of scholars and other interested parties, maintains a considerable staff, has installed a computer, provides facilities for occasional users of their resources, and other amenities (Wolf and Jorgensen, 1970: 30).

The TRC, with its "computer" and its support for scholars of all kinds, was supposed to be at the epicentre of a scandalous relationship between anthropologists and counterinsurgency efforts.

Established in 1964 with funding from the Southeast Asian Treaty Organisation (SEATO), the TRC was intended to support ethnographic research in the highlands to inform Thai government policy in dealing with the 'hill tribe problem' (Buadaeng, 2006; Geddes, 1967). The Centre was staffed by Thai researchers and foreign advisors whose presence was supported by SEATO and whose role was both to conduct research on the highlands and, through their partnership with Thai colleagues, help train local experts in social research. Its aim of contributing to policy certainly linked the TRC with the purposes of the Thai government, but more sinister security links were difficult to prove.

What appears to have most agitated Wolf and Jorgensen was the suggestion that researchers were cooperating with government personnel on the collection and storage of data on the highlands and highland communities. They highlighted plans to develop:

> a reference centre with in-house study facilities for use by scholars *and concerned government and nongovernment agencies and personnel* (Dean of Faculty of Social Sciences, Chiang Mai University, quoted by Wolf and Jorgensen, 1970: 30; emphasis in the original).

The suggestion that anthropologists and ethnographers were collaborating with government and sharing the results of research undermined the expectation that professional subjects should act outside of politics as advocates and defenders of traditional communities. Amidst the volatile political atmosphere generated by the Vietnam War and the very strong anti-war feeling on both US and Australian university campuses, any cooperation between anthropologists and government authorities was suspect. Suspicions were fuelled by the revelation that one of the villages in which an Australian anthropologist, Douglas Miles, had been working was later bombed by the Thai military. At this time the Thai government often launched air strikes against highland communities and any government involvement in ethnic communities was assumed to be potentially harmful. Thus cooperation between ethnographers and agents of the state, especially the military, was seen as a betrayal of the ethical code prescribing that the professional subject should work 'for the people'.

While the concerns of Wolf and Jorgenson and others who fuelled the controversy are understandable, these were not adequately investigated and the accusations were without foundation. None of the work undertaken at the TRC was classified and no international or domestic agency concerned with counter-insurgency was directly involved with work at the Centre. The computers that were supposed to store detailed data of highland villages did not exist (John McKinnon, pers. comm., Jan. 2002). In the 1970s there were covert operatives based in northern Thailand and some of them did write pseudo-anthropological manuals assessing highland groups for the likelihood that they might join an armed revolt or be recruited to covert operations in the hills. None of the anthropologists accused, however, were conducting this kind of research. In the end the substance of the controversy rested on the fact that the TRC had been founded with SEATO money. All its operations were therefore assumed to be tainted by the geopolitical objectives of the Treaty.

The accusations were deeply upsetting for many of the researchers at the centre of the crisis and the debate soon became personal, with rifts opening up between former colleagues. Some have chosen never to speak publicly about it while others prolonged their debate over decades — the Thailand Controversy still comes up for discussion in the departments of anthropology in Australia (Hinton, 2002, Miles, 2008). The AAA investigation that followed largely exonerated members working in Thailand of any unethical practice. Although the reputation of the TRC and its associated researchers was tarnished for several years, most of the American and Australian researchers accused of misdeeds went on to good academic careers. For the Thai staff, however, the ramifications were more serious. The Director of the Center, Wanat Bhruksasri, for example, was never able to move to a regular academic job, despite the fact that he was one of only a few trained Thai researchers and had chosen to take a stand against the most harmful Thai government policies in the highlands. Because of its reputation, my father, John McKinnon, was advised against taking up a post at the TRC in the mid-1970s; he went regardless to find out for himself how true the accusations were. He was drawn into the controversy several years later when students in New Zealand made the connection between his TRC appointment and the controversy and accused him of acting as a government spy.

For anthropology as a discipline and the practice of ethnographic field research in general, the controversy marked a turning point. The committee established by the AAA to investigate the controversy, chaired by the famous Margaret Mead, concluded that there was a new ethical dilemma facing anthropological researchers, namely "that the publication of routine socio-cultural data about identified village communities…might be used for the annihilation by bombing or other forms of warfare of whole communities, as such data lend themselves to computerization and mass depersonalisation of communities marked for destruction" (Mead *et al.*, 1992). The controversy made it clear that even apparently neutral research activities were nevertheless embedded in volatile political contexts. Researchers could not therefore ignore the context, regardless of how innocent the topic of their research or its intended uses might be.

The immediate effect on the research community was that researchers were expected to choose sides. Either they were seen to be supportive of the clandestine operations of the military, or they had to disassociate themselves from the controversy and any hint of military or political funding and explicitly state their political opposition to the Vietnam War and associated conflict in mainland Southeast Asia. For Douglas Miles, the bombings in northern Thailand were intimately connected with the Vietnam War: his conduct during the controversy and stance in subsequent debates were part of an explicit rejection of US and Australian involvement in the conflict (Miles, 2008). For those affected by the controversy, however, the situation was not so simple. Peter Hinton, Bill Geddes, Charles Keyes and others drawn into the controversy, including my father, were also strongly opposed to the war in Vietnam and associated conflicts but did not feel that their role was necessarily being corrupted by the sources of funding they were receiving.

A second and, I would argue, more important effect of the controversy was that it provided an opportunity for debate over the ethics of anthropological research and foreign involvement in the highlands. Peter Hinton, who served at the TRC between 1966 and 1969, was drawn into the controversy on his return to Sydney University. In an interview with John McKinnon in 1976, he stated that:

> Outside the more hysterical claims, which got most public attention, there has been a far more constructive underlying debate which has focused on the general issue of Western aid to the Third World, and the role of visiting specialists. Quite rightly the general ethical standing of aid was being questioned (Hinton quoted by McKinnon, 1976: 3).[1]

Anthropologist Charles Keyes, who worked on Karen history,[2] recalls that researchers were acutely aware of the political situation but there

---

[1] For more on Hinton's response to the accusations of Wolf and Jorgenson, as well as comments from Delmos Jones (who was also implicated in the controversy), George M. Foster, A.J.F. Koebben and Wolf and Jorgenson, refer to "Anthropology on the warpath: an exchange" in *The New York Review of Books* 17(1) 1971, and 16(6) 1971. See also Hinton (2002).

[2] See Keyes, 1979a, 1979b, 1993.

was little questioning of the role that researchers might inadvertently be playing. The Thai military "really was [waging] *war* against the Hmong" based on the accusation that they were planning a communist rebellion (Keyes, pers. comm., July 2001). In Keyes' view, the controversy served to remedy "naïveté on the part of people working [in northern Thailand]" and draw their awareness to the care with which they must handle their data lest it impact negatively on the communities they were working with (Keyes, pers. comm., July 2001). Amidst fears of a domino effect spreading communism throughout Southeast Asia, funding was made available for all kinds of research activities in Thailand, just as funding priorities now revolve around the geopolitical concerns of the day, be it terrorism, the global financial crisis or climate change. Researchers could not isolate themselves from these political dynamics — although they could refuse to contribute by not publishing their results (as Delmos Jones chose to do, see Adams and Jones, 1971). Ultimately, the controversy highlighted that researchers are always, as Hinton put it, "political men [sic]" whose actions as a professional must also be tied to his or her "political conscience" (Hinton, 1971) .

However 'apolitical' a research project might have been, the controversy made clear that social research could not go untouched by the political climate of the times. No longer was it possible to assume that simply by being 'for the people', ethnographic research could serve a universal moral good of respect, preservation and understanding. It became clear that researchers were not autonomous agents and had only limited power over how their data might be used and limited choice of funding. Western countries were providing research funding for work in Southeast Asia precisely because of strategic interests tied to Cold War politics. Whether or not it came through military channels, research moneys were tainted by this desire for social research in 'risk' areas. Researchers wanting to be entirely free of the ethical dilemmas this presented would have to move their work to new regions.

Some of the issues that arose from the Thailand Controversy are now much dated. Thirty years on, government-funded development projects routinely employ anthropologists as consultants. Thailand itself has been so extensively mapped that it is unlikely any village remains unmarked in military records. Much of the information sought from social scientists in the 1960s and 1970s can now be gathered from routine surveillance via satellites. In this age of satellite imagery and personal computers, the fears expressed around "infrared photography and miniaturised microphones" and their possible use to "provide exact descriptions of areas and people, while computers [were] used to store and retrieve information on command" seem irrelevant (Wolf and Jorgensen, 1970: 24). In practical terms, the potential impact of such descriptive data has declined, just as the political potency of researchers' familiarity with remote areas has lessened in this age of satellite surveillance and easy international communications.

Yet, other aspects of the controversy are still relevant, especially the recognition that the privileged knowledge of researchers may do harm. As Kathy Robinson notes, the ethical debate that rose out of the controversy "reminded us of the power of the words we produce, and their potential to damage lives" (Robinson, 2004: 398). The Thailand Controversy was the first serious challenge to the ethical practices of researchers working in northern Thailand, particularly those associated with the Tribal Research Centre. As the moral standing of these researchers was called into question, professionals became seen not only as agents who protect the people they work with, as envisioned by Malinowski, but also at times as complicit partners, aiding and assisting state oppression and facilitating the imposition of Cold War political agendas. These revelations created the conditions for re-imagining the professional subject around more nuanced ethical debates of professionalism and professional responsibility.

Guarding against the Damaging Professional

The possibility that professionals could be a harmful presence contributed to the shape of ethical debates in the community of US anthropologists for many years and helped to shape the AAA Code of Ethics that remains in place today (Fluehr-Lobban, 1991). The most recent revision to the code, adopted in June 1998, emphasises that researchers' primary ethical obligation is to "the people, species, and materials they study and to the people with whom they work" (AAA, 1998). Most recently that responsibility has been threatened by the new practice of 'embedding' anthropologists with military units in Afghanistan. The AAA has considered amending the Code of Ethics to "guard against the ethical perils that may be encountered through certain positions with US military, intelligence and security organisations" (AAA press release, 20 March 2007). From the early

1970s to the present day, the core concern is still that researchers should ensure as far as possible that their research does no harm either to the physical well-being or to the dignity of their research subjects.

The issue that remains at the heart of these ethical debates is how to ameliorate the imbalance of power between the professional and the local people. As Wolf and Jorgensen asked in the midst of the Thailand Controversy:

> By what right do social scientists invade the privacy of powerless people, in order to pass on information to powerful third parties for purposes beyond the control of both the anthropologist and his unwitting informants? (Wolf and Jorgensen, 1971: 45).

Since the earliest days of anthropology as a discipline, ethnographic research has been critiqued as a process of investigation by the powerful of the powerless. Levi-Strauss (1966a: 126) viewed anthropology as the "daughter" of a colonial "era of violence". For some scholars the imperialistic origins of anthropology continue to shape an unequal relationship between the researcher and the researched: "there is always in the background of anthropological work an unequal status between the observer and the observed" (Godelier, quoted in Eiss and Wolfe, 2004). These sentiments have been explored by a range of authors who problematise the uneven relationship between researcher and researched, and between the development professional and the beneficiaries of development. This is an issue that has been of particular concern to scholars influenced by the work of post-colonialists, who share the aim of analysing the disempowering effects of Western colonial discourses.[3] Linda Tuhiwai Smith (1999), for example, offers an uncompromising critique of the role of the professional ethnographer as a translator between cultures in the case of New Zealand/ Aotearoa. For Smith, the translator subject is reimagined as an exploitative subject. The researcher in colonised or Third World communities is always a powerful thief, extracting and then laying claim to indigenous knowledge in ways that delegitimise the subaltern's own practices and understandings. In a similar vein, Linda Alcoff argues that speaking for less privileged others is "discursively dangerous":

---

[3] Such as Asad, 1973; Bhabha, 1994; Hooks, 1992, 1994; Said, 1978, 1993; Spivak, 1985, 1999.

"the effect of the practice of speaking for others is often, though not always, erasure and a reinscription of sexual, national, and other kinds of hierarchies" (Alcoff, 1991: 7, 29). For these scholars it is difficult, if not impossible, to escape the imbalance of power and the exploitative relationships that characterise research in Third World or indigenous communities.

Researchers have sought to address the problems arising from uneven relationships of power by adhering closely to ethical codes and by actively problematising the researcher's position throughout the research process. The 'colonising professional' and the 'thief' are problematic because they are seen to appropriate the knowledge of the subaltern subjects and to presume to speak on behalf of others. Feminist post-colonial critiques of positivism and objectivity in the social sciences have led to the emergence of reflexive approaches to field research, in which the role of researchers and their impacts on the data is acknowledged and discussed. This body of literature encourages scholars to reflect on their role in the production of knowledge and to position themselves in the text in ways that demystify the authority of the author (Cosgrove and Domosh, 1993; see also D'Amico-Samuels, 1991; England, 1994; Kobayashi, 1994). Action research is another approach that repositions researchers as partners in projects where investigations are led by community members and mutual learning and knowledge sharing is often the main aim (Stringer *et al.*, 2008). Advocates of these approaches hope that by carrying out research differently, professionals may escape the binds of a colonial heritage and the possibility of thievery that enters into research conducted according to the standard norms of social science.

In the field of development studies, the concern is not that the professional is a thief but an 'expert': here the problematic professional is the expert who does not accept that they need to learn from the local community. The expert enters communities with knowledge, skills and resources that local people do not have but are assumed to need if they are to escape the circumstances of their underdevelopment. Numerous critics have argued that this model of development often delivers solutions that are inappropriate or even harmful. The knowledge and advice of the expert is often ill suited to local ecological, cultural or social circumstances. Worse still the assumption that outside knowledge is necessarily better devalues indigenous knowledge and innovation, both in the eyes of the funders and often in the eyes of the locals themselves, who come to believe they cannot progress without outside assistance and technologies. Copious studies have shown how development programs assuming the need for outside expertise often fail to deliver long-term benefit. Introduced technologies break down because locals do not know how to maintain them; introduced systems do not take root because they conflict with local custom; temporary improvements cease when the project ends and the team of experts packs up and moves on.

Placed in opposition to the development-as-expert has been a very different vision of the professional as a 'facilitator' of a participatory process of change. According to the participatory approach, the professional is obliged to 'put the people first', to prioritise local needs and perspectives, to act in partnership with communities, and to place local development 'beneficiaries' in the position of leaders and decision-makers about their own development.

Participatory approaches themselves are not beyond criticism. It has been pointed out that participation may become just another conduit to imposing outside interests on communities, not empowering them but incorporating them into modernity in ways they may or may not desire, that it may facilitate an unjust exercise of power, and that development institutions are rarely able to conduct truly participatory programs (Bryant, 2002, Cleaver, 2001, Cooke and Kothari, 2001, Henkel and Stirrat, 2001). While participatory discourses value local knowledge above 'expert' knowledge, and seek to empower locals, this still demands the presence of an expert, an outsider with special skills and technologies for drawing out new perspectives and possibilities for change (Triantafillou and Nielson, 2001). The reaction to each of these critiques has been to reiterate how important it is that development should be genuinely 'of the people' and, by implication, that it is the job of development professionals to make sure that the work they do is *genuinely* assisting local people to meet their needs and realise their desires and aspirations, whether or not these fit with a conventional notion of what 'development' or 'progress' should be about. This has been channelled into efforts to create tools and approaches which could be more genuinely participatory. Some examples include Asset Based Community Development approaches, reconfigured participatory toolkits focusing on learning and action, and emerging tools such as Mobile Interactive Geographic Information Systems (MIGIS), a method which integrates participatory research techniques with GIS technology (McKinnon & McKinnon, 2005).

All these discourses of professionalism ultimately return to a belief in the local. In debates about social research and development practice, the ideal professional is consistently identified as someone who works for the people. Past models of professional conduct — the anthropologist as saviour, the colonial administrator as a civilising force — have been challenged and rejected. Yet the basic sentiment that professionals should act in the interests of local communities remains the underpinning moral standard. In its contemporary form, this discourse assigns 'the local' a central role in determining what its own best interests are. The ideal professional must give ethical priority to the needs, desires and perspectives of the local people and avoid doing any harm through their innate power and privilege. For advocates of the participatory approach, this ideal finds expression in a language of putting the last first, and the first last (Chambers, 1983, 1997). For feminist ethnographers, privileging the local means abandoning the claim to be able to represent objective truth. For some post-colonial authors, it means that one should not attempt to speak for others from "less privileged" backgrounds (Alcoff, 1991). And, for all ethnographers who subscribe to the ethical standards of organisations like the AAA, the emphasis on the local means owing ultimate responsibility to the researched, the participants and informants. The combined response to the challenges presented by ethical debates around the politics of development and ethnographic research, and the responsibilities of the professional, has been to rephrase the universalising discourse of a benevolent professional working 'for the people'. This reconfigured ideal is the 'pro-local' professional subject for whom definitions of ethical practice are closely related to an approach that is "of the community for the community" (Crespo *et al.*, 2006: 63).

Conclusion

The pro-local professional is the latest in a long line of discursively constituted and interrelated professional subjects. I have identified a few of these: the people's professional, revolutionary leader, transforming agent, expert, facilitator/catalyst, thief, translator/interpreter, powerful subject, naive subject, exploitative subject, reflexive and conversing subject, complicit subject, neo-colonial subject, participatory professional and, finally, pro-local subject. Through ongoing debates, the role of the development professional is consistently cast as one of a subject who helps, assists, enlightens and understands a local other who should be properly valued and respected. These are the origins of a mythical, pro-local professional subject, an ideal figure embodying the ethical and moral standards to which any professional must aspire.

The idea of the local, and the sense of the professional responsibility towards the local, are themselves constructs. 'The local' represents a mythical site of truth, an ideologically configured point to which the professional must attach loyalty, thus guaranteeing his or her moral standing as an ethical practitioner. Just who is that 'local' and how diverse and often conflicting interests of local communities may come to the fore is constantly debated. Yet it is local people who underpin professional identities, not least because without a local community needing assistance, the professional has no reason to exist. Thus alongside the mythical professional is an equally mythical 'other', constructed variously: (in archaic discourses) as the native, the primitive, the oriental, the oppressed; (in contemporary discourses) as the underdeveloped, the indigenous, the disadvantaged; and finally (in critical discourses) as the knowledgeable participant, the respected informant.

The ideal of doing good and helping the local shapes the ways in which professionals see themselves, but it also shapes the way they see the locals whom they are supposed to help. In Thailand, the broad debates about professional responsibility have had a significant role in shaping professional identities. Just as important, however, are the local discourses that have shaped the highlands. The way that local communities in the highlands have been constructed as needy and problematic, and the role development professionals have played in creating and contesting this discourse, have in turn shaped the professional identities that have emerged in that context. In my next chapter I go on to discuss how these needy subjects, and the problematic spaces they occupied, were first called into being.

3

The 'Hill Tribe Problem'

Until the 1950s, the highlands of northern Thailand were mostly inaccessible and highland villages had very little contact with the Thai authorities. Although they had been drawn into Thai territory half a century before, little had been done to extend formal Thai control. The highlanders were allowed to live independently and autonomously, as they had for centuries. In 1959, however, all that was set to change. The Thai government took the decision to develop a policy on how to deal with the highlands. Their first step was to commission a survey to gather population data on highland communities. This survey was carried out in 1961 and 1962 with funding and 'expert' assistance from the United Nations in the form of German anthropologist Hans Manndorff. As Manndorff noted:

> [it was no longer] possible for the government to leave these ethnic minorities in the hills alone. It is the inevitable logic of events in our time that administration and modernisation is extended even into those remote parts of the country which were traditionally self-sufficient (Manndorff, 1965: 7).

The survey was the first step in extending Thai administration and modernisation into the highlands. Development would become the main tool for these efforts as both the Thai state and foreign donors turned their attentions to the region.

Why did highlanders become the object of development? The answer is not that they were desperately impoverished and in need of outside assistance. In the 1960s most highland communities were still subsistence-based economies, with very little cash income to provide a buffer against a bad season or to enable the purchase of modern luxuries such as a radio or — for those communities close to town — modern medicines. Many highland villages were remote from main roads and cities, accessible only on foot, and health indicators like life expectancy and infant mortality were certainly much worse than today. Nevertheless highland villages were not isolated. Most communities maintained close contact with neighbouring groups and villages throughout the mountains and traded with lowland towns. The northern Thai dialect was widely spoken.[1] Furthermore, highland communities maintained a rich set of cultural practices tied to the seasons, the growing cycle of rice crops, and the marking of key events in people's lives such as birth, marriage and death. Villages had functioning leadership systems, social and economic inequalities were minimal, and shamans, healers and spirit mediums worked to ensure the health and well-being of all. In other words, while highland communities were materially poor, by most early anthropological accounts, they were also healthy, functional and culturally and spiritually rich in many other ways. Thus the need for development assistance did not emerge from any sense of need within mountain communities.

The imperative for development came instead from the political interests of the Thai state in securing its borders and putting in place a modern form of sovereignty over all Thai territory. Development has long been entangled with questions of national sovereignty and the political complexities of progress (Sidaway, 2007). The conditions through which development programs were introduced to the mountains is no different. When development professionals first ventured into highland communities in the 1960s and 1970s, they entered a political landscape being reshaped by the geopolitical movements of previous decades. Since the early 1900s the way highland villages were conceptualised in relation to the state authorities had changed dramatically. The mapping of state borders had placed the highlands clearly inside Thai territory; a new order had been introduced based on European models of the nation-state; and a new Thai national subject was being constructed, one which excluded highland groups from national belonging (Renard, 2000; Thongchai, 1994, 2000). By the time of the first development programs, Thailand's

---

[1] Northern Thai, or Kham Meuang, is closely related to central Thai and Lao and is spoken widely in the provinces of Chiang Mai, Chiang Rai and Mae Hong Son.

population was exploding, putting increasing pressure on land (Hirsch, 1997). Furthermore, the rise of communism and fears that a 'red wave' was about to engulf Southeast Asia had brought the Cold War to the region, with conflict in Korea and Vietnam, and communism gaining power in Laos and Cambodia. There were fears that high-landers might join a communist rebellion in Thailand and that the people of the borderlands could become a potential threat to the newly emerging Thai nation-state.

As highlanders were reimagined as a threat, development, and the ministrations of the development professional, became necessary. In the space of just a few years, highlanders went from being ignored by the Thai administration to being the highly problematic object for extensive development programs. In this chapter I trace how the highlands were reconfigured as a problematic space, inhabited by problematic populations of 'hill tribes'. Together these created both a site and a subject in need of development and thus the conditions necessary for development programs to be introduced.

Modern Thai Territoriality

The highlands would not have been reimagined as problematic but for the introduction of the modern nation-state system. Conventional histories of Thailand portray the nation as founded upon an ancient line of kings who ruled the land dating from the Kingdom of Sukhothai in the thirteenth century. In fact, as recent work by South-east Asian historians such as Thongchai Winichakul (1994) and Ron Renard (2000) shows, the nation and territory of Thailand has emerged only over the last 150 years and took its shape largely in response to the influence of colonial powers on the geopolitics of the region. In the terms of Benedict Anderson (1991), it is an "imagined community" founded on the myth of a shared ethnic and cultural heritage that was brought into being only very recently. A contemporary vision of the nation — a unified group of people with rights to a particular territory — as something defined by birth is vastly different from the system in place during the pre-colonial era.

Before the colonial period, state relations were mediated by a much looser sense of territoriality. The state system that predominated in Southeast Asia at that time was focused around networks of vassal states. Chiang Mai was the centre of the northern Lanna Kingdom; Ayutthaya (and subsequently Bangkok) the centre of the Siamese

Kingdom in what is now central and southern Thailand.[2] From centres like Chiang Mai and Ayutthaya, rule was established not so much by the conquest of territory but through the formation of allegiances. Rule was therefore not uniform across contiguous space (Bowie, 2000; Osborne, 2002; Renard, 2000; Thongchai, 1994). Instead, there were pockets of state spaces in which individual tenants, agricultural communities and towns maintained allegiances with the lords of the land who, in turn, were aligned with the rulers of the vassal states. Within this system, state subjects and state territories were less intimately linked than in the contemporary nation-state system. It was possible for a farming family to pay rent on their land to one lord while being the bonded subject of another. Thus, allegiance and loyalty to particular rulers were not necessarily determined by geography (Thongchai, 1994: 164). The spatiality of this pre-colonial system was a diffuse web of allegiances between separate spaces of rule, tied to a powerful centre that provided protection, both military and cosmic. In between these governed and protected spaces lay forests and mountains that were subject to more local modes of rule within individual villages and communities. These were ostensibly non-state spaces that were a refuge for bandits and refugees and the domain of autonomous self-governing societies of highlanders (Scott, 2000, 2010).

Along with this distinct territorial arrangement, the pre-colonial state had a very different relationship with its subjects. In pre-colonial Siam, relationship to the state was not defined on the basis of descent. Instead subjects were labelled according to whether they were seen to be part of a system of state allegiances (*tai*) or whether they existed outside it (*kha*) (Renard, 2000). The terms *tai* and *kha* are of unknown origin but appear in various chronicles kept by the royal courts of Sukhothai and Ayutthaya about key events such as battles and journeys during the king's reign (Renard, 2000: 66).

---

[2] The capital moved to Bangkok under King Rama I (1782–1809) following the Burmese sacking of Ayutthaya in 1767 (Wyatt, 1984). In the colonial era, Siam would gain dominance over neighbouring city-states and begin to establish the united territory that is now Thailand. After several centuries of allegiance with Burmese states, Chiang Mai became a vassal state of Siam in 1794 and was eventually incorporated under the direct rule of Siam in 1874 (Wood, 1965: 118).

The *tai-kha* distinction was not based on any concept of nationality, race or ethnicity; the terms were more negotiable identifications that distinguished subjects on the basis of perceived levels of civility (Renard, 2000). Civility was in turn determined by social and spatial proximity and degree of incorporation into a given polity. Unlike contemporary concepts of ethnicity, in which identity is endowed by birth or descent, it was possible to move between the identity designations of *tai* and *kha*. Movement between groups was a matter of moving between the spaces of wildness and civilisation, between faraway forests and the city states (Leach, 1954; Renard, 2000; Scott, 2000; Thongchai, 2000a).

The shift away from mobile understandings of identity (and belonging) began with the arrival of British and French colonial power in the region in the nineteenth century (Osborne, 2002). Siam had maintained relationships with European powers since the seventeenth century (Tachard, 1981 [1688]), but in the nineteenth century Europe began to have a much greater influence over developments in local politics, introducing a new vision of the state with a different understanding of spatiality and the subject. Europeans were puzzled by the indigenous state formation in which power was a matter of control over subjects rather than land (Thongchai, 2000: 164) and established power through a more familiar system of laying claim to contiguous territories and subjects who dwelt within them. In the mid-to-late nineteenth century, the Kingdom of Siam, with its capital in Bangkok, began to negotiate its borders with the colonial powers and their cartographers, and the contemporary Thai geo-body began to take shape (Thongchai, 1994). The reigns of King Mongkhut (1851–68), his son Chulalongkorn (1868–1910) and grandson Vajiravudh (1910–25) were pivotal in the modernisation of Siam. They responded to the challenges presented by colonial forces in neighbouring Burma and Indochina with a range of strategies that helped to avoid colonial occupation. Nevertheless the consequence has been described as a form of indirect colonisation, where Siam's rulers set about introducing many of the reforms that colonial authorities were imposing elsewhere (Osborne, 2002; Tarling, 1998; Wyatt, 1984).

In characterising Siam's kings as the centre of a colonising Siamese 'empire', there is the risk of overstating the dominance of the state centre at the expense of the power of the periphery and its active engagement with the centre. Although my analysis in this chapter is focused on how discourses of the state centre construct subjects at the periphery, it is important to acknowledge that northern cities such as Chiang Mai, as well as highland villages, have been active centres of power in themselves and were not merely the passive recipients of Siamese reforms. Thongchai's account of the formation of the modern Thai nation-state, along with other 'Bangkok-centric' accounts of regional politics (such as Keyes, 1993; Penth, 1994; Stott, 1991; Tambiah, 1985; Wijeyewardene, 1991) has been critiqued by Andrew Walker, (1998: 6–10) for being overly reliant on historical accounts from the centre. Walker's studies of the Laos-Thai borderlands provide an account of life in the 'margins' counterpoised to Thongchai's Bangkok-centric view, exploring how the introduction of modern modes of spatial control "had to *contend with* — rather than simply conquer — local practices and perceptions that had quite different frames of reference" (Walker 2008; see also 1998).

The Siamese also had to contend with the genuine threat of colonial occupation, which it avoided by making concessions to colonial powers. Territory was ceded under duress to the French on Siam's eastern border with Indochina and trade concessions were granted such as those given to the British under the Bowring Treaty of 1855 (Wyatt, 1984: 183). Realising the importance of laying claim to territory in the face of pressures from the British in Burma and French forces in Indochina, Siamese rulers cooperated with European surveyors to map the borders of the state. As Thongchai (1994) argues, the process of mapping introduced an entirely new idea of state and territory. When the British and French sought to establish a precise border between territories, they had to contend with Siamese and Burmese perceptions of what a border was. For both the Siamese and Burmese, the mountains and forests were understood as natural markers of the spatial divisions of their states. A Siamese official who was part of the team negotiating with the British envoy to the court of Siam made this clear:

> The boundaries between the Siamese and Burmese consisted of a tract of mountains and forest, which is several miles wide and which could not be said to belong to either nation. Each had detachments on the look out to seize any person of the other party found straying within the tract (*The Burney Papers*, quoted by Thongchai, 1994: 64).

These wide tracts of mountains and forests were effectively un-governed, non-state spaces that formed a buffer between the Siamese-and Burmese-controlled lands. The adjacent colonial authorities, however, pushed for a boundary *line*. The exact location of this carto-graphic line was not fixed until decades later. Even then, laying claim to the territory was not the same thing as being able to govern every inch inside the national boundary — that would come much later.

Introducing Thai Nationalism

Within the new state boundaries, a new nation also started to take shape. In response to pressures from its colonial European neigh-bours, Siam began to adopt new social, cultural and political norms as if they had indeed been colonised. Under the leadership of King Mongkhut and his son Chulalongkorn, Siam began a program of reforms designed to reconfigure Thai political structures along Euro-pean lines and to create an integrated state made up of "many peoples, both Tai speaking and others who had little previous connection with the Kingdom of Siam" (Wyatt, 1984: 181). Where loyalties had been due to one's immediate patron or master, reform shifted these allegiances to the Siamese king. Slavery was abolished and bonded labour dramatically reduced, while village monasteries and schools were founded across the country. Political reforms introduced a much more centralised system of government, enabling the Bangkok court and bureaucracy to exercise direct control of government in the outer provinces (Wyatt, 1984). All these changes "reinforced the idea that all inhabitants of Siam were subjects of a single King, members of the single body politic" (Wyatt, 1984: 217). Through this period Siam began to change into something that more closely resembled the European states of the time.[3]

For the people of the borderlands, mountains and forests, these changes meant their position in relation to the state also shifted when the places they inhabited were reimagined as state rather than

---

[3] The imposition of new modes of rule did not take place without considerable resistance. There is still ongoing resistance in Southern Thailand where Muslims are agitating for secession from the Kingdom. For discussion of the resistance to Siamese rule of the hinterland, see Nartsupha (1984), Ramsay (1976) and Tanabe (1984).

non-state spaces. The earliest evidence of this appears to be in the rise of amateur ethnologies undertaken by Bangkok elites in the Siamese hinterlands, pointing to a fundamental transformation of the *tai-kha* relationships of old (Thongchai, 2000). In place of a more fluid *tai-kha* relationship, difference was re-presented in terms of essentialist notions of culture and race. As in Europe, where domestic ethnology was one of the many new forms of knowledge enabling modern modes of rule (Godelier, 1997), the ethnological writings of Bangkok elites helped to make the highland subject, hitherto largely absent from a Bangkok-centric view of the nation, a known and recognised subject. In these new discourses, highlanders entered the consciousness of Bangkok elites as racialised 'others', examples of primitive peoples who were juxtaposed with the sophistication and civilisation of the Siamese. Over time, as European ideas of the nation-state became more pervasive, highlanders would become more and more sharply defined against an emerging Thai nation and their 'otherness' increasingly set in ethnic and racial terms.

The idea of a unified Thai nation, and the inspiration for how to bring such a thing into being, was first introduced in the early twentieth century as the children of Siamese elites returned home from studies in Europe. They brought back with them a European notion of the nation-state, predicated upon a vision of a unity of people, land and government. The uniting force was nationalism: "a myth that provides the empty signifiers of 'the nation' and 'the people' with a particular, substantial embodiment ... [and constructs] the nation-as-this and the people-as-one" (Torfing, 1999: 193). A vision of the unity of nation, state and territory first took root among the ruling elite of Bangkok in the early 1900s. King Vajiravudh (1910–25) is credited with popularising the idea of the 'Thai nation' (Wyatt, 1984: 229). Vajiravudh had studied at Sandhurst and Oxford from 1893 to 1903 and returned to Siam with ideas of the nation-state as envisioned in Europe at the time — one territory, one nation, one race. The idea gained support and after Siam had been renamed *Prathet Thai* (Thailand) in 1939, the government of the day under Prime Minister Phibun began actively promoting the idea of a Thai national identity to the population of the fledgling nation-state. During this period that Wyatt (1984: 252) refers to as "mass nationalism", the population learned to start using the national Thai 'we' and conform, as required by law, to the practices stipulated by government commissions on Thai culture. Stipulations for appropriate 'Thai conduct' penetrated the school system, media, domestic realm and practices of everyday life. Along with a school curriculum that taught Thais 'to be Thai', the introduction of the census and the establishment of new state institutions such as the Department of Public Welfare, edicts were issued against the chewing of betel nut and wearing of traditional clothing (Thongchai, 1994). It was also due to Phibun that the national anthem continues to be played daily in public spaces at 6 am and 6 pm. Until the late 1980s traffic in the cities would come to a standstill as people stopped their cars and got out to stand and honour their country. These measures ensured that over time the idea of Thai-ness, of such a thing as the Thai nation, came to be taken for granted. These days the idea of a Thai identity even reaches across national borders as the ethnic and cultural grouping of 'Tai' spread across Burma, Thailand, Laos and Southern China is "promoted as a cultural foundation for regional integration in a globalising world" (Walker, 2009: 3).

Although the program of introducing a Thai identity was well underway in the 1930s, legislative definition and identification of Thai nationals would not come about until the 1950s. Only then did the deliberate exclusion of highlanders from the Thai nation become apparent. The 1956 household registration program was the first step towards creating a comprehensive and centralised registration of all Thai citizens. This was the first piece of legislation which "set down in law the procedure for classifying between Thai and non-Thai people" (Chainarong and Suppachai, 1999). Because of the inaccessibility of many mountain communities, the majority of highlanders were not registered. While the 'wild' and 'backward' subjects of turn-of-the-century ethnologies were a recognised and documented presence within the Kingdom, no steps had been taken to formally identify these subjects as either 'insiders' or 'outsiders' of the nation. Anthropologist Peter Hinton (pers. comm., Sept. 2002) suggests that this could have been due to the lack of resources and the difficulty of navigating the mountainous terrain where there were still few roads. It could also be that geopolitical circumstances did not give rise to any urgent need for Thai authorities to gain access to the highlands. Whatever the reason, while lowland Thais were being registered, highlanders remained a documented subject but one outside the regulating gaze of the state.

Reimagining the Highlands as a Threat

Thai nationalism and modern Thai territoriality put highlanders in a contradictory position: they were within the boundaries of the Thai state but ostensibly excluded as legitimate subjects of that state. For a time the contradiction did not matter because most communities remained inaccessible and had little to do with state authorities. For all intents and purposes the borderlands remained non-state space, beyond the regulatory authority of the Thai state. In the late 1950s and early 1960s, however, the Thai government began to bring the border territories under state control. The highlands started to be considered a problematic zone and highlanders themselves were reimagined as a potential threat to the Thai Kingdom.

The shift came with changed geopolitical circumstances and the growing fear of a communist takeover in Southeast Asia. The defeat of the French at Dien Ben Phu in 1954 marked a dramatic turning point. The United States had become involved in Vietnam in an 'advisory' role before the French defeat and now took on a greater role in the region, motivated by an anti-communist agenda. With communist governments being established in China, North Korea and Vietnam, and the beginnings of the war against communist forces in South Vietnam, it was feared that Thailand would be the next domino to fall. The borderlands came to be seen as vulnerable to communist infiltration. At last the Thai state moved to actualise a vision of the nation-state as a contiguous and uniformly governed territory within the existing boundary lines.

In the highlands, national and international concerns with the region's vulnerability to communist takeover translated into concerns about the prospect of communist forces forging alliances with high-landers. It was recognised that highlanders had an intimate knowledge of the borderlands and exceptional communication channels between scattered mountain settlements across state borders. According to Saihoo, lecturer in social anthropology at Chulalongkorn University in Bangkok, in the absence of a strong sense of 'national loyalty', it was feared that

> Given adequate support and encouragement from outside, the hill tribes in a particular country may easily engage themselves in subversive activities to further their own ends or to put up resistance to the national authority which seeks to impose some control contrary to their interests (Saihoo, 1963: 16–17).

Highlanders thus became seen as a potential threat to national security because they had not yet been wholly incorporated into the Thai state and had not been included in the process of national identity-building that had occurred in mainstream Thai society in the preceding decades.

The concern that the highlands could be a sphere for communist insurgency against the Thai government did eventually seem to be justified in the highlands to the east of the northern province of Nan. In 1967 a sizable contingent of Hmong rose in open rebellion against the state (Hanks and Hanks, 2001). The Thai government was quick to identify it as a communist uprising though the Hmong involved in the events that precipitated the 'uprising' made no such ideological claim. The Thai authorities saw the conflict as a "[Hmong] conspiracy cooked up by outside communists and directed from headquarters in Laos" (Cooper, 1979: 325–6). According to Jane and Lucien Hanks (2001), anthropologists who conducted several extensive surveys with highlanders in the region between 1969 and 1979, the insurrection was a response to repeated attempts by Thai officials to exact fines for cutting trees without permission. As was usual under these circumstances, the Hmong paid 'hush money' to the first set of officials, "but when the next day another provincial policeman arrived to profit from the same infraction the headman lost patience" (Hanks and Hanks, 2001: 194). This policeman was driven from the village by gunfire. In response a party of 50 provincial police raided the village the next day, only to be ambushed on the path. One policeman was killed and several wounded. Several days later, in retaliation, the police burned the village to the ground (Race, cited by Hanks and Hanks, 2001: 194–5). Robert Cooper, an anthropologist who worked with Hmong communities in the region, provides a different account. According to him "police patrols were only ambushed after they had destroyed Hmong villages which refused to pay an increase in the unofficial tax that is levied on opium cultivation in some areas" (Cooper, 1979: 325–6). Regardless of the underlying causes, the Thai government responded as if it was a communist-inspired uprising. The Thai army began to clear out Hmong and Yao villages in the area as the air force began bombing raids in the mountains. According to Tapp (1989), 40 per cent of the upland population had become homeless by 1968. Cabinet declared the area a free-fire zone and it remained so into the 1970s. All villages in the free-fire zone were evacuated and anyone remaining in the hills was considered a communist. At some point during this time the insurrection became a reality and Thai army units in the hills were targeted by rebels — even the governor of Chiang Rai and his police chief were killed in an ambush on a mountain road (Hanks and Hanks, 2001). The Hanks' interviews with Hmong who lived in the region at the time make it clear that by now Pathet Lao — the eventually triumphant communist faction in the Laos Civil War — was recruiting among Hmong across the Thai border and supporting the insurrection with arms and ammunition (Hanks and Hanks, 2001: 196). If the rebellion had not started out with an ideological component, it had certainly acquired one along the way.

At the same time as the highlands became a focus of national security, the region also began to draw attention in relation to opium production, a practice which had been made illegal in 1958. Opium has been grown in the region for centuries for its medicinal qualities. During the two Opium Wars of 1839–1842 and 1858 between Britain and China, and after the Chinese government's subsequent legalisation of the trade, opium became an important cash crop in China. Hmong and Yao farmers cultivated the crop in China's remote southern highlands of Yunnan. As these people moved south to escape the fighting that erupted after the first Opium War, they took their crop with them and thereby introduced cash cropping of opium to Thailand (Renard, 2001: 1). Opium cultivation was legalised in Thailand in 1855 and the supply was regulated by the Royal Opium Department. The processed opium was sold at exorbitant prices at licensed opium dens. A profitable black-market business thrived alongside but official trade earned a good revenue for the state (Renard, 2001). When the sale and consumption of opium was finally banned, it was in response to international pressure and only took place after many years of internal negotiation in the ranks of the leading military and police personnel (McCoy, 1972). According to Ajhan Chupinit Kesmanee of Srinakharinwirot University in Bangkok, in 1957 Field Marshall Sarit launched a campaign to make opium illegal across the board, but was persuaded that the opium revenue was still vital to secure the ongoing loyalty of his subordinates (Chupinit, pers. comm., 2001). By the time opium was finally made illegal in 1958, the opium poppies, which were ideally suited to the difficult terrain and touchy soils of the mountains, were well established as an important cash crop supplementing the livelihoods

of many communities in the highlands (Geddes, 1976).[4] The continuing production of opium by highland farmers despite its illegality
thus became an additional problem in the view of Thai authorities.

In addition to concerns of national security and opium production, the highlands also began to draw attention because of highlanders' land-use practices that were thought to be causing environmental damage and deforestation. At that time the dominant form
of agricultural production in the highlands was swidden farming.
Also known as 'slash and burn' or shifting cultivation, swiddening
is commonly used in tropical upland areas where irrigation systems
cannot be built due to unreliable water supply or hilly terrain. Fields
are cleared in the forest, burned and planted with rice and vegetables.
When yields start to decrease, the fields are either left fallow for up
to 12 years so that the soil may recover its nutrient value or abandoned altogether, leaving the forest to reclaim the fields. As illustrated in Plate 2, the resulting landscape is a pattern of mixed land
use in which virgin or second-growth forests, fallow fields, and fields
in production dot the hillside. This land-use system could be characterised in the case of Akha in northern Thailand and southern China
by the term "landscape plasticity" to describe the responsiveness to
the changing conditions of production and the ongoing need to
sustain both village households and the land (Sturgeon, 2005).[5] The
problem was that the system was thought to compromise the health
of the soil, thereby stunting forest regeneration, and to require a
degree of clearing that was quickly depleting Thailand's precious rainforest reserves and exacerbating seasonal flooding in the lowlands.

In fact, the data upon which such assumptions rested was not
particularly strong. Very little good research had been conducted on
the environmental impact of swidden farming. The assumption that
swidden agriculture was a bad thing was probably based firstly on the
norms set by dominant forest management paradigms as well as the
links that were being made between swiddening and other concerns
about opium and national security.

---

[4] Opium was made illegal by the Proclamation of the Revolutionary Party, No. 37,
9 Dec. 1958 (Wanat 1989: 13).
[5] Sturgeon's study included two case study villages: one located in southern
Yunnan province in China and the other in Mae Faluang district in northern
Thailand. From her results she extrapolates to Akha land use in general.

Plate 2   Highland swidden landscape (Mae Suai, 2005)

According to historian Ronald Renard, anti-swiddening prejudices may have been introduced to Thailand from British colonial authorities in Burma (Renard, pers. comm., July 2001). The Royal Forest Department of Siam was established in 1896 under the leadership of Herbert Slade, an Englishman trained in German forestry (Usher, 2009). The Royal Forest Department was charged with the responsibility of managing the forested highlands, territories officially owned by the state. The ethos of the organisation was to produce more teak — the wonder wood for ship building. The approach was to create carefully managed single species plantation forests clearly separated from agriculture, whose proper place was in the lowland valleys. The existence of agricultural lands scattered through the forests was an affront to the German forestry system of clearly delineated and carefully managed forestlands. When teak production was the aim, any clearance of forest by swidden farmers was considered to be a wasteful use of resources (Saihoo, 1963). According to Saihoo, the earliest ethnologies of the highlands remarked on the extent of forest destruction by highlanders (Saihoo, 1963). For example Blofield, who published his account in 1955, described their method of agriculture as wasteful, entailing the systematic destruction of valuable jungle. Blofield did not consider the matter particularly serious at the time "in view of the enormous area of jungle in Thailand which has hitherto been put to no use whatever" (Blofield, quoted in Saihoo, 1963: 21). As Scott (1998) discusses, the complex usage of forest resources by swiddeners was simply not legible to dominant perspectives of the time that remained enthralled by the orderly and exact production of plantation forests under the German forestry system.

As the priority for the Royal Forest Department shifted from teak production to forest preservation, the perception of the problem shifted from swiddening as a wasteful practice to swiddening as a destructive practice. The Department of Public Welfare identified the major cause of forest and watershed destruction as "the shifting cultivation practised by the hill tribes" (Department of Public Welfare, 1964). Despite the lack of accurate data, the Department estimated in 1964 that hill tribe activity had destroyed two-thirds of the forest in Chiang Mai and Lamphun provinces. Shifting cultivation was seen to be such a damaging practice that it was outlawed. By 1960, when the first highland Land Settlement Projects were established, so-called 'slash-and-burn' agriculture had been made illegal (Manndorff, 1967: 533).

Although the concern in the 1950s and early 1960s focused on the risk that shifting cultivators posed to virgin forest, by 1969 broader environmental concerns began to emerge, many of which were closely related to the cultivation of opium. Although, as mentioned above, opium had been banned in 1958, little direct action was taken against opium producers who continued to grow it both for domestic use and as a cash crop. Opium could be grown on marginal land which was either very steep or had poor soils. Even on otherwise productive land, opium was an excellent crop for when the soil fertility and weed invasion became a problem. In these cases planting an opium crop was an effective way to continue to create an income from land. As a crop that could be planted in otherwise unproductive sites, opium worked well with the swiddening system and provided producers with a cash income to supplement a subsistence farming livelihood. From an environmental point of view, the problem was that the cultivation of opium on very steep land was believed to be causing erosion and subsequent siltation of streams, which in turn was affecting lowland water supplies (Grandstaff, 1980).

In addition, because opium will still thrive in soils no longer fertile enough for cultivating rice, this further use of the land was thought to be severely depleting soil fertility. As a result, the only plant that would grow over the fallow or abandoned fields was imperata grass, which was thought to inhibit regeneration of forest (Keen, 1972). Opium production therefore was believed to be leaving swathes of the highlands irrevocably denuded of precious rainforests.

Finally, swidden farming systems allowed people to move through the hills. Opium production was believed to be a key element in the livelihoods of 'pioneer swiddening' groups, communities that would periodically relocate to find new land rather than rotating the same fields through the production cycle. The pioneer swiddeners — Hmong, Akha, Lisu and Lahu — were considered to be the main opium producers and their periodic relocation added to national security concerns. This movement was unregulated by state authorities and often led communities across state borders. Under the modern form of territoriality, such unauthorised movement constituted a violation of state sovereignty and the integrity of national borders. In the 1960s and 1970s, this was believed to carry the added risk that communist ideologies might also travel alongside farming communities.

The Threefold 'Hill Tribe Problem'

By the early 1960s the three issues of national security, opium and swidden farming were rolled together as 'the hill tribe problem'. It was under the rubric of the 'hill tribe problem' that the Thai state sought increasing engagement with highland communities. In the process highlanders themselves became redefined by the governing gaze of the state.

The first important act of redefinition came with the introduction of the term 'hill tribe' (*chao khao*) to describe highland peoples. The term was adopted as the Thai state began formally to engage with highland communities after the establishment of the Hill Tribe Development and Welfare Program of the Department of Public Welfare in 1959. From this point on, 'hill tribe' became the term most widely used to refer to highland groups. This had the effect of grouping together as a singular population a diverse range of groups, ignoring the wealth of ethnic, cultural and linguistic diversity of these ten officially recognised highland peoples: the Karen, Hmong,

Mien, Akha, Lisu, Lahu, H'tin, Lu and Khamu. Furthermore, the 'hill' designation also glossed over the extent of interrelationships with valley people as recognised since Leach's groundbreaking research in the 1940s (Leach, 1954; Jonsson, 2005; Toyota, 1998, 2003). As 'hill tribes', highlanders became part of a state discourse as a singular entity that was defined by its distinction from lowland Thai groups. Highland peoples thereby entered both popular Thai consciousness and the attentions of state authorities not as a range of culturally rich additions to the nation but as the 'other' to an emerging Thai national identity. 'Hill tribes', seen as strange, dirty, primitive, could not be more distant from the supposed sophistication of the modern Thai.

Official definitions of 'hill tribes' are exemplified by this following extract from a Department of Public Welfare brief on the Hill Tribe Development and Welfare Program (1964). It is an example that has not dated at all:

> It is estimated that there are between 200,000–300,000 hill peoples living interspersedly in the densely forested hill ranges of Northern Thailand. These people belong to various tribes having their own distinguished languages, cultures, traditions, beliefs etc. Most of them raise and sell opium, practice shifting cultivation and always keep on moving to hunt for new pieces of land for cultivation which have greatly resulted in the forest and watershed destruction. These hill tribes are generally illiterate, have ill health and are economically deprived and could become the victims of [communist] infiltration so easily. These lead to the problems of social economic development, administration and political security of the nation which therefore demand the most urgent solution (Department of Public Welfare, 1964: 1).

In this picture, the 'hill tribes' are identified by their primitiveness, illiteracy, ill health and economic deprivation, and by their destructive agricultural practices, for which they must "always keep on moving". This discourse of the 'hill tribe' subject attributed a single identity to diverse and widespread communities on the basis of a shared 'problem' they presented to the Thai state. By defining highlanders in this way, a homogeneous identity was brought into being that was fundamentally abnormal and, like the development subjects discussed by Escobar (1995), could be treated and reformed through the development process.

The Thai state had a clear interest in representing highlanders in this way. Long-standing prejudices aside, the new discourse of 'hill tribes' made perfect sense in the context of the emerging need to govern the highlands more effectively. Being rendered a singularity had the convenient effect of rendering hill tribes no longer mobile, diverse and complex peoples but a single population that could become the object of policy-making and state-policing. The discourse created, in theory at least, a population that could become a manageable group and the object of special legislation. It created a knowable and at the same time, governable subject, and was part of the state's attempt to make highland societies legible in order to control them (Scott, 1998).

The first efforts to govern highlanders established a pattern that would characterise highland-state relationships for the coming decades. Although the terms 'welfare' and 'development' embedded in the title of the Hill Tribe Development and Welfare Program denoted a rather benign approach, alongside the stated aim of promoting socioeconomic standards the Program's objectives built on negative stereotypes about highlanders and approached them from the outset as being a problem. As stated in 1964, its objectives were:

1. To promote and develop the socio-economic standard of the hill tribes by ways of promoting their occupation, education and health as well as helping develop their own communities.
2. To prevent forest and watershed destruction by way of introducing stabilized farming.
3. To abolish opium production by way of introducing other occupations to replace opium raising.
4. To guarantee the public safety in border provinces by way of promoting mutual understanding and loyalty (Department of Public Welfare 1964).

These objectives held true to popular beliefs about highlanders at the time but were without basis in any extensive or critical research. As anthropologist Saihoo (1963: 15) recognised, and although there was not yet any "complete data or results of specific studies", by 1963 the three interrelated issues of swidden farming, national security and opium were well entrenched as a 'hill tribe problem' that needed to be addressed urgently. Saihoo characterised these three issues (quoted verbatim) as follows:

It is by now generally agreed among persons interested in Thailand hill tribes that they invite careful consideration in three important respects:

1. Their shifting cultivation which involves the destruction of extensive areas of the forests on the mountains and moving the villages in search of new fields with possible consequences of soil erosion and damage to watersheds which would affect the supply of water for the lowland Thai cultivators.
2. Their little recognition of international boundaries and national authority and control with possible consequences of border insecurity, especially in the present world political situations, for the country in which they reside.
3. The production of raw opium of some tribes which supplies the country and the world with an illegal and harmful product in various forms.

No complete data or result of specific studies exist on all these matters, but we believe that these points are based on reliable observations of those who are in well-qualified positions (Saihoo, 1963: 15).

In the absence of hard data, trust was placed in the "reliable observations of those who are in well-qualified positions" (Saihoo, 1963: 15). In practice such knowledge could be traced back to observations by colonial explorers such as Pendleton and Blofield, supplemented by the preliminary results of the first broad social survey in the highlands. The first comprehensive survey was carried out by a UN team led by anthropologist Hans Manndorff (see Manndorff, 1965). The survey itself was not designed to question the basis for the threefold hill tribe problem but to gather data describing the extent of the issues (see further discussion in Chapter Three). On this tenuous basis the 'hill tribe problem' would form the cornerstone of development and research policy from the 1960s and remains a powerful driving force behind much state policy until the present day.

Belief that highlanders posed a serious security threat, supplied narcotics and threatened precious old-growth forests also shaped the development strategies of the international community. From the early 1970s, Thai efforts to address the hill tribe problem would be bolstered by foreign development assistance also focused on issues of opium production, national security and preservation of forests.

Why was the hill tribe problem so compelling despite the absence of any foundation of substantive research? The most plausible explanation has little to do with the welfare of highland peoples. What seems most likely is that there was an accepted geopolitical imperative for Thailand to secure its borders. Development interventions were one conduit towards achieving this while seeming to act in a benign and altruistic way. The core 'problems' for which aid was required coincided with national and international geopolitical concerns of the day. The possibility that highlanders could threaten national security fitted neatly with Cold War paranoia about the 'Red Wave' of communism sweeping through Asia. Concerns with opium production coincided with rising rates of heroin addiction in Western cities and increasing attention being given to finding strategies to limit, if not eliminate, supply (McCoy, 1972). At the same time, there was burgeoning interest in the value of old-growth forests and the need to preserve them. As highland development programs were aimed at addressing all three of these overlapping concerns, few were motivated to find out if the investment of aid money was in fact justified.

The circumstances in which Thailand negotiated the first bilateral highland development programs support this view. International involvement in the drug eradication process in Thailand came out of an international conference on drugs held at UN offices in Geneva in 1958. At the time of the conference, the United States was the sole donor country negotiating with the Thai government to introduce opium eradication programs. In an interview with his replacement as chief advisor to the Tribal Research Centre, anthropologist Bill Geddes gave his account of how negotiations at the conference took place. He reported that under agreement with the United States, Thai representatives at the conference were underreporting opium production figures as part of a strategy to keep other donor countries out of opium eradication efforts in Thailand. In the course of proceedings, however, the Thai contingent rethought this arrangement. Overnight the reported figures for opium production in Thailand increased dramatically, and the Thai delegation was able to recruit international support for crop eradication programs (Geddes, pers. comm. with John McKinnon, July 1987). The process of negotiating development assistance was always more than simply identifying an appropriate way to deal with real problems. For the United States, sole charge of the opium eradication programs could allow unique access on the ground at a time when the border regions were still beyond direct government of the Thai state. Given Thailand's reliance on US aid money, it is hardly surprising that the government was initially supportive. The final decision to negotiate for development assistance with a broad range of international powers, including Germany, the Netherlands, Australia and the United Nations was an astute move to ensure that no single international power gained too much of a foothold in the borderlands.

Conclusion

This chapter has traced the ways in which highland development has been bound up with processes of nation-building and the management of international geopolitics. The introduction of development to the highlands coincided with a belated push to realise a vision of the Thai nation-state in which control would spread from the centre at Bangkok out to the edges of the cartographic line that contained it. As part of this process, the highlands and highland peoples came to be understood in terms of the problems they presented and the need they had for the ministrations of the development industry. Development was thus introduced to the highlands as a tool for transforming remote mountains into accessible Thai territory and making it possible for the state to administer the highland population.

The discourse of the 'hill tribe problem' was a key element in this transition. Through it the highlands were reconstituted negatively in terms of their lawlessness, distance from the state, and damaging otherness to the Thai nation. Constructed as a peripheral and disadvantaged space inhabited by 'dangerous' and 'deficient' subjects, the highlands became the space of 'problems' that could then be 'fixed' through outside intervention. In the process, the highlands became known and governed in new ways, transforming remote and largely ungoverned highland communities into governable spaces and governable subjects. The discourse of the 'hill tribe problem' thus found a place for highlanders within hegemonic discourses of the nation-state. Simultaneously, it worked to continue to locate this new 'hill tribe' subject outside the Thai national body. As problematic and potentially dangerous, hill tribes remained 'the other' to Thai national identity.

By manipulating international geopolitical concerns, the Thai state gained the cooperation of foreign governments in bilateral development programs in the mountains. Tapping into international concerns allowed new spaces of development to be called into being, along with both a problematic hill tribe subject and an international professional subject who would be brought in to find a remedy. These co-dependent subjects — the problem and its remedy — were inevitably constituted on a landscape already shaped by politics, and thus were bound together in processes of governmentality and nation-building.

Highland development efforts were to be characterised by the belief that the highlands were a problematic region and that the interventions of professionals could bring redress. The highlands and highlanders became understood as problematic and in need of aid. The problematic highland subject and the able development professional entered into a co-dependent relationship, each relying on the other. Without a problematic population needing help, the developer had no reason to exist. Without the developer ready to remedy deficiencies, the problematic highlander might not be considered in need at all. In the interrelationship between the two, and the development discourses making possible their mutual existence, a new kind of space emerged in northern Thailand, a space given to development.

4

Experts and Advocates

> Now life has changed everywhere. Today village life is more diffi-
> cult because there is less and less land and the soil has become bad
> [because] now we cannot move anymore…. Government people
> have taken over good land and forest. That's why people in the
> village are not happy because there is less and less work in the
> fields (Deuleu Choopoh in Deuleu and Næss, 1997: 200).

> People with ideals usually quit … the system chews them up or
> spits them out…. Bureaucracy needs as much research atten-
> tion as cancer (Thomas, pers. comm., Sept. 2001).

The modern Thai state saw the highlands and its people as a 'problem'
and treated them accordingly, offering functional remedies rather than
establishing relationships on the basis of mutual respect. The remedies
came in the form of highland development programs staffed by teams
of Thai and foreign development experts who entered the field in the
late 1960s and early 1970s knowing little about highland communities. What they did know was that they had come to help solve the
problems of the highlands. They entered the field believing that they
had come to do good and to make life better for highland peoples.
Within a few years, however, it became apparent to many that addressing the so-called 'hill tribe problem' was not necessarily benefiting
highlanders at all.

By the mid-1970s many professionals were beginning to question whether the 'hill tribe problem' was indeed an appropriate focus
for highland development. My own father was one of these, arriving
to work at the Tribal Research Centre a decade after the first highland
development programs had been established. By then it was apparent
that there were big gaps in the research upon which highland development programs were based. Moreover there was a good deal of

slippage between the geopolitical concerns of the Cold War and the genuine needs and aspirations of mountain communities. My father became part of a cohort of professionals who were beginning to critique development policy and practice and to take a stand on behalf of highlanders who were being marginalised and dispossessed. Bringing contemporary critiques of development and research to bear on their own work, they began to challenge not only the practices of the projects they were involved in but also the basic understandings of highland societies and ecology. As they got to know the highland communities they worked in, this cohort began to question the legitimacy of the 'hill tribe problem'.

These professionals suggested that the development industry and policy-makers needed better knowledge and new modes of intervention that would place highlanders rather than politics at the centre of the process. Many saw a way forward in participatory approaches that placed local community's needs and knowledges at the centre of the development process. Accordingly, these professionals started introducing participatory approaches in their work and struggled to get their colleagues and the bureaucracy of the aid industry behind them.

Perhaps inevitably, these efforts to displace established policy had only limited success. Many of the 'old hands' I interviewed dwelled on stories of failed efforts to create change and registered their deep disappointment. These stories were familiar to me from years of dinner-table conversations over the frustrations of trying to advocate a more people-centred approach to development. However, as I listened more carefully to the stories I was being told in Chiang Mai, another theme emerged. Although professionals were fond of telling disaster stories, in fact time had shown that their efforts had not been entirely wasted. These professionals had laid the foundations for a set of competing discourses about highlanders and begun to facilitate a process through which highlanders would be able to contest the negative stereotypes they had been assigned, thereby creating new opportunities for themselves.

In this chapter I argue that in dealing with early disappointment and failure, this first generation of development professionals began to reconfigure their professional identities and, at the same time, reshape their understandings of highlander identities. In doing so they created new discourses that have shaped highland development ever since. To show what led professionals to challenge the status quo, I begin the chapter with a discussion of the first development programs that were put in place to remedy the 'hill tribe problem' and the ways this discourse of 'problems' started to be challenged by young professionals in the 1970s and 1980s. Through their writings, these professionals acted as public advocates for highlanders at a time when highlanders were less able to speak for themselves. Turning next to ethnographic data from my interviews and observations with professionals working in Chiang Mai in the 1970s and 1980s, I explore how their critical writings and advocacy were based on an understanding of themselves as 'pro-local' subjects with primary duties and responsibilities to highland communities. Finally, I discuss how in the 1980s this sense of responsibility gained official endorsement through a new discourse of participation. I explore the implications through a close examination of the story of one professional and his involvement with the Thai-Australia highland development program. These examples show how professionals who sought to intervene on behalf of highlanders, and to remedy the mistakes and failures of the past, made space for new configurations of professional and local subjects.

Early Remedies for the 'Hill Tribe Problem'

The Thai government's initial efforts to address the 'hill tribe problem' were characterised by a schizophrenic approach in which sometimes heavy-handed policing clashed with efforts to establish friendly relations. In 1955 the Thai Border Patrol Police (BPP) was the first agency to be given the work of securing the highlands. It was formed with the assistance of the United States Central Intelligence Agency and operated as a semi-autonomous unit within the Royal Thai Police. In northern Thailand the BPP's main role was to bring the borderlands within the circle of government surveillance and control. It was assigned the task of patrolling remote hill areas and forging contacts with hill people. In its work with highland communities, the BPP focused on establishing friendly relationships. It was often located in villages and promoted the idea that the people of the hills were under the care and protection of the Thai state and the patronage of the Thai king. It also established schools and distributed medical and agricultural equipment (Manndorff, 1967: 531). Yet, while the BPP was working to extend state power in the hills through these relatively benign interventions, there were also reports of violence and abuse. While some units wooed the population, others used intimidation to ensure highlanders did not infringe state security. It was not unknown for the BPP to shoot dogs and livestock or to rape village women as part of its tactics of intimidation (Suwannarat, pers. comm., Aug. 2001).

The BPP's two-pronged approach would prove to be typical of the Thai government's management of the highlands. Security concerns were spoken of alongside aims to promote socioeconomic development and bring highlanders within the protective embrace of the state. Thus the ongoing process to develop the highlands involved a blend of policing, the establishment of links between state institutions and highland villages, and the introduction of Thai schools and health services.

The first steps taken by the BPP were intended to eliminate any possible threat posed by highlanders and began to establish highlanders as an official presence inside the Thai state. As insiders, highlanders could be distinguished from and used as a defence against a new external threat — the communist insurgent. Bringing villagers under the auspices of the state was a step towards ensuring their loyalty to the Kingdom and lessening the likelihood that they might be recruited by communists.

Within just a few years, the work of fostering loyalty and diminishing any potential threat would be carried out by welfare agencies rather than police forces. The Hill Tribe Development and Welfare Program (hereafter Hill Tribe Welfare Program) of the Department of Public Welfare (DPW) was established in 1959. The BPP continued to operate in the highlands but this new body would take the lead in terms of highland development. The Hill Tribe Welfare Program did, however, continue to focus on the apparent risk of insurgency, as is evident in this excerpt from its 1964 brief:

> The hill tribes do not count themselves as citizens of Thailand, even though they were born and live in the Kingdom of Thailand yet they do not feel that they belong to this country. Loyalty cannot be found in the mind of these hill tribes. They do not have a sense of belonging to any-body nor institution and might become easily the victims of communist aggression ... groups of tribal people always travel crossing the border lines just for a social visit. Nobody can guarantee that these people will not be the communist agent. Any of them might easily be exploited by such agent for the purpose of propaganda (Department of Public Welfare, 1964).

This statement clearly identifies hill tribes as dangerous and suspicious subjects whose lack of a sense of citizenship is in some way their own doing. The hill tribe described here is incapable of loyalty to the Kingdom, dangerously mobile and potentially subversive or revolutionary. With the growing threat of communist insurgency, the ambiguous position of highlanders in relation to the Thai state became precarious. If highlanders were not loyal and pro-Kingdom, they could quite possibly be persuaded to work against it. In terms of the dominant political discourse of the time, this meant assisting communist aggressors.

The unregulated cross-border movement of highlanders was seen as one of the most disturbing features of this population. In the 1960s pioneer swidden communities still periodically relocated in search of new farmland and many communities maintained links across state borders. Encouraging highlanders to relocate to permanent communities was thus one of the first measures taken by the Hill Tribe Welfare Program. Land resettlement projects were established in the same year as the Hill Tribe Welfare Program itself and sought to bring highlanders within the circle of government surveillance and control:

> The primary purpose was to settle hill tribes in locations suited for them, by means of establishing 'settlement areas' (*Nikhom*) on the ridges and high plateaus which are the most favoured sites of the hill peoples, and by encouraging the tribes to migrate to the settlement areas (Manndorff, 1967: 531–2).

Through the land settlements the government hoped to address its most urgent concerns. Creating permanent settlements would reduce the national security risk posed by an ungoverned and mobile population. At the same time, the Nikhom would oversee a transition to new agricultural practices that would ensure ongoing cultivation and eliminate swidden agriculture and opium cultivation. The Nikhom program aimed as much to enable effective governance and surveillance of highland communities as to encourage socio-economic development.

This same blend of objectives characterised the first comprehensive survey of the highlands carried out in 1961 and 1962 under the direction of the Department of Public Welfare. The survey took place with funding and 'expert' assistance from the United Nations in the form of German anthropologist Hans Manndorff. Its aims were to gather population data on highland communities so that the state could begin to develop appropriate policies for the region. As Manndorff noted:

> [It was no longer] possible for the government to leave these ethnic minorities in the hills alone. It is the inevitable logic of events in our time that administration and modernisation is extended even into those remote parts of the country which were traditionally self-sufficient (Manndorff, 1965: 7).

Under a modern state system it had become untenable to allow an unregistered and unregulated population to exist within national borders. The survey was therefore an important step towards extending administration and modernisation into remote parts of the country. Highlanders could no longer be left to manage their communities as they wished.

The results of the survey confirmed that the 'hill tribe problem' of national security, opium and deforestation was indeed a serious matter. This was hardly unexpected because the survey was designed not to investigate whether these were actual problems but to determine their extent. As well as attempting to "give a comprehensive account of the ethnic and socio-economic situation in the hills", the survey "discussed the major problems, including: 1) promoting a more stabilised economy; 2) replacing opium growing by developing new cash crops; and 3) administration and control in the remote hills and frontier regions" (Manndorff, 1967: 534–5). This list of problems was central to both the design of the survey and the recommendations made after its completion.

Following the recommendations of the 1961–62 Department of Public Welfare survey, the state presence in the hills continued to expand. The BPP was strengthened and, after some setbacks, the land settlement projects (Nikhom) were reconfigured as demonstration plots and home bases for newly established Mobile Development Teams:

> Since it would be unrealistic to expect that those tribesmen scattered over the hills would migrate into the sphere of the settlements (or even visit and study their demonstration plots), the hill tribes should be approached in their own villages ... in their own world, in their own physical and social environment (Manndorff, 1967: 537).

Manndorff's research team recognised that highland farming systems and social and political structures actually sustained their villages well. Few were so desperate for a new way of doing things that they would voluntarily resettle at the established Nikhom. The Mobile Development Teams were therefore given the responsibility of trying to persuade highlanders that their current way of life did indeed need to change, but they would allow the process of negotiation to be on highlanders' terms, leaving aside the intimidatory tactics used by some branches of the BPP.

The staff on the Mobile Teams were young, with very little knowledge of highland culture and very little practical experience, which hardly prepared them to transform highland communities and draw them more closely within the embrace of the state. Team members were Public Welfare Department recruits, all lowland Thais who had been employed straight out of tertiary education. The three-member teams consisted of a leader, who had usually completed an undergraduate degree in social science; an agricultural extension worker who had studied at agriculture college; and a sanitary worker with at least three years of high school and hospital training (Chupinit, pers. comm., April 2001). Ajhan Chupinit Kesmanee, a former team leader and now lecturer at Srinakharinwirot University, recalls how going into the mountains in those times was like "going to another country" (Chupinit, pers. comm., April 2001). Most villages could be reached only on foot and teams would often spend weeks at a time walking from village to village. The food was different and so was the language. All this was in stark contrast with the contemporary situation in which most villages have road access, Thai television and a shop selling a range of instant noodles, sweets, Coca-Cola and the ubiquitous Red Bull energy drink (see Plate 3). In this setting, the Teams' practical duties were to promote agricultural systems as alternatives to shifting cultivation and opium crops; to provide a primary health care service; and to provide identification documents such as household registration, birth, death and marriage certificates, as well as travel permits. The presence of the Mobile Teams in this remote and unfamiliar place began a process through which the highlands would become less like 'another country' and more like part of Thailand.

In 1969 King Bhumibol boosted efforts to address the 'hill tribe problem' by establishing the Royal Project Foundation, which aimed to persuade highlanders to abandon opium production and change

Plate 3   Most highland villages now have electricity (Saen Charoen village, 2005)

their farming practices. The involvement of His Majesty in highland development had the important effect of making highland development a serious and respected way of trying to deal with the 'hill tribe problem', especially at a time when it seemed that the military could easily choose to deal with the problem in harsher ways. Nevertheless, the Royal Project was based on the same perception of a problematic highland population. Since 1969 its four central objectives have been:

1. Offer a helping hand to all humankind.
2. Ensure natural resources for conserving a sustainable future.
3. Eradicate opium poppy cultivation and opium derived addiction problems.
4. Encourage a wise and proper balance in utilising and conserving land and forest resources (Royal Project, 1996).

The Royal Project is still in operation and as such is the longest-running highland development program. It has maintained a commitment to "help the hill tribes to help themselves in growing useful crops which enable them to have a better standard of living" (Royal Project, 1996).

The BPP, the Mobile Development Teams and the Royal Project were the first steps in what would become a much more extensive process involving internationally funded bilateral development programs and teams of international researchers. Over the next two decades, the United Nations and the governments of the United States, Australia, New Zealand, the Netherlands and Germany, among others, would establish bilateral development programs in the highlands. Hans Manndorff was only the first of many foreign experts to be called in to assist with managing the highlands.

The Public Welfare Department survey, which Manndorff led, also recommended the establishment of a Research Centre to provide a focal point for research into highland communities and to serve as a permanent advisory institution to the government. The Tribal Research Centre was thus established in 1964 (see further discussion of the TRC in Chapter Three). Support was provided by SEATO in the form of anthropological advisors from Australia, the United States, Britain and New Zealand, and funding for the library and photographic and recording equipment from Britain and the United States (Geddes *et al.*, 1967). The non-Thai anthropologists would provide leadership for the Centre until Thai researchers, apprenticed to the trained anthropologists, received enough training to take over. The Centre was established on the campus of Chiang Mai University and though not formally linked with the University then, it contributed to an emerging community of social researchers. This growing community was expected to contribute to policy, as noted by the Deputy Undersecretary for the Ministry of the Interior in 1967:

> The ideas of the social scientists working in the north of our country can be of vital assistance to our administrators in their search for ways and means of extending government services and administration to the people who live in the less accessible areas of northern provinces (Malai, 1967).

Research was therefore a tool for making the highlands governable and, as Kwanchewan (2006) notes, for dealing with 'hill tribe problems'. Foreign support reflected growing international interest in the 'problems' the Centre was designed to address. It was also an indication that the project of gathering knowledge about the highlands and thereby transforming them from a remote and ungoverned zone into a space occupied by known and controllable communities was a project that required foreign expertise.

Foreign expertise was also required for practical development interventions. The first international development project was the Joint Thai-United Nations Program for Drug Abuse Control that began in 1972. This project was the first of many bilateral programs aimed at finding new cash crops to replace opium and persuading highland farmers to grow them. While replacing the opium crop was often the central focus of these projects, the process of finding alternative cash crops was expected simultaneously to address issues of national security and deforestation. National security would be improved through increased contact between highland communities and state officials, while the introduction of permanent cropping systems would eliminate swidden farming practices and establish permanent settlement. The Thai-German Highland Development Program (TGHDP), the longest running of the bilateral projects, provides a good example of these broad-ranging aims. The TGHDP aimed to accomplish five central objectives:

1. Improvement of subsistence in cash farming practices supporting more sustainable farming systems.
2. Conservation, development and efficient utilisation of the natural resources in the highlands, in particular forest, soil and water.
3. Improvement of social services in the highlands, as well as communications and infrastructures.
4. Furthering the stability and security of highland areas through rural development measures.
5. Facilitation of integration of the highland population into the mainstream of the Thai nation (Dirksen, 1993: 4).

Embedded in these aims were a set of 'abnormalities' that were seen to need attention: the disadvantaged ethnic minority, shifting cultivation, inefficient utilisation of natural resources, opium cultivation, security and stability, integration of the highland population in the Thai mainstream, community stability, sanitation and education, and access to Royal Thai Government support (Brandenberg, 1982).

There was broad consensus across the Department of Public Welfare, United Nations Drug Control Program (UNDCP) and international partners in bilateral highland development programs that these 'hill tribe problems' could be addressed by improving farming methods and replacing opium with alternative cash crops. Improvements meant moving to permanent fields of paddy rice, fruit orchards or cabbages, while simultaneously preventing the destruction of more forests for swidden farming, reducing erosion by moving to more intensive cropping on less steep land, and replacing opium production with 'harmless' crops such as coffee, kidney beans and cabbages. These cash crops did not fit in with the rotations of the swidden agricultural system. As a result, it was expected that, in taking up such permanent crops, highland settlements would also become permanent and people would cease to periodically migrate to new village sites and new fields in the mountains (Geddes, 1967; Manndorff, 1965, 1967; Wanat, 1989). As well as ensuring that no more virgin forest was cleared for fields, permanent settlements would be much easier for state institutions to regulate and administer.

Changes to farming systems and settlement patterns were also intended to produce a reformed hill tribe subject, one who no longer presented a problem to the state. This new subject would practise permanent agriculture, use new technologies to eliminate erosion, preserve and nurture the forest, grow cash crops other than opium and would not use or traffic narcotics. The new highlanders would live in permanent settlements easily accessible by Thai government authorities and headed by a Thai-approved headman and village council, and send their children to Thai schools. Above all this reformed subject would be loyal to the nation and be governed by the state.

Emerging Challenges to the 'Hill Tribe Problem'

While early interventions sought to remedy the 'hill tribe problem', one of the real problems left unacknowledged was that understanding of this 'problem' was based on very little empirical evidence or substantive research. It did not take long before those employed to work on the first highland development programs began to realise the dubious foundation for many aspects of highland development policy. This led to their beginning to challenge the discourse of the 'hill tribe problem' and to question the merit of the intended outcomes of development programs. Together with colleagues working as researchers in the north, this cohort of critical professionals began to look more deeply into the assumptions that lay behind the 'hill tribe problem'.

Plate 4 Peter Hinton and his daughters in Dong Luang, Mae Sariang, 1976 (courtesy of John McKinnon)

Some research was already available to provide a counterpoint to mainstream assumptions about highland people. One important piece of work was the anthropological research conducted by Edmund Leach in the 1940s, which challenged the simple assumption that hill people and valley people were fundamentally different from each other. Leach argued that efforts to describe "distinct 'tribes' distributed about the map in orderly fashion with clear-cut boundaries between them" were "in a sense, ethnographic fictions" (Leach, 1954: 290–1). Leach's discussion of "ethnographic fictions" and his muddying of an accepted narrative of differentiated hill-valley societies has never been widely accepted among social scientists working in the highlands of Thailand. His influence, however, is clear in the work of scholars who questioned the premises for intervention in highland communities. One who took his work seriously was Peter Hinton, an Australian anthropologist and early advisor to the TRC, who argued that policy decisions and research agendas overemphasised differences between 'Thai' and 'hill tribe'. Hinton (pictured in Plate 4), like Leach, argued that "the social realities of the highlands [are] far more subtle, complex, and fluid than any ethnic classifier could ever conceive" (Hinton, 1983: 165).

Similar critiques were raised in subsequent years by other researchers in the north. Many of these alternative views were brought together in a book compiled by my father (then in an advisory position at the TRC) and Wanat Bhruksasri (director of the TRC) (McKinnon and Wanat, 1983). The book was an attempt to establish a counter-discourse to the 'hill tribe problem'. One important contribution was by Yves Conrad (pictured in Plate 5), a French anthropologist who worked with the Lisu. Conrad picked up on Leach's theme of "ethnographic fictions" and Hinton's critique of ethnic boundaries, as well as the increasing attention being given in the discipline to Edward Said's work on the productive power of discourse. Conrad argued that:

> the very enterprise of attempting to differentiate peoples in a systematic way rests on the implicit postulate that they are significantly different from one another. This focus on difference ensures that differences will be found and implies that their relevance should be taken for granted (Conrad, 1989: 192–3).

For Conrad, the delineation of difference produces the reality it seeks to describe. Together with Hinton and others, Conrad was part of a cohort of scholars critical of a discourse of ethnic division and who challenged the validity of an assumption of difference that was basic to the formulation of highland policy.[1] They argued that such misconceptions subjected highlanders to "the increasing suspicion, dislocation and alienation which accompany structural assimilation as a policy by default" (McKinnon, 1989: 350).

An emerging critique of the ethnographic 'truth' of a distinct hill tribe entity developed alongside increasingly strong criticism of the perceived 'problems' that shaped the policies of the Department of Public Welfare towards the highlands. In his 1969 report to the Department, Hinton (1969: 4) argued that "issues which have previously been regarded as crucial, such as 'the hill tribe problem', the welfare of impoverished tribesmen, the suppression of opium cultivation, the preservation of forests and watershed from swidden cultivators", were based on inaccurate assessments of the real issues faced

---

[1] See, for example, Jonsson (1998, 2000a), Kampe (1992, 1997a, 1997b), Kampe and McCaskill (1997), Kunstadter and Chapman (1978), McKinnon (1992), McKinnon and Vienne (1989), Sturgeon (1997) and Tapp (1989, 2003).

Plate 5   Yves Conrad
with Lisu children, c. 1987
(courtesy of John McKinnon)

by highlanders. With regard to opium, Hinton claimed that 90 per cent of opium passing through the Kingdom actually came from elsewhere and thus was not a problem of the highlands at all. Hinton also claimed that the environmental risk of swidden farming had been much exaggerated. His assertion was backed up by other researchers who argued that swidden farming was in fact "a *stabilised* system of agriculture" (Miles, 1967: 93; emphasis in original), which seldom encroached on virgin forest and was not a cause of erosion, soil degradation, siltation of waterways and the loss of Thailand's watershed forests (Grandstaff, 1980).

As professionals began to question the assumptions behind the discourse of the 'hill tribe problem', they also started to speak of their own responsibility to focus on issues of importance to highlanders themselves. They reframed the issue of narcotics and deforestation "not as 'the hill tribe problem' or even as the problems of the hill tribes but rather as the problems of the entire nation which can only be solved by highlanders and lowlanders in cooperation" (Kammerer, 1989: 289–90).

Through their critique of the stereotypical hill tribe subject and associated 'problems', this cohort of professionals working in the 1970s and 1980s sought to overturn inaccurate assumptions based on inadequate knowledge and understanding. In their work, a critical professional subject emerges whose role is to question accepted knowledge and approaches, to challenge "established wisdom" and "provide alternatives to current practices" (McKinnon and Vienne, 1989: xxvii, xxv). The motivation for mounting such a challenge had much to do with a perceived injustice in the treatment many highlanders were receiving.

Only a handful of professionals, however, published their concerns about apparent injustices (Kammerer, 1988, 1989; Kampe, 1992; and McKinnon, 1989 were particularly direct in speaking about the situation as unjust). Those who did voice direct criticism were invariably in a privileged position as outsiders. Although many Thais were involved in professional development and research work in the hills, few were able to publicly criticise the beliefs that were driving government policy. In the 1970s there were few Thais with a graduate education in social sciences who could make such radical claims. Until the early 1990s, when political reform allowed for greater public debate, any Thai who voiced public criticism of state practices could be putting him/herself and his/her family at risk. Rather than publishing their critiques, Thai professionals who held similar views often preferred to work quietly within their institutions and government departments to bring about change. Some like Ajhan Chupinit, who began his work in the mountains as a member of the Mobile Development Teams, would later become active and outspoken advocates for highlanders.

Through both the vocal critique of those in a position to speak out and the quiet advocacy of Thai colleagues, a critical professional subject took shape in the north. This professional rejected accepted truths about the highlands and instead sought to create more accurate knowledge and develop more effective ways to work for the people. These professionals sought a way past the injustices of existing policy by pursuing a critical perspective that they believed could access a truer picture of the highlands, and thus find a better path forward.

The New Pro-local Professional

As criticisms of the status quo took shape, what emerged in the north was a new kind of professional subject that drew on discourses of participatory research and development methods informed by the ethical debates of the 1970s. Scholars who had arrived in northern Thailand around the late 1960s, such as Douglas Miles, Peter Kunstadter and Peter Hinton, had either directly or indirectly been implicated in the scandal of unethical practice surrounding the Thailand Controversy (see Chapter Two). As such, they and their colleagues were acutely aware of ethical codes such as the American Anthropological Association Code of Ethics, a code that became formalised in the aftermath of the controversy and in which the responsibility of the researcher to the researched was held to be paramount. In the late 1970s and early 1980s, a parallel discourse of ethical responsibility began to gain prominence in mainstream development discourses under the rubric of participation.

The idea of participatory practices was nothing new but by the early 1980s participation had begun to be associated with formal 'tool kits' disseminated through an increasing number of manuals of participatory development practice. Work done in Thailand on Rapid Rural Appraisal was an important part of this movement (Grandstaff and Grandstaff, 1987 [1985]). It was the work of Robert Chambers, however, that really captured the attention of development professionals worldwide. He developed the method that continues to be the cornerstone of community development practice, namely Participatory Rural Appraisal (PRA). Chambers (1983) argued that it is the duty of development professionals to witness the extent of rural poverty and change it by understanding the poor and putting their needs and priorities first. Doing this, he argued, requires working against biases embedded within development institutions and challenging accepted practices. The moral imperative to act for the poor, and the tools and techniques professionals should use, were codified in countless PRA manuals. This became a powerful movement, informing research methods through participatory action research[2]

---

[2] Action research is a social research method that is intended to enact change in the commmunity being researched and often engages community members as co-researchers. For some good examples of action research see Attwood and Gaventa (1997), Berardi (2002), Gibson and Cameron (2001), Gladwin and Peterson (2002), Krimerman (2000), Martin and Sherington (1997) and Stoecker (1999).

inspiring dozens of manuals as PRA 'tool kits' for development professionals to use in the field[3] and is now the cornerstone of Participatory Learning and Action (PLA), an umbrella term for a range of participatory development methods.

In the early 2000s, participation was a topic that came up again and again in my conversations with professionals in the field. An important component of these conversations — especially with those who had arrived in Thailand in the 1970s and 1980s — was the sense of a moral imperative to work for the people and the need to struggle against entrenched perspectives and practices in the development industry. In my interviews with these senior professionals, I asked them to remember what it had been like to work in the highlands when they first began working there, and how things had changed over the years. I asked them about how they first came to northern Thailand, how they remembered the work they did then and the methods they used at the time. These early days were remembered as a problematic time, in sharp contrast to the kind of work done now. Prompted by my questions, many of my interviewees told stories that invoked a sense of a battle between themselves and 'the system'. They described a process of trying to combat the failures of development programs — both the failures to meet program objectives and the failures to work in the best interests of the people.

This sense of having to battle against 'the system' was most clearly articulated in my conversations with David Thomas, an experienced development worker who had been involved in development programs in northern Thailand since the 1970s (see also Dialogues, p. 196). David was one of a handful of community development professionals who arrived in Chiang Mai after having fought for the United States in the Vietnam War. These professionals had for various reasons remained in Thailand but shared a certain rejection of their American origins and a desire to work for the people in remote and poor highland villages.

I first met David at a workshop held by the Uplands Program on "Participatory Technology Development". It was an opportunity for many of the 'old guard' to gather together again and reminisce on what Chiang Mai used to be like in the 1970s and 1980s, on how greatly the city had changed while the issues and challenges for

---

[3] For some good examples of the PRA 'tool kit', see Davis-Case (1989), de Negri *et al.* (1998a, 1998b), Goldman and Abbot (2004) and Pretty *et al.* (1995).

development practitioners had remained much the same. My father introduced me to David at the welcoming event on the first day. The conference was held in Mae Sa valley, a narrow valley about 40 minutes' drive away from Chiang Mai that used to be farmland. While a few villages remained, in recent years the land had slowly been taken over by resorts, elite international schools and luxurious conference centres. The manicured and well-irrigated gardens seemed incongruous with the focus of the conference on village-level participatory work. This incongruity was a starting point for discussion.

I spoke further with David at a later date. In my second interview, I asked him questions about how he had first come to Chiang Mai and why he had become involved in development work. For him, as for others among his contemporaries, the move to Thailand was made possible in part through his participation in the Vietnam War. Drafted into the US Army, David had become a soldier on the front line. During our informal conversation at the conference he had spoken of how that experience made him never want to return to the United States and had influenced him to find ways to stay in Thailand and do something more positive. I asked David to reflect on the course of his career in the north and the shifting policies and approaches of development agencies. He spoke with passion against the "patronising attitudes" of an old top-down style of project management that conceived of villagers as "ignorant" and needing education. This is what is different in participatory work — "the respect for the fact that this is their place, and must be about their decisions" (Thomas, pers. comm., Sept. 2001). He was very sceptical of the success of a participatory approach in transforming institutionalised interventions in the mountains. David observed that, while individual practitioners had learned much over the years, the problem was how to translate this into an institutional setting, how to bring change to 'the system':

> People with ideals usually quit…. The system chews them up or
> spits them out…. Bureaucracy needs as much research attention
> as cancer (Thomas, pers. comm., Sept. 2001).

David implied that people are 'chewed up by the system' when they fall back into the role of the 'expert', that is, somebody who thinks that he/she knows how to fix a situation of underdevelopment and disadvantage. In his view, it is much better for professionals to act as someone who will help local communities to find their own solutions to their problems. Nevertheless, he observed that in order for development professionals to continue to find work, they must continue to be represented as 'the expert':

> The term 'lesser developed countries' is a classic. Professional people wherever, for them it is a career. Without someone to patronise, they are out of a career (Thomas, pers. comm., Sept. 2001).

In my conversations with David, a sense of professional integrity was identified through the ongoing need to struggle against the demands of 'the system' for professionals to be 'experts'. By 'the system', he was referring to the operations of the mainstream development industry, one that demands quarterly reporting on project aims and objectives, hires specialist consultants, and is ruled by the funding cycle. In this system there is little room for flexible programs shaped around community rhythms and relationships, where objectives might need to shift, spending patterns might not be predictable, and outside consultants are not the central decision-makers. Many of those I interviewed recalled their battles with this system as they tried to make room for local knowledge, priorities and decision-making in the early highland development programs. They represented their efforts as a battle against the top-down development styles in order to work with and for the people. Through these struggles, professionals like David started to form their own identities around a particular set of ideals. They rejected patronising, top-down practices and approaches in order to become a more ethical and effective professional subject.

The question of effectiveness is just as important as the sense of a pro-local ethical responsibility. Not only were participatory approaches supposed to entail a greater respect for communities and give greater power to those at whom development programs were targeted; they also become popular because they were supposed to be much more effective. This belief was evident in the many stories I heard about the failures of early bilateral programs, whose less ethical and effective approaches contrasted with a contemporary sense of ethical and effective practice based on a pro-local participatory approach.

Participatory Solutions: New Methods, New Subjects

The early bilateral programs are perceived to have failed in a number of ways in their first years of operation. Among the examples most often discussed by my informants in Chiang Mai were those which had sought to introduce inappropriate innovations in agricultural systems or failed to educate villagers on how to care for the new crops introduced by the program. One example of this was the Thai-Australia program's first attempt to introduce coffee. Coffee was considered an appropriate crop for the soil type and climate of the highlands and has since become a successful cash crop for some communities. The program's first attempt to introduce coffee, however, was not so successful. A certain amount had been allocated in the annual budget for the purchase and distribution of coffee seedlings (Hoare, pers. comm., March 2001). The coffee was distributed as planned without consulting farmers on whether they might want to plant the trees on their land or any training on how to tend to them. The result was that most of the trees sat where they had been put, in the bags in which they had been delivered, until they died several months later.

The Thai-Australia program was not the only bilateral program to make such mistakes. Many of the first attempts to introduce opium replacement crops were disastrous: local anecdotes report that the first kidney bean harvests had to be delivered by helicopter because no one had appreciated the lack of road access. The harvest then sat in a warehouse in Chiang Mai because there was no market for the crop. Observers elsewhere reported driving past piles of cabbages left to rot by the side of mountain roads. The programs were also thought to have had little actual impact on reducing opium production. Cropping did not cease until much harsher measures were introduced, when the Thai military set about burning poppy fields before the opium could be harvested (Renard, 2001). In addition to these kinds of technical failures, the programs have been accused of causing serious harm to highland communities as a whole. The bilateral programs have been connected with processes through which hill people were forced out of their homes to make way for national parks, forest reserves or resorts, and have been accused of contributing to the loss of traditional cultural practices and knowledge.

Ironically, the bilateral programs may even have contributed to the spread of heroin in the hills. Chupinit and Gebert (1993), for example, in a report to the TGHDP on drug abuse in project villages suggested that project interventions themselves may have contributed to escalating addiction rates. Addiction was particularly evident in villages where traditional leadership structures had been replaced by

Thai-speaking leaders who were approved by the Thai government and performed the role of liason between the village and the state. These were often younger men and in some communities had entirely usurped the role of a traditional village council of elders. It appeared that the breakdown of traditional leadership structures by the project was linked to social disintegration and, in turn, rising levels of drug abuse.

The most clearly recognised failures at the early stage were episodes like the Thai-Australia program's unsuccessful attempt to introduce coffee. These were failures in technology transfer and were easily identified as problems because they absorbed a large part of project funds and the time of personnel. In an attempt to avoid further failures, participatory approaches were then adopted by nearly every bilateral highland development project. The Thai-Australia program was no exception. Peter Hoare, who worked on the Thai-Australia programs in the 1970s and 1980s, claims that in the early 1980s the program was one of the first to bring in participatory planning on a large scale, introducing it across at least six project villages (Hoare, pers. comm., March 2001).

The Thai-Australia program first got underway in 1972 with the Thai-Australia Highland Agronomy Project (TAHAP). The objectives of TAHAP included developing "an agricultural extension methodology which will be effective among the hill tribe people" (TAHAP, 1979: 2). In 1981 TAHAP was replaced with the Thai-Australia Highland Agricultural and Social Development Project (TA-HASD). HASD had four main development components: agricultural development, social and community development, institutional development, and management and information. Its overall goals were "to generate sustainable improvements in the environmental, social and economic welfare of highland people in Northern Thailand" (Bull, 1993: 9).

HASD adopted a participatory approach with the 'problem census' method (Hoare, pers. comm., 2001; also Hoare, 1986). The problem census involved a long period of discussion and consultation between project staff and village people. Meetings would be held in the evenings with men and women from the village to talk through and prioritise the needs and desires of the community and identify key problems that ought to be addressed. Further meetings were then held to discuss problems that lay within the realm of project capabilities and negotiate solutions that could be implemented with the help of the project. Extension officers would run the meetings and were meant to facilitate discussion rather than try to direct the community towards any predetermined outcomes. Nonetheless, the starting point for their approach was to persuade farmers to change their practices by helping them to recognise certain issues as problems that intervening projects could help them to solve.

This contradiction reflected the origins of the problem census tool that was developed to enable more successful interventions to improve farming practices. The problem census approach acknowledged that traditional agricultural extension, which assumed that the extension officer had all the knowledge and all the answers, was not having much success in changing farming practices. Originally developed in Papua New Guinea by University of Queensland professors, Joan Tully and Bruce Crouch, it was developed as a method for technology transfer in agricultural extension work (Crouch, 1984; Tully, 1966).

Tully focused on how information about new agricultural practices spread through farming communities and was able to show that farmers made rational decisions within their own meaningful social context. She argued that information provided by agricultural extension workers did not always match the needs and priorities of farmers. Farmers made use of new technologies and information only when it was clear that new technologies were relevant, could be utilised within their existing resources, or provided a means to further prioritise goals (Tully, 1966: 402). She argued that project 'beneficiaries' were embedded in communities and social networks "with their own value systems and norms, and sanctions to enforce them" (Tully, 1966: 402). The problem census narrative thus constructed a 'beneficiary' subject who thought through decisions on the basis of local knowledge and understanding, and through the multiple roles and responsibilities they held within local social networks.

Tully's work in the 1960s marked an important shift towards recognising that extension work needed to start with farmers' own perceptions and needs. It was the beginning of a movement away from thinking of the professional as the expert, always able to access better knowledge, and towards a concept of valuing local knowledge. Later innovations developed this emphasis on farmers as the starting point and developed the problem census approach based on the assertion that "it is more efficient, and sociologically more meaningful, to use the natural (informal) groups that exist within the village community to collectively identify problems and to decide on what should be done about them" (Crouch, 1984: 7). This shift to a concern for locally guided intervention took place alongside an increasingly influential discourse of participatory development that was emerging internationally as the work of those such as Robert Chambers (1983) gained popularity.

Through a discourse of participation and the introduction of tools like the problem census, both professional and highland subjects began to be recast in the development spaces of the highlands. By the early 1980s when the Thai-Australia project began using the problem census, the approach was not just about improving the rate of adoption of agricultural innovations but about designing projects in partnership with farmers. Farmers were thus being asked to take on a different role in development — becoming partners in a shared effort to institute projects that would best suit their needs and priorities. The problem census had been transformed from a method for technology transfer, in which the agriculture extension officer still possessed the best knowledge, to a method of participatory development, in which the knowledge of the farmers was also respected. This transformation was important but had its limitations. The problem census was still governed by the central aim of finding more effective ways to promote more productive farming practices. It still conceptualised a highland subject as a "project beneficiary" (in Tully's terms), but highlanders were also being recast as *partners* in planning rather than as mere recipients of an already defined 'treatment'.

The person assigned the responsibility for making sure the planning process resulted in benefits and improvements to the 'beneficiaries' was still a trained professional, armed with the tool of the census. Although working as facilitators, the problem census professionals still occupied the role of 'expert', albeit one trained in the techniques of the problem census, of effective participatory planning rather than in the details of agricultural practices. This participatory professional subject would help highlanders to recognise 'problems' and think about 'solutions'. This expertise was no longer specialist technical knowledge or the wisdom of the developed world but the ability to draw out local knowledge and understanding. The participatory professional acquired a new expertise of working as a partner in a development process closely tailored to the problems and priorities defined by the local community.

As bilateral projects relied increasingly on participatory approaches, the individual professional became recognised in project documents as the key to success. In project documents, the professionals themselves are largely invisible as independent decision-makers beneath the umbrella of generalised aims, objectives and methods. It is 'the project', 'project staff' or 'advisors' rather than named individuals who act to achieve the aims and objectives of the project. Yet, within a discourse of participation, it is these unnamed professionals upon whom success depends. They are the "outsiders" of Chambers (1997), the "revolutionary leaders" of Freire (1970), the "educators" of Yen (Buck 1945), the "developers with a deep sense of mission" of Mayfield (1985). At the completion seminar for the Thai-Australia program, which in 1993 presented the successes and failures of the program and outlined the lessons learned, the dedicated and participatory professional was identified as the vital component in project success:

> The success of any participatory approach is totally dependent upon the dedication, interests and motivation of the staff involved. Staff must forego the widely held perception of the dictatorial role of government offices and start to work WITH villagers. Not all staff can make this change, wish to live and work extensively in the villages or are supported and encouraged to make these changes by senior or supervising staff. In addition living conditions in the villages are usually difficult for non-Hill Tribe people, salaries and per diems are minimal and promotion does not necessarily flow from achievements at the village level (Bull, 1993: 183; emphasis in original).

The professional who is capable of working with villagers was here represented as a rare creature: a subject who must be tough, motivated and dedicated. As shown above, it was the professional subject's toughness and dedication upon which success depends.

A New Participatory Orthodoxy

As the idea that professionals were 'doing good' began to be challenged and signs of project failures became clear, the discourse of participation located exactly why things were going wrong: failures could be explained by the flaws of a top-down development approach. At a discursive level, locating the problem allowed renewed faith in ideas of intervention and improvement — it was not the whole project of improvement that was problematic, just the way it was done. A discourse of participation allowed professionals to reject old, ineffective and potentially harmful top-down methods in favour of a grassroots approach that would achieve the positive transformations they hoped for.

Participation thereby emerged as *the* approach that professionals should use if they hoped to be successful and the means through which development intervention could continue to be regarded as positive. Participatory approaches came to be seen as the only way for projects to overcome early failures and succeed in attaining the objectives of improved livelihoods and empowerment in the highlands. Furthermore, it was not just the tools that were seen as the key to success but people and relationships. The new subjects envisaged by a discourse of participation — the participatory professional and the knowledgeable local partner — have displaced the idea that technological innovation or expert knowledge are the keys to a successful project. The new orthodoxy was most visible in the stories of failure recounted by professionals in the Chiang Mai community. These narratives blamed project failures or shortcomings on a lack of true participation and the absence of the dedicated participatory professional who would make sure interventions were appropriate and effective. To illustrate this, I turn to an example that I came across often in my interviews with senior professionals: the Australian grass strips.

Among the stories of project disasters that still circulate among Chiang Mai professionals, one came up repeatedly. This was the story of the Thai-Australia project's failed attempt to introduce an erosion control measure known colloquially as 'grass stripping'. HASD's agricultural development objectives were to "improve food production, increase cash generation and progressively replace slash-and-burn with permanent farming systems based on preserving soil fertility and minimising soil erosion" (Bull, 1993: 11–12). Because fertility in mountain soils is quickly depleted, the traditional method for dealing with the problem had been to leave the fields fallow for long periods to allow the forest to regenerate and soils to regain nutrients. Pressure on highland resources, along with outlawing of the swidden farming methods, put pressure on highland farmers to find alternative production methods. The grass strips were intended to maintain soil fertility and reduce erosion in highland fields. Grass was planted in narrow strips along the contour lines across rain-fed highland fields of dry rice, legumes or corn. In theory the strips would act as a barrier to run-off and help to fix nutrients in the soil, allowing continuous farming with sustained yields.

Things did not work out as planned. All the accounts of this programme shared a tendency to attribute failure to a lack of participation and the inability of the Australian professionals to recognise in the 'project beneficiary' a knowing subject and planning partner. The most compelling account came from Peter Hoare who was forced out of his job due to his objections to the planning procedures behind the grass strips.

Peter had worked with the Thai-Australia program in its early incarnation as TAHAP. He was a team leader for project components such as baseline surveys of highland farming systems, developing a highland agricultural credit program, investigating opportunities for paddy development and contributing to the highland extension manual. Peter was also brought on board as an agricultural extension officer for HASD. Alongside this professional role, he undertook research for a Masters thesis on rural development methodologies with the Department of Agriculture at the University of Queensland (Hoare, 1986). In 2001 I spoke often with Peter about his experiences of highland development and travelled with him to villages that in the 1980s had been part of the Thai-Australia program.

We drove north out of Chiang Mai on the highway that traces the western side of the valley. As the hills began to close in, we turned west into the mountains, winding our way up steep narrow roads in Peter's four-wheel drive vehicle, while he interpreted the development history of the landscape on the way. We spent the day catching up on changes in the area and chatting with old acquaintances. As we began our descent back down to the valley, Peter began to tell the story of how the Thai-Australia project had introduced grass strips as a method of erosion control in this area. The erosion problem had been a focus of discussion from the initial planning meetings in project communities. The project's suggested solution was to put in bench terraces. An entire year was spent working with project communities to discuss the introduction of bench terracing and agree upon the assistance that the project would give to those farmers who chose to test it out on their land.

At the end of the year, when the consultation was complete and plans in place to go ahead with bench terracing, the project staff held an internal meeting to discuss how the budget would be allocated for the coming year and to finalise the amount that would go into the extension plans that had emerged through community planning meetings. At this meeting, the project agronomists announced that they had decided the project was not going to introduce bench terracing after all. Instead they wanted to deal with erosion issues by introducing grass strips, planted along contour lines at intervals through upland fields. The grass strip method had been used before by the Thai-German program with some success and the agronomists were keen to try it out using an Australian species of grass that could also be used as livestock fodder.

As one of the extension officers who had just spent the previous year working with project communities to devise a plan around bench terracing, Peter stood up and said, "Well, if that's what you want to do then we need to go back to the villages and check it out with them first and find out if they are happy with that or not. If they're not happy then we might have to rethink our approach" (Hoare, pers. comm., March 2001). Peter left Chiang Mai the following day for a three-week trip. When he returned he was met at the airport by the Australian accountant of the project with a letter telling him that his services were no longer required. The reason given for his dismissal was that he had publicly criticised the project, the 'public' being all the project staff present at the meeting. After his departure from the project, the grass strips project went ahead with disastrous results. While the type of grass had been chosen because it could double as fodder for stock, the stock refused to eat it. Even worse, the grass was impossible to manage. It spread beyond the strips and took over entire fields, rendering the land useless for cropping. Nothing that farmers did seemed to get rid of it.

An Australian species of grass taking over highland fields and rendering them completely unproductive remains a popular metaphor for the worst failures of development. It circulated in the development community of Chiang Mai as a cautionary tale about what happens when programs fail to engage true participation. The problem census method was introduced in the Thai-Australia project in order to achieve more effective intervention, which would lead to a better life for the farmers. Participatory methods were supposed to get more farmers to adopt extension technologies as well as ensure that extension work was more suited to the target community (Hoare, pers. comm., March 2001). The method should have prevented a situation whereby a decision to change from bench terraces to grass strips would be made without consultation and cooperative decision-making, and with potentially detrimental results.

When I asked Peter to explain how things had gone astray, he replied that he thought the agronomists working on the project did not understand the point of the participatory approach. He underlined his point with another story of a conflict over the extent to which farmers should be included in a decision-making process. Looking out the window at the passing fields, Peter pointed out how the lychee trees were planted in the valley and the annual rotational crop, such as rice and legumes, were planted on the hillsides. He said his old agronomist colleague would look at that crop pattern and say that the farmers were doing it all wrong: tree crops should go on the hills where they promoted soil stability and annual crops in the valleys. The farmers, however, have good reason to follow their own system: lychee is their main cash crop and planting it in the more fertile soil of the valley will yield better-quality fruit. Peter remembered a time when one of the farmers he was working with had started to plant lychee trees in the valley. The agronomist spotted it and stormed up to Peter saying, "Why did you let that farmer do that?" Peter shook his head and laughed at the memory. "It's the farmer's decision what to plant where on his own land" (Hoare, pers. comm., March 2001).

Peter and the agronomist's disagreements over how to manage the participation and decision-making of the highland farmers had its roots in conflicting notions of what participation is and what it is supposed to achieve. Both, in their own way, were seeking the outcome they thought best for the farmer. For one it was the success of anti-erosion measures; for the other it was empowering local decision-making. Through their conflict, each was calling on a different kind of professional identity. As Peter recalled, the agronomist's question of "Why did you let the farmer do that?" evoked a highland subject who needed the expert assistance of a trained agronomist as he was not capable of making the best decision and did not have the right to make the decision about what happened to his own land. In this story the agronomist, as the trained expert with specialised knowledge, was the 'expert' professional subject. As such, it was his knowledge, not the farmer's, that would have the best outcome for the farmer. Opposed to this was Peter, who embodied the participatory professional subject for whom the highlander was the respected and knowledgeable other. This highland subject was not a deficient subject in need of 'treatment' or expert assistance but was instead a rational subject with proprietary rights that entitled him or her to make decisions about his or her own land. In Peter's clash with the agronomist, it became evident that each man's understanding of participation was very different even though they were working on the same project and, ultimately, for the same goals and objectives.

Among the professionals who were my informants, similar stories were told in ways that invoked a moral imperative for professionals to work in 'truly' participatory ways. In Peter's telling, the problem was that the HASD agronomist lacked a proper understanding of participation. Proper participation was represented as the key to ensuring interventions did not result in harm. Doing true participation meant being the anti-establishment professional, working against the system, and focusing on being a facilitator for the people.

While the story of the grass strips is often told as a cautionary tale, the ending of the story is not widely known. On the same day that I travelled with Peter up to some of the fields where the Australian grass had gone rampant, I discovered that the effects of the project's intervention had not been all detrimental. The reflection on the saga by the farmers Peter and I met told a different story — one of the adaptability and resilience of local communities to the mistakes of professional intervention.

One of our stops was in Huay Tatd village, where we were invited to share a cup of tea with Khun Djabu, who had worked with Peter many years ago at one of the first agricultural research sites established under Thai and Australian cooperation. As we sat sipping his Oolong tea, Djabu brought up the issue of the grass strips. Saying little of the impact of the original grass introduced by HASD, he spoke about how the old grass was no longer being used. Instead a different variety, one given to them by the Royal Project, was being planted. He also said that the grass strips allowed people in the village to farm their fields continuously. They would plant rice one year, red beans the next, and so on. When we left, Peter and I drove away from Huay Tatd skirting around fields in which we could see Royal Project grass planted in neat strips along the contours of the hill (see Plate 6).

Our last stop on the way down into the valley was at a village that had been established 17 years ago as a satellite to Huay Tatd. We had stepped out of the car for less than a minute when a woman who had approached us exclaimed, "It's Ajhan Peter!" Again we were

Plate 6   Mae Taman grass strips, 2001

invited in and ended up once more discussing the grass strips. The man in this household said that they had grown the Australian grass but it had been impossible. It grew very tall and spilled over the strips, becoming a weed that spread over the whole field. "It was good as cattle feed though," he remembered. Now, like his neighbours, he had started using a different variety of grass in the same strip formation. He did not say that the variety they had planted was from the Royal Project — in fact he said there were no Royal Project activities in this village — but the strips meant they could also farm the fields continuously, alternating between rice and legumes without a drop in productivity.

The idea of grass strips itself had been brought to these farmers by the agronomists on the Australian project. Even though the idea had been poorly conceived and badly implemented, once modified, the grass strips ended up doing what they were intended to do, that is, retaining the fertility of the soil and allowing farmers to farm continuously on their highland plots. As a story about subjects, this postscript to a disaster is the story of a capable, adaptive and self-sufficient highland subject who was clearly able to make the most of a good idea and who did not need professional intervention to raise awareness, educate or persuade.

Stories of success in highland development programs are often stories of highlanders being treated as capable and knowledgeable partners rather than problematic and in need of education or persuasion. Peter, for example, spoke of a recent project in Nan Province that had succeeded in persuading the Royal Forest Department to respect and subsequently adopt village environmental management systems. At issue was the risk of fire damage to forested areas. Over many months of meetings between project staff and village representatives, the staff began to understand that each of the villages already had fire management strategies in place. They then worked to record and formalise village management strategies and negotiated with the Royal Forest Department to give these strategies formal recognition. The final product was a document entitled "Village Watershed Network Rules and Regulations", which included detailed guidelines and an agreed system of fines that now apply at the district government level. Peter discussed this success with evident pleasure and pride. Compiling community management strategies that clearly originated in and were owned by the villagers themselves was seen as an achievement. Even more so was the success in obtaining formal recognition of the strategy from the Royal Forest Department (RFD):

> One of the most satisfying results of the project to me was to observe the changes in RFD watershed management chiefs who at the beginning of the project were using 'top down planning and implementation' … [but by the end of the project] were saying to me, "Of course we have to work with the village people if we want to have effective fire management (Hoare, pers. comm., Nov. 2006).

Peter's pride in the project came from shifting the focus of RFD from an agenda of limiting and controlling village activity to a sense of partnership and a greater respect for village skills and knowledge.

Peter's stories of negotiating with the Royal Forest Department for the adoption of village fire management strategies invoked the theme of the moral, pro-local professional battling against the system. In this hopeful narrative, the practice of participatory approaches — in this case in an agricultural development context — could bring into being the participatory professional subject, as well as that subject's other, the knowledgeable, respected, decision-making highlander.

Through the practice of participation, particular relationships between project staff, villagers and Royal Forest Department officials were nurtured and opportunities created for a certain set of decisions to become possible. Project staff were able to put themselves in the role of facilitators, guiding negotiations between villages, as well as between villages and the Royal Forest Department. The expertise they brought to the project was mainly in how to facilitate a participatory process rather than seeking to educate the farmers or persuade them to adopt new technologies. In this example it was the Forest Department personnel who were educated. As a result, the project saw a reversal of the norm in which regulations decided by the state are imposed on villages. In this case, a set of governing practices decided upon at the village level also came to be adopted by a branch of the state, one especially powerful in the highlands of the north.

Conclusion

Taken at face value, the story of Peter's success with the fire management project in Nan Province is an example of how to carry out participation well and of what kind of professional conduct is necessary. Yet the significance of this story, and the other narratives of failure and success recounted in this chapter, does not lie with the lessons they may impart on how to do development. Rather they are significant for how they track the emergence of a new ideal of professionalism that has since become *the* ideal against which the success of development practice is measured, at least by the group of professionals I encountered in northern Thailand. This ideal emerged out of disillusionment with existing knowledge and practice and was meant to supply a remedy, not for the hill tribe problem but for the ills of the development industry. First the 'hill tribe problem' which underpinned highland development programs was severely challenged. At the same time, the early failures of bilateral programs and the emergence of a discourse of participation led to the problematisation of top-down approaches and a search for alternatives. In these complementary critiques, new kinds of professional subjects emerged: the critical subject, who is a remedy for inaccurate assumptions and inadequate knowledge, has a better grasp of reality and points the way to alternative approaches and deeper understanding; the battling subject, who offers a critical reassessment, works against the rigid and unmalleable system; the professional who mobilises the people and works against the colonising forces of the state; and the participatory professional, who is in partnership with local communities and acts as a facilitator and guide in a mutual process of decision-making. Alongside these multiple (mythical) professional subjects are multiple (equally mythical) 'hill tribe' subjects, whose transformation from a deficient, underdeveloped and problematic subject to a knowledgeable partner or equal participant has also been an essential process in the reconfiguration of the professional.

Through stories like that of the grass strips, these subjects, and their embattled origins, continue to be remembered by this group of professionals in Chiang Mai. A participatory professional subject is identified in and through a discourse of its contrast with the past, a past marked by blunders and failures. The participatory ideal to which Peter Hoare and David Thomas refer, brings into being a certain kind of professional subject, defined by its distinction from, and opposition to, top-down approaches. For these professionals, a top-down approach is equated with development interventions that seldom helped but often harmed; approaches that allowed — if not fostered — complicity with the aggressive policies of the state; research that can now be read as theft of indigenous knowledge; and development that acted as an instrument of colonisation. Being the participatory professional subject then is to identify with a certain sense of due process, the democratic idea of everyman's right to speak, and the right of 'the other' to take part in making decisions and formulating representations of themselves. The participatory subjects that emerge are nevertheless subjects who continue to be formed in relation to a founding myth of improvement, of doing good for the impoverished other.

5

New Discourses, New Subjects

We cannot use the paradigms thought of by foreigners (*farang*).[1]

Much has changed in the highlands since the 1980s. While high-landers are still among the poorest and most marginalised of Thailand's residents, decades of development work have brought some benefits. In his review of the opium crop replacement programs in northern Thailand, historian Ronald Renard (2001) sets out how little high-landers gained as a result of such programs. Towards the end of his book, however, he concludes that the advocacy role played by many of these professionals was one of their most important contributions to the well-being of highlanders :

> In the 1970s when the Thai Third Army spent more time in firefights with hill people than in cooperating with them in development work, the UN projects and the Royal Project were the only influential friends the hill people had…. It was better for the hill people that [the bilateral] projects specifically trying to improve conditions for the hilltribes [*sic*] reached them before other projects. Although the project teams were inexperienced in hill work and unfamiliar with the highland customs, they were nonetheless trying to work with the hill people to create a higher standard of living (Renard, 2001: 158).

Renard suggests that what mattered was not so much what the pro-grams did or did not achieve but the fact that they brought in a group of people who genuinely sought to represent the best interests

---

[1] Participant, Watershed Management Symposium, Chiang Mai, 2001.

of highlanders. Many professionals in the highlands took on the role of speaking out for highland people, and because of the close ties between branches of the Thai government and many of these programs, they were able to have some impact. Development professionals have thereby helped to slowly transform relations between highlanders and the state.

The changing relationships between highlanders and the Thai state is also due to broader transformations that have taken place in Thailand since the earliest highland development programs of the 1970s and 1980s. De-agrarianisation and the rise of neoliberalism has reshaped the economic, social, cultural and environmental dynamics of the Thai countryside (Rigg, 2001, 2003; Rigg and Sakunee, 2001). In many communities, subsistence farming has given way to monocropping of new crops like lychees, flowers, coffee and cabbages. Tourism interests, commercial forestry and lowland farmers looking for new land have placed increasing pressure on highland resources. With improved transport and communications networks, highland communities are increasingly closely linked with lowland towns and cities, evidenced in the mountains by the prevalence of the Thai language, reliance on consumer goods from the lowland markets, and high levels of out-migration as young highlanders seek employment in the cities. With the expansion of these links, highlanders have become more a part of mainstream Thailand and have come to see themselves as Thai.

At the same time, highlanders have become more politically active, taking advantage of increasing political freedom to fight for their rights as members of the nation. This has been possible largely because of political transformations that have taken place across Thailand in the last two decades. Fears of communist rebellion declined through the 1980s as the state slowly opened up to increasing political freedom. By 1992 a civilian government was voted to replace the successive military-led regimes that had dominated national politics through the century. As a result, more room opened up for free debate and political dissent in the country (Pasuk and Baker 2002, 2004). Since the first decade of the twenty-first century, the fragile democratic system has been plagued by government corruption, a recent example of which is the military coup that removed the Thaksin government from power in 2006. Nevertheless, the post-1992 democratisation process has continued to ensure greater room for political dissent than in the past. In contemporary Thailand a much wider range of political views is now acceptable and community contributions to public debate are the norm. While highlanders are still seen to be problematic in many ways, they now have much greater space to assert themselves in their relations with both government and non-governmental agencies.

The last two decades have also seen significant shifts in the context of highland development. Participatory approaches and a rhetoric of community-led development have now become mainstream. The 'hill tribe problem' is no longer such a defining factor in development programs, although it continues to shape popular perceptions of highlanders along with new concerns about environmental management. Development professionals have continued to work as advocates for highlanders, but increasingly their interventions are not necessary. Indeed, one of the major shifts in recent decades is the emergence of a new set of development professionals — highlanders as development professionals, their own advocates who speak for themselves.

I begin this chapter with a brief account of some of the main political shifts that in the last two decades have ushered in an era of NGO-based civil society in Thailand. I discuss the role of development professionals in supporting the emergence of highlanders' own development-oriented organisations and explain how the discourse of the 'hill tribe problem' has shifted since the 1980s with counter-discourses emerging to contest negative stereotypes of highlanders. Finally, I explore how all these discourses continue to compete and how the differently positioned subjects they produce still confront one another through public debate. Using a two-day symposium that gathered together proponents from all sides of the debates, I consider how drastically the discursive arena has shifted (even though so much has stayed the same).

The Rise of Civil Society

In Thailand and across much of Southeast Asia, civil society has arisen only in the last two decades. Although Thailand has ostensibly been a parliamentary democracy since 1932, in practice government was mostly in the hands of the military up until the early 1990s. Elections tended to be either rigged or hopelessly inconclusive and from the end of World War II until the early 1990s the country experienced a military coup on average every three years (Wright, 1992:

418). In the early 1970s a popular pro-democracy movement emerged, focused on removing the military from positions of political power. Student-led protests in Bangkok in October 1973 resulted in a brief period of civilian-led government until 1976, when renewed demonstrations protesting against a resurgence of military control were brutally put down.[2] The protestors were labelled communists and the military, along with rural patriots exhorted by Thai army radio to "kill communists", launched a violent attack against protestors in the capital in which hundreds were slaughtered (Wyatt, 1984: 302). The military opened fire on protestors from helicopters and students were beaten, lynched and burned alive. Many of the students who survived fled to the hills in the north or sought amnesty overseas. After this violent repression, little space was allowed for any independent non-government groups. Thailand returned to strict authoritarian rule in which military strongmen dominated and dissent was not tolerated. Through the late 1980s and early 1990s, however, the situation eased and civil society groups began to spring up throughout the country. The Cold War was on the wane internationally. In Europe the Soviet bloc was crumbling. In Asia the formerly closed economies of China and Vietnam were introducing reforms to open their economies to global markets, while in Thailand concerns for a communist uprising faded following the amnesty offered to insurgents in 1982 by the then Prime Minister, General Prem Tinsulanonda. In response to domestic and international pressure, there was a gradual institutionalisation of electoral politics (McCargo, 2004).

This slow transition to a more tolerant and democratic system was threatened by a military coup in 1991 but massive public protest ensured that military rule would not persist. Within a year of the coup, pro-democracy protesters were again on the streets. Huge crowds of up to 150,000 began to gather outside Parliament in Bangkok and protests spread to regional capitals across the country. This time the demonstrators came from a much broader cross-section of the community than in the 1970s and garnered widespread support from rural areas as well as the urban upper and middle classes. As the protestors marched through the streets on 17 May 1992,

---

[2] More extensive discussion of the events of October 1973 and its causes and effects can be found in Matthews (2003), McCargo (2002, 2004), Missingham (2002), Wyatt (1984), and Ungpakhorn and Millikin (1977).

they met a military blockade. When the crowd did not disperse, the soldiers began firing, sparking four days of running battles in the streets of Bangkok during which many unarmed protesters were gunned down (Wright, 1992). The official toll of casualties is 100 but this number continues to be disputed by scores of families who have close relatives among those still missing. Eventually King Bhumibol used his immense informal power to step in and obtain assurances of an end to the violence from the leaders of both sides. New elections brought in a civilian prime minister and the government began to slowly introduce greater political freedoms and gradually erode a long tradition of military patronage — a process which continues, though not unhindered, to the present day.

The increasingly liberal political climate of the 1990s, along with the rise of a new middle class, saw a burgeoning of civil society (Connors, 2002; McCargo, 2004). As was the case elsewhere in the region, such as in Indonesia and the Philippines, political openness and a process of democratisation created new spaces for non-government organisations of various kinds to be involved in political processes (Acharya, 2003; Callahan, 2000; Clammer, 2003; Clarke, 1998; Pathmanand, 2001; Weller, 2005). Civil society in Thailand now consists of a broad range of non-government organisations (NGOs) addressing a wide range of social issues, from campaigns for greater democracy, support for AIDs sufferers, to the care of street dogs in the cities. Also in the mix are the numerous organisations that focus their work on the highlands, be they tribal-based NGOs, church missions, or small groups started by concerned individuals from Chiang Mai, Bangkok or abroad. The proliferation of NGOs now operating in Thailand testifies to the emergence of a political climate in which NGOs, as representatives of community interests, are able to comment on government policy and use public protest as a means of influencing government policy. A significant example of the new powers of popular protest is the rural-based people's organisation, the Assembly of the Poor, which staged a three-month-long demonstration in central Bangkok from January to May 1997 (Missingham, 2002). During this time "ordinary villagers from marginalised communities spoke on national TV, were quoted in the daily newspapers and negotiated face-to-face with senior government bureaucrats, cabinet ministers and Prime Minister Chavalit Yongchaiyudh" (Missingham, 2002: 1647). The Assembly succeeded in obtaining promises from the government to address many of their concerns. More recently, the power of civil groups has been amply demonstrated in the frequent public protests by red-shirt and yellow-shirt protesters in the political turmoil that followed the ousting of the Thaksin government in 2006.

In northern Thailand, the increasing openness to political debate and dissent and the growth of civil society have contributed to the emergence of an activist movement led by highlanders themselves. One organisation that has become an important part of the movement is the Highland NGO.[3] The history of this organisation supports Renard's (2001) assertion that the presence of aid projects and professionals with a genuine concern for the well-being of highland people played an important role in improving the circumstances of highlanders. In the case of the Highland NGO, the support provided by development professionals helped to bring the organisation into existence and to support it through its early years of operation. These professionals thus helped to establish what is now one of a handful of highland-managed NGOs that advocate and campaign on behalf of their highland compatriots.

The Highland NGO originated as an offshoot of the Mountain People's Organisation (MPO), the very first highland-based NGO. The MPO was established in the late 1980s, when participatory development approaches had begun to dominate discourses of development intervention in the highlands. By the mid-to-late 1980s many professionals had established firm relationships with highland communities and leaders. At the same time, there was increasing interest in moving towards more participatory practices. It now became possible for researchers and development professionals who had built strong working relationships with highland village leaders and collaborators to think about establishing viable hill-tribe organisations. Thus, in 1988 Thai and foreign academics, development professionals and highland leaders came together to establish one of the first highland NGOs — the Mountain People's Organisation.

Despite the focus on establishing an organisation 'by and for' highlanders, the MPO was not yet entirely controlled by its highland members. The chairman was a European, who stepped down only after a near mutiny of MPO staff and other foreign advisors seeking greater decision-making power for highlanders. While foreign and

---

[3] 'The Highland NGO' and the 'Mountain People's Organisation' are both pseudonyms.

Thai professionals initially played an important role in advocacy, in light of the emerging orthodoxy of participatory practices, these same professionals demanded that their role be reduced once their patronage was no longer needed. With the encouragement of the majority of board members and advisors, by 1991 the funders demanded a restructuring to ensure that the organisation was fully in the hands of its highlander staff members. The Highland NGO was thus formed that year as a new pan-tribal association, under the control of highlanders representing each tribal group.

The newly formed Highland NGO built participation and democratic decision-making into the structures of the organisation. The new leadership put in place a participatory management structure where leadership would come from the grassroots. While the Highland NGO has maintained a good relationship with former Thai and foreign advisors, and continues to have Thai involvement in the management board, the leadership of the organisation is made up almost entirely of highlanders. It now has official status as a state-certified NGO and is one of a network of highland-managed NGOs that undertake community development work and public advocacy on behalf of their members.

By the early 2000s the success of the Highland NGO in establishing itself as an influential organisation with good links to state authorities was evidenced by the fact that the Highland NGO leadership sat on advisory boards to the Thai government, including those of the National Security Council, which oversees border security and anti-trafficking efforts, as well as broader non-governmental advocacy groups such as the Assembly of Indigenous and Tribal Peoples established in 1998. Increased political liberalism and the growing participatory orthodoxy in northern Thailand and worldwide have thus allowed what was in the late 1980s a very small movement of highland activism supported by a handful of pro-local professionals to emerge as a significant and independent voice in national-level debates.

New Discourses of the Highlands

By the early 1990s there were important shifts in the nature of national-level debates about the highlands, even though a negative image of highlanders persisted. By the end of the 1980s Kammerer noted that "the image of highlander as insurgent" was gradually being replaced with "the image of the highlander as destroyer of the nation's forests and watersheds ... and trafficking in illegal drugs" (Kammerer, 1989: 288). Through the next decades this was set to continue. National security, environment and drugs remain central in public discourses of a problematic hill tribe and continue to support a discourse that, Gillogly (2004: 141) argues, "allowed the opportunity for Thais to play the role of the kind and wise older brother, therefore to develop the hill tribes by leading them out of their backwardness, and provided the Thai middle class with appropriate objects of charity". Building on a sense of highlanders as "appropriate objects of charity", the emerging movement of highland activism, supported by pro-highland advocacy from prominent Thai academics and journalists, has presented new positive representations of highlanders to compete with negative stereotypes of old.

A prominent issue in recent debate about national security is the designation of many highlanders as illegal aliens. Highlanders have long been described as recent arrivals in Thailand who followed migration patterns south from China and arrived in the Kingdom from neighbouring Laos and Burma. Those who reached Thai land before the first citizenship legislation was passed in 1956 have a rightful claim to citizenship (see Chapter Seven). The difficulty is that many lack the appropriate documentation and it is difficult for authorities to distinguish between long-term residents and more recent arrivals. Highland people continue to cross the border into Thailand today, escaping high levels of poverty and the repressive state regime in Myanmar. Activists seeking citizenship for highlanders work hard to distinguish legitimate 'Thai hill tribes' and to combat the view that these highlanders are foreigners who do not belong in Thailand. The fact that English-language newspapers, *The Nation* and the *Bangkok Post*, have continued to highlight the issue over the past decade gives some indication of the public nature of the debate. Opinion pieces in these papers have mostly been sympathetic to the cause of highland citizenship, with commentators like Sanitsuda Ekachai and Mukdawan Sakboon writing in support of giving citizenship to highlanders.[4]

In 2000–01 another national security issue was raised in the Thai media following claims made by a provincial newspaper (*Nakhon*

---

[4] Ekachai has long been sympathetic to the plight of marginalised groups in Thailand, as evidenced by the publication of her book *Seeds of Hope, Local Initiatives in Thailand* (1994), which focuses on community level action in the highlands and elsewhere.

Chiang Rai) that Hmong in the province of Nan, to the east of Chiang Mai, were amassing weapons and nourished long-term hopes of establishing a Hmong homeland in the region (*Bangkok Post*, 5 July 2001). These claims were related to an incident in Nan province in August 2000 in which lowland villagers, with the support of local police officers, had raided the orchards of their Hmong neighbours, destroying more than 50,000 lychee trees. The motivations for destroying the trees were unclear because many of the orchards had been around for 15 years and the Hmong had lived there for much longer. The attack and the ensuing debate articulated a growing concern about water consumption and the pollution of waterways by highland farmers using chemical fertilisers and pesticides on their crops.

The possible impact of fertilisers and pesticides is one of the more ironic legacies of the push to get highland farmers to grow cash crops in permanent fields, instead of practising traditional swidden or rotational agricultural methods. The new cash crops adopted by many highland communities, such as cabbage, coffee and lychee, tend to require the regular application of fertiliser. Since the new crops are not resistant to local pests, it is claimed that farmers have also had to resort to chemical pesticides. There is as yet very little research to substantiate the accusation that chemicals are leaching into water-ways, but farmers are certainly made more reliant on chemicals. Lowland Thai farmers have also accused highlanders of excessive water consumption.

The violence in Nan mirrored similar conflicts elsewhere in which the environmental impact of new highland agricultural prac-tices have become another cause of conflict. New 'deep green' conser-vation groups (so called for their uncompromising environmentalism) are fighting for the removal of highland communities, reflecting a northern Thai example of the complex politics of the environment and environmentalism (Hirsch and Warren, 1998; see also Pinkaew, 2001). The fact that conservationists have focused on highlanders rather than other groups present in the mountains reflects what Vandergeest (2003) identifies as the racialisation of resource and land tenure conflicts. In Chom Thong, an area bordering on Doi Inthanon National Park to the south of Chiang Mai, conservation groups, the Royal Forest Department, and Karen and Hmong villagers clashed over resource use in the late 1990s. Lowland Thai accused highland farmers of polluting waterways with chemicals from their farms and cutting down trees in the national park. The Chom Thong Conservation Group backed the lowland Thai farmers and insisted that all hill tribe communities be relocated out of forest areas. The Royal Forest Department supported this call and threatened to relocate the Karen and Hmong villages, while highland leaders and NGOs tried desperately to intervene to prevent forced relocation (Hargreaves, pers. comm., Aug 1998; see also Hargreaves, 1999). Elsewhere, flash floods and mudslides have been attributed to the "shifting cultivation of Hmong villagers" (*Bangkok Post*, 28 August 2001). In each of these cases, the agricultural practices of highlanders, particularly the Hmong, "are said to be causing droughts in lowlying areas and contaminating waterways" (*Bangkok Post*, 24 August 2000). Resource conflict between upstream and downstream farmers is framed in these instances as ethnic conflict in which Hmong are characterised as "invaders" in the Thai mountains and are accused of damaging the environment (*Bangkok Post*, 24 August 2000).

A final aspect of the contemporary discourse of a 'hill tribe problem' is the shift from representations of highlanders as opium suppliers to drug traffickers and addicts. Drugs remain a central part of the Thai public's perception of highlanders. Even more pro-highlander newspapers such as the *Bangkok Post* and *The Nation* frequently discuss drug trafficking and highlanders in the same breath. The drug in question is no longer opium, or even the heroin manufactured from it, but increasingly speed and *yaa baa* (methamphetamines, literally 'crazy medicine') (Chouvy and Meissonnier, 2004; Sattah *et al.*, 2002). Both are produced in large quantities in facilities on the borders of Burma, Thailand and Laos, and are transported into Thailand to satisfy a huge domestic market or shipped overseas.

The drug issue even became conflated with an old discourse of national security. In June 2000 the *Bangkok Post* ran a story about how Thai authorities were anticipating 600 million methamphetamine tablets to enter the country. Efforts to stem a flow of illicit drugs focused on increased surveillance of "tribes people". The same day, editorial commentary pointed to the inevitability that the drug influx would "shake morals, destroy communities, intensify social problems, and criminalise Thai politics". One of the ways in which the government sought to address the perceived problem of highlander involvement with trafficking was to introduce legislation enabling Thai authorities to strip those convicted of drug offences of Thai citizenship. Such legislation was targeted at highlanders who had recently been granted citizenship. A high-ranking military officer was quoted as saying, "They are aliens. Only our national unity counts" (*Bangkok Post*, 29 June 2000). This approach was to become even more harshly stated after the announcement of a new 'war on drugs' by the Thaksin government in February 2003. Over the next three years, several thousand alleged drug runners were killed by the Thai police. Anecdotal evidence from the north suggests that a disproportionate number of them were highlanders (multiple informants, Chiang Mai, May 2007). The international group Human Rights Watch claims that by the Thaksin government's own count "more than 2,275 people were killed in the three months after the campaign was launched" (*AsiaViews*, Aug. 2007). In August 2007 government conduct during the war and the actions of alleged extra-judicial killing squads became the subject of Thai Ministry of Justice investigations. As reported in *The Nation* newspaper, the fact-finding panel found that "of 2,500 deaths in the government's war on drugs in 2003 … more than half were not involved in drugs at all" (*The Nation*, 27 Nov. 2007).

Another, largely informal, discourse of problematic hill tribe subjects focuses on highlanders as a source of the AIDS epidemic in Thailand.[5] I have not found reference to this in any written sources, but on several occasions in casual conversations with Thais, I found myself being told that it was highlanders who had brought AIDS into the country. In Mae Hong Son, for example, I met a retired Border Patrol policeman who insisted that this was so. He told me that the problem was particularly bad among the Lahu and Lisu of Mae Hong Son because of their promiscuity — "they are 'free sex'" he said, using the English term (field notes, Dec. 2000).

Thus environmental damage, drugs and the threats posed to the health and well-being of the Thai nation still characterise dominant public representations of highlanders. Set against this contemporary version of the problematic hill tribe, a counter-discourse has arisen which tends to place highlanders in the role of ecologically friendly indigenes. This counter-discourse has been most successfully applied to the Karen, who have been recast in popular discourse as 'natural

---

[5] On the AIDS epidemic, see also Singhanetra-Renard (1997) and Ruxrungtham and Phanuphak (2001).

conservationists' whose traditional land management systems are an example of sustainable resource use and an ethic of conservation. Andrew Walker (2001, 2004) has argued that the result is the emergence of a 'Karen consensus' in which "the Karen represent a fragile ideal of mutually beneficial interaction between culture and nature" (Walker, 2001: 145). The Karen consensus is visible in the public domain in the work of journalists like Sanitsuda Ekachai. An example of her work is the article "Tribal truths" (*Bangkok Post*, 19 Dec. 2000) in which Karen are described as "forest communities" who are "working together to realise their constitutional rights in natural resource management — and to fight against public prejudice".[6] These representations of highlanders as caretakers of the forest have been called upon in debates around the Community Forestry Bill. The bill proposes to hand some responsibility for managing Thailand's watershed forests to local highland communities through a form of community-based forest management. The exact shape of that community responsibility has been the subject of much debate.[7] After more than a decade the Community Forestry Bill was passed in 2007 but remains contentious as this book goes to press in 2011.

These new discourses of the highlands have brought significant change to the context of development work in the highlands. New issues revolving around citizenship, Karen conservationists, *yaa baa*, pesticide use in cash cropping and Hmong nationalism sit alongside the remnants of a discourse of the 'hill tribe problem' (national security, environmental destruction and drugs). Thus hill tribes continue to be represented as damaging and dangerous and in need of outside help. In the contemporary era, however, dissent has become much more widespread, as evidenced by the Karen consensus. A contingent of new pro-highland advocates has emerged from the ranks of Thai academics, journalists and highland NGO workers. In addition, along

---

[6] Walker challenges the factual basis for such claims of the Karen as 'forest communities' and argues that the selective focus of the 'Karen consensus' on rotational farming and forest stewardship denies legitimacy to the wide diversity of contemporary Karen experience and ethnic identity. Walker's argument, the critique of his paper by Yos Santasombat (2004), and Walker's rebuttal (2004) are discussed further in Chapter Six.

[7] For more detailed discussion of the bill, refer to Chusak and Dearden (1999), Forsyth and Walker (2008), Johnson and Forsyth (2002) and Walker (2004).

with the emergence of new highland organisations, the highlanders staffing those organisations have emerged as a new kind of professional subject — the highland professional. Organisations such as the Assembly of the Poor and the Highland NGO have created space for highlanders and the poor (the former voiceless beneficiaries of development interventions and objects of research) to gain an independent public voice without the mediating presence of foreign professionals. As nationalism plays an increasingly important role in the discourse of new local pro-highland professionals, foreign professionals have been relegated to a more marginal position in new debates over watershed management, cash cropping and forest conservation.

A Slice of the Debate: The Watershed Management Symposium

The event that for me brought into focus the new dynamics of debates about highland development was the Watershed Management Symposium held in Chiang Mai in 2001. It was no coincidence that new debates about highlanders and 'hill tribe problems' became clear at a symposium on watershed management. As Forsyth and Walker (2008: 9) discuss, "the 'environment' has become a new ideological battleground in the north", one that pulls issues of national identity, belonging and race into debates about forest management. The symposium provided the perfect context for the drawing of contemporary battle lines.

While much of the discussion during the symposium appeared to be an apolitical debate about 'facts', the arguments voiced could be located along a trajectory that ran from a pro-local and pro-highland discourse of participation and local knowledge to a conservation discourse in defence of forestry policy and 'natural law'. The political implications of the debate between these two broad alliances were signalled by the frequent references to the question of highlanders' status as either indigenous (pro-highland position) or outsiders (a more hostile and often 'deep green' conservationist position). Repeated interjections on this theme located a background debate around the issue of whether or not highlanders have a legitimate place in the forests of the north, or indeed in Thailand itself.

The stated aim of the symposium was to be a "forum for substantive discussion of issues relating to watershed management", to propose principles that should guide it, and to bring together different parties concerned to discuss issues, approaches and possibilities for policy directions (Chayan, 2001). The symposium was convened by Dr Chayan Vaddhanaphuti, the founding director of the Regional Center for Social Science and Sustainable Development at Chiang Mai University. Like most conferences, it was structured with panels of three or four speakers and time afterwards for questions and discussion. The time given over to discussion was quite lengthy, often taking as much time as the presentations. As an observer, I attended all sessions, taking copious notes and observing the range of views presented. In the course of presentations, questions, responses and rebuttals, there emerged a wide spectrum of views and political projects, and also some unexpected alignments between them. My account of the symposium draws both on my notes and on written versions of the presentations that were distributed at the venue.

The introductory speeches located the central issues of watershed management policy in a context of larger, longstanding issues surrounding the highlands and highlanders. The political divisions in the room were immediately apparent. In her opening address, Professor Pasuk Pongpaichit, a political economist at the prestigious Chulalongkorn University and an outspoken public intellectual, spoke of the need for Thais to change their attitudes to highlanders, to rethink who has rights to land in the mountains and who is Thai. Her speech placed broad questions of national identities and the legal status of highlanders at the centre of debates about watershed management and also showed where she stood in this politically divided audience. With her stood the majority of the other speakers, as well as the symposium organisers. On the other side of the political divide was the Royal Forest Department representative, who teased in his presentation that at first he thought the invitation to speak must be a joke.

The politics of the room were thus transparent to most of those attending. On one side were the workshop organisers and their allies. These were left-leaning academics, activists, development workers and public intellectuals who supported local knowledge and local decision-making together with representatives from highland villages. On the other side were the Royal Forest Department, the conservation groups, and the handful of academics who remained loyal to a discourse of scientific truth, expert knowledge, and a reconfigured, though still recognisable, discourse of the 'hill tribe problem'. Most of these participants had been working in and writing about the highlands for many years and some had begun their work in the region as long ago as the 1970s and 1980s. Others were representatives from highland villages and spoke from personal experience. My account of the symposium focuses on three main themes in the exchanges between these different protagonists who revealed their competing positions in the discourses they called upon in support.

Local Community and the Marginalisation of 'Western Science'

In the battle between the two opposing views of the highlands and highlanders' land management practices, the first weapon to be used by both sides was a discourse of community. In the opening presentations and discussions, both sides used a pro-local discourse of participation and rights to support their very different views. In these discussions, the impact of a pro-local orthodoxy was apparent as both sides appealed to the interests of 'the community' and placed the local in opposition to the interference of outsiders and foreigners.

The first speaker, Professor Somsak, Director of the Regional Community Forestry Training Centre at Kasetsart University, focused on the importance of a participatory approach in watershed management strategies. He argued that professionals must be placed in the role of facilitators rather than experts, shifting away from techno-centric styles of development and management strategies, to interventions that worked with practices and knowledge already present in the local communities. Somsak's speech drew on a familiar discourse of participatory practices and the responsibilities of professionals. As we have seen, the idea of shifting from techno-centric styles of development and the concept of development workers as experts has a longstanding presence in the community of highland professionals. The facilitator is the ideal, fair, professional subject of this vision while the highlander is not a deficient subject in need of help but a knowledgeable and capable local in partnership with the professional.

Following Professor Somsak, Dr Shwan Thanhikorn spoke as the representative of the Royal Forest Department. Shwan emphasised that as an arm of the government, the RFD had a responsibility and a commitment to the people and that it shared a common goal with delegates attending the symposium, that is, to preserve natural resources and preserve biodiversity while allowing production and, most importantly, supporting people's livelihoods. He stated that he had come to gain an understanding of the attitudes of the community and the new ideas for management options and explained that the priority must be to "preserve the natural resource at the same time as thinking about the rights of the community".

Shwan's reference to the "rights of the community" showed how a discourse of 'the local' had increasingly been adopted by government offices like the Royal Forest Department. In the past the Department has been associated with a discourse of the 'hill tribe problem' and at times been involved in forced relocations of hill tribe villages out of the mountains. 'The community' to which Shwan was now referring was a wider Thai community, so that the "rights of the community" were not necessarily the rights of the highland community. However, the language he was using also provided the opening for highland subjects, invoked in Pasuk's opening address, to be considered legitimately Thai and part of that Thai community, and to have their rights acknowledged alongside those of lowland Thais.

The final presentation on the opening panel elaborated on themes of participation, community and the value of local knowledge but introduced a new theme, that of Western science as a form of imperialism. Professor Anan Ganjapan, a Thai anthropologist at Chiang Mai University and an experienced consultant and commentator on the progress of development in the mountains, spoke on the problematic influences of "Western knowledge" and "scientific knowledge". He argued that Western science had introduced problematic understandings of the highlands and led to problematic watershed management policy. Anan's argument drew a sharp distinction between Western scientific approaches and local wisdom and knowledge. He stated that the root of many of the problems with watershed management policy grew from what he termed "linear thinking" — a "colonial mentality" leaning towards an interest in the exploitation of resources, the domination of scientific knowledge and a devaluing of local indigenous knowledge. Anan called for a new approach that would take a more complex view, allow a diversity that a "linear" system closed off, and learn from local people and local management practices.

Anan's critique of Western scientific knowledge became a narrative through which the problematic policies of the past could be explained and allegiances with the local community be declared. As a member of the audience commented the following day:

> We cannot use the paradigms thought of by *farangs* [foreigners]. It
> is not enough to rely upon the use of Western science. I worked

as a researcher on the Thai-Japan and the Thai-Australian project and after 16 years of working we still have not found a solution to the watershed problem ... we need to review the policies ... we need more involvement of local people in policy formulation in order to find solutions (anonymous comment from the audience, Watershed Symposium, 2001).

The opposition established here between science (as Western and colonial) and local or indigenous knowledge imbues both forms of knowledge with moral value. In this discourse, knowledge of the local ranks ahead of the (scientific) knowledge of the West and is more useful in terms of finding solutions to social problems.

The discussion that followed this first session was dominated by exchanges between Forestry Department officials and their opponents. Combative assertions of a rural-urban divide in terms of rights and responsibilities were aired. Responding to Shwan's evocation of the responsibilities that both the Royal Forest Department and highland people had to the broader population, Khun Wandii, a representative from the Highland NGO, stood up and demanded to know why highland people were the only ones charged with the responsibility of conservation when their resource use was so small compared with urban uses. She stated that in the North, "we have more forest because of *chao khao* [hill tribe] yet mountain people are blamed for forest destruction, blamed for drugs". She pointed out that only 20 to 30 per cent of Akha have citizenship, yet mountain people recognise that this is a shared responsibility and are willing to cooperate. Shwan responded with an attempt to smooth the issue over, recognising that there were problems while pleading his own, and the Royal Forest Department's, innocence:

> We don't ask the hill tribe people to answer the problem for everybody. The hill tribe people still live on the mountains which proves that we don't need to move them. Now we're trying to think freshly about how to do things in the government. The hill tribes live close to the watershed so they might feel a little bit under pressure ... but we don't want to repeat the mistakes from other countries. We don't want people from other countries to tell us what to do when they have hurt their own people. There are many ways to look at the problem.... Please don't think that government institutions don't try to do their best. I came to listen both to blame and advice. I'm mostly getting blame but that's OK too....

In Shwan's response can be seen several of the emerging themes of the morning. In his declaration that "we don't want people from other countries to tell us what to do when they have hurt their own people", there is simultaneously a parallel drawn between "their own people" (indigenous populations) and highlanders, and an emerging narrative of what "people from other countries" do and the advice they give. Without explicitly responding to Wandii's criticisms, Shwan used an emerging narrative in which the "paradigms thought of by *farangs* [foreigners]" became an explanation for past mistakes and Western science emerged as problematic. The solution to watershed issues was thus to be found in local knowledge, that is, the knowledge of Thai communities, both lowland and highland.

Critical Science — Questioning Fact

Western science was used in a very different way in a later series of presentations that sought to debunk the assumptions of conservationists and the RFD.[8] In these discussions, science did not marginalise local knowledge but supported its validity. Building on research undertaken in the 1980s and 1990s, a series of mostly non-Thai researchers presented 'scientific data' that challenged the factual premises of much past watershed policy and the assumption of a clear relationship between the presence of highland communities and damage to the environment (Fisher and Hirsch, 2008; Hirsch, 1987, 1990). Jefferson Fox, an environmental studies professor at the East-West Centre at the University of Hawaii, opened the ground for this critical discourse by arguing in his presentation that swidden farming could not be blamed for deforestation (2000; Fox *et al.*, 2001). Dr Nibhon was asked to respond to Fox's points as a government official:

> There may be some things that I have overlooked. As Dr Somchai says, we have learned from Western countries.... We have to make people in the uplands understand the problems of people in the lowlands so that we can live together.

---

[8] This debate bears some resemblance to the debate on land degradation in the Himalayas. Refer to Ives and Masserli (1989) for examples of a similar debate around the 'facts' of environmental degradation in that region.

Nibhon chose to accept the critique with very little rebuttal and suggested that it might be what was "learned from Western countries" that could be at fault. Nibhon appeared to be picking up on an emerging narrative in the symposium that shifted responsibility for what was called misinformation or 'bad science' to Western knowledge and Western learning that had somehow tainted local approaches. Earlier Chayan had sought to ease emerging conflict by pointing out that the two parties spoke from different perspectives and that both must remember that rural and urban people together have responsibility to help solve problems: "It is not just rural people who must sacrifice everything." There was an emerging notion of an inclusive Thai subject, encompassing both the highlands and the lowlands, with the concept of the 'local' forming an alliance between the two. Nibhon's emphasis on the importance of people of the uplands and the lowlands working together was also an appeal to a consolidated local in the face of the West. This inclusive subject posited both the professional and the highlander as partners in a project to find new watershed policy. At the same time, the narrative was creating a new outsider — the *farang* outsider, the Western scientist tapping into a colonial knowledge system and creating problems in the highlands.

That afternoon three more papers were given that made similar 'scientific' challenges to the basic knowledge that had shaped watershed management policy over the years. Two papers challenged beliefs about the effect hill tribe agricultural practices were thought to have on soil erosion (Giambelluca *et al.*, 2001) and forest fires (Achara, 2001). Two more sought to debunk common understandings of highland ecology, in particular the relationship between watershed forest and rainfall (Forsyth, 2001; Walker and Scoccimarro, 2001). Both papers argued that there was very little evidence for a relationship between rainfall and good forest cover in watershed areas and questioned whether forest clearing had any bearing on water supply.

British geographer Tim Forsyth put forward a list of the assumptions that had driven Royal Forest Department policy over recent decades and considered the evidence. He argued that the claim that forests make rain and increase downstream water flow is not backed up by data. Forsyth also evaluated the belief that forests regulate dry-season water flows, decrease erosion and reduce floods in the lowlands, declaring that although these assumptions were the foundation of Royal Forest Department policy, research provided no definitive answer. Finally, he discussed the accusation that total forest cover had decreased dramatically in northern Thailand and argued that, in terms of overall cover, not much had changed since the 1950s, even though the proportions of plantation forest, secondary forest and virgin forest were now very different. Forsyth addressed directly the assumption in Thailand that fixing water supply problems was a matter of fixing the watershed:

> If the concern is with water shortages, [farmers and conservationists] need to be aware that there are many causes of water shortages and simply planting trees will not address the cause of the problem.... There is a lack of adequate concern for water use, especially in terms of irrigated agriculture in the low-lands.

Forsyth's paper thereby challenged the basic 'facts' that policy makers and conservation groups had put forward to argue for the removal of highland communities from watershed areas.

There was a dramatic response to Forsyth's efforts to debunk these entrenched myths. He was criticised by several speakers for lacking the credentials, being a social scientist, to discuss data belonging to the field of physical sciences. The representative from the Royal Forest Department was adamant that Forsyth was simply wrong. "It is dangerous to say these things. They are not true...", he said, before launching into a reiteration of the accepted state discourse that "forests help the rainfall... deforestation increases erosion for certain". Professor Sutira, a staff member at Payap University in Chiang Mai and the representative from the Chom Thong Watershed Conservation Group, agreed. She responded to a panel on soil erosion, forestry management and rainfall by touching on indigeneity:

> The problem is that it is not clear who are the traditional, local people. We use the term 'indigenous' but the term comes from imperialism and colonialism. Colonial authorities called the local people indigenous. But in Thailand there is no imperialism, so who is indigenous?

Such conflation of arguments over ethnicity and watershed ecology ran throughout the symposium. It was particularly evident in the comments made by representatives of groups such as the Royal Forest Department and the Chom Thong Watershed Conservation Group, who in other forums supported the view that highlanders should not be allowed to make their homes within national park or forest reserve boundaries.

In this forum, however, representatives of highland communities were given as much speaking time as representatives of such conservative groups. The result was an exchange that would have been impossible in an earlier era. For example, Sutira went on from her discussion of indigeneity to speak about the damage that highland communities could cause as forests regenerate:

> As regards the issue of forest regeneration, the cattle kept by local people is a problem because cattle eat the leaves of the new trees. It's very simple to calculate — how many leaves do you think one cow eats in one day — and it is easy to see how much damage could be caused to regrowth in secondary forests.

In reply to the professor, a Karen villager stood up to say:

> I'm just a villager from the mountains, and I don't know much, but I do cultivate cattle. In my experience cattle don't eat leaves at all, just grass on the ground. I know this because I take care of them myself.

At this point he was interrupted by cheers and applause from a large majority of the audience, a clear sign of which contingent formed the majority at the event. He continued:

> I am sorry that people name shifting cultivators and hill tribes as a cause of deforestation. I live on the mountain and I don't know anything about state policy. We don't study books but we know everything about the forest. But when we start to be exploited by the state we have no choice but to come down and learn.

Another villager stood and said in agreement:

> The laws are complex and we don't always understand them. Some people are good at talking to us, some are just not interested. Some come and talk with us, some talk impolitely. State officials and NGOs should think well about participatory planning.... The state in some areas can't take care of the forest well and they should talk to the local people.... It's easy to talk. Come and talk to us, make the law understandable to us, talk with us about how to make it concrete. In order to solve these problems we must talk to each other.

This exchange between the conservationist academic and the representatives of two highland villages was a confrontation between two discourses of subjectivity in practice. Sutira engaged a familiar discourse of a problematic hill tribe — the non-indigenous migrant, the destructive farmer — and called upon a discourse of the knowledgeable academic (herself) who could easily calculate the damage done by this problematic subject to regenerating forest. In response, a new highland subject spoke. This new subject was not only a local highlander subject who was acknowledged by others as being knowledgeable and rational but a highlander who spoke out for the community. The confrontation between these two discursive practices illuminated the power that the knowing local subject can wield in contemporary Thailand. Highland leaders, notably Karen elder Joni Odochao and NGO activist Prasert Trakansuphakon, now occupy prominent positions within national-level debates about the highlands. Even the ordinary highlander, standing behind a microphone and speaking to an audience made up of foreign and Thai academics, government officials and development professionals, could have a voice that reached political players.

New Subjects, New Possibilities — Outcomes of the Symposium

The newfound power of outspoken highland leaders, along with acknowledgement of the importance of community interests and local knowledge, point to important shifts in the highlands debate. While some parties may have been merely paying lip service to local concerns, by the end of the symposium it was clear that highlanders were no longer going to accept being excluded from the debate. Balance and reconciliation became the central themes. In the final speech of the symposium, organiser Dr Chayan Vaddhanaphuti, summed up the mood:

> Science has provided the main direction for finding answers and providing ideas about the best way to manage resources. This has ignored local wisdom. The problem with relying on scientific knowledge for policy is that this knowledge is not complete. Policy must also consider cultural dynamics. A new attitude should integrate science, local wisdom and social science as a new body of knowledge that will correspond better to reality.

This conciliatory speech pulled together diverse themes from the discussion over the previous two days, introducing a rhetoric of balance and integrating different perspectives and different kinds of knowledge.

He highlighted the importance of recognising the interconnectedness of different populations and the shared responsibility of watershed management, and commented that regulation needed to be culturally appropriate. In responding to Chayan's summary, the speakers reiterated the importance of working together, recognising cultural and ethnic diversity, establishing relationships between communities and the state, and sharing knowledge and learning. As the symposium drew to a close, the rhetoric emphasised balance and compromise and the need to reach truer understanding and better and fairer management strategies through a partnership of local and scientific knowledge, highland villagers and professionals.

Not all disagreements were nullified by this conciliatory rhetoric. A stubborn point of contention emerged around the conservationists' uncompromising stance on forest preservation and the belief that highlanders were responsible for forest degradation. After Chayan's conciliatory speech, Sutira took the opportunity to make the following speech:

> It is our traditional right to make the life of Inthanon [National Park] longer.... I disagree with Prof. Chayan's first point — please excuse me — the foremost principle in watershed management must be nature and natural laws. When you act against the laws of nature, the balance is upset. You can talk about people, about society and culture, but the laws of nature are final. The laws of nature take precedence over human law. When we run out of water ... this is the law of nature telling us that things are getting worse. Before there is any other discussion we must respect Mother Nature.... As for local wisdom of the people, they do have wisdom but the different pressures make it impossible for communities to retain that wisdom.... Chayan says that upstream and downstream people must work together. I agree. Upstream people have a responsibility to conserve the watershed. Lowland people also have a responsibility. To ignore this is a cause of conflict. We concentrate too much on the uplands — areas that you want to take as community forest are watershed for us. Community participation is problematic.... Sometimes villagers must be punished and the law must step in.

Sutira's appeal to the primacy of "natural laws" and the need for state law to "step in" to punish villagers perpetuated a discourse of an untrustworthy and damaging hill tribe subject, who requires the intervention of a knowing professional to safeguard the "traditional rights" of the wider community. These statements repeated a discourse of the 'hill tribe problem', though with subtle shifts. Although her syntax distinguished between lowland Thais and communities of the uplands, this upland subject was at the same time presented as a wise local subject, signalling a new kind of hill tribe presence that could be responsible and rational and able to participate as a partner in negotiations over forest management. Sutira's primary concern remains, quite clearly, with "natural law" and a belief in the need to discipline villagers against harmful practices, but there was a softening of the discourse here and some space emerging for a new kind of highlander subject.

That knowing and vocal highlander subject was a vibrant presence at the symposium. Indeed, in response to Sutira's point about "natural law", a man in the audience who identified himself as a Karen villager argued that:

> If nature has a fixed law, it should apply to the whole watershed, including urban areas.... One professor said that science is simply composed of local wisdom gathered over generations. If it is applied to natural resource management, science and local wisdom should be linked and equal status given to both.

Like Chayan, this speaker pointed to the possibility of better knowledge and understanding emerging from a synthesis of local knowledge and science. The mere presence of a highland villager speaking in such a public context in support of linking facts and data with local wisdom was in itself materialising a new hill tribe subject who was wise and who jointly produces better knowledge alongside the scientist and the scholar. The highlander subject who found his voice in the symposium was not only a local subject but also one with local wisdom, who should be included in decision-making practices within development interventions such as HASD and in the broader formulation of national-level policy. The appeal for locals, academics and the state to work together to create a better society was not a new or challenging discourse; what was novel was the fact that the appeal was being made by village representatives to an audience of government representatives, academics and NGOs. Unlike the highland subject participating in a development project initiated by someone else, here were vocal, lobbying highland subjects who wanted to "work together to make a good society" and were interested in how they could "become good citizens and contribute to a better society"

(Hmong representative from Doi Pui, speaking during the closing session).

Conclusion

With the shift to a more open democratic political system in Thailand and the rise of civil society, critical discourses of participation became part of mainstream discourse. These shifts also opened up the possibility for a new range of subjects to emerge and began to break down 'the professional and the people' binary through which traditional development subjects had operated. An emerging highland NGO movement was able to engage with reconfigured discourses of a 'hill tribe problem' and to support new, more positive representations of highlanders as 'natural conservationists' and caretakers of the forest. In this changed context, new kinds of subjects have taken shape around the development spaces of the highlands.

These new discourses and the subjects they bring into being were very much present at the Watershed Symposium of 2001. Much of the debate during the symposium revolved around the question of what constituted legitimate knowledge and, beneath this, whose knowledge was better — the local's or the scientist's? The debate echoed a discourse of dissent that had surfaced in the late 1970s and 1980s. To some extent it remains a debate about truth and who has access to 'better knowledge'. In this case, however, the debate was more clearly a competition between two factions: on one side, the pro-highland professionals and local representatives, who positioned themselves as working for the people and respectful of local knowledge, and, on the other side, the conservation groups, conservative academics and, Royal Forest Department officials who found themselves using the same arguments around natural laws and ecological imperatives, though for varying political purposes.

The competition between these two broad groups became polarised in a competition between two kinds of knowledge, 'scientific' and 'local'. The designations had little to do with the knowledge each side used to bolster its arguments. Anan was as willing to use knowledge generated by well-respected social science methods as the conservationists were to use anecdotal 'local' evidence to support their views. All sides represented at the symposium used a discourse of local knowledge and community and invoked professional identities in line with a participatory professional subject, one working in partnership, respecting science and local wisdom equally, and bringing both together for the sake of a better future. The fact that these opposing groups both adopted a participatory discourse demonstrated the degree to which a pro-local discourse had achieved the status of orthodoxy across the political spectrum.

The symposium also saw new openings in the discourses employed by both a pro-highland camp and the opposing Royal Forest Department and conservation representatives. Both sides appealed to a discourse of conciliation, compromise, and joint understanding and opened space for seeing all parties in attendance — hill tribes, policymakers, development professionals and academics — as equal and potentially united voices. The new sense of reconciliation and partnership was certainly assisted by an emerging discourse of a problematic and imperialistic 'Western knowledge' that denied foreigners legitimacy in the debate while creating a new alliance between locals in ways that reimagined highlanders and lowlanders, hill tribes and urban officials, as equally Thai.

What emerged was a contingent of pro-highland professionals, including foreigners, Thai and highlanders, arguing in favour of community management of watersheds and advocating highlanders' rights to land and citizenship. Beside these new pro-highland professionals, who may well themselves be from the highlands, a new non-professional highland subject was emerging as an outspoken participant in political debate. The villagers who spoke at the symposium represented a new kind of 'beneficiary' subject in the development spaces of the highlands, one who no longer required the mediating presence of any professional, foreign or local, in order to speak out.

6

Policing Participation

Ultimately one loves one's desires and not that which is desired
(Nietzche, 1973 [1886]: 175).

A rhetoric of participation and respect of indigenous knowledge and
support for community-led interventions now prevails in highland
development. The idea that good development must be participatory
constitutes a new and largely uncontested set of parameters against
which development programs are judged. While the rhetoric is widespread, few of the professionals I spoke with in Chiang Mai believed
that participatory approaches were being well implemented. As I
engaged in successive conversations about what was going wrong
with highland development — and hearing very little about what was
going right — it became apparent that while everyone seemed to be
talking about participatory approaches, they also agreed that very few
professionals were actually doing it.

When I conducted my interviews in 2001, one of the programs
that was the subject of much discussion about whether a participatory
approach was really being followed was the Uplands Program. It was
the first year of the program's operations in the north and the professionals I was working with, whether or not they were involved in the
program itself, watched and commented on the process of initiating
a range of sub-projects and establishing relationships with study communities. I am in no position to judge the validity of their criticism
and it is not what interests me here. Rather my focus is on the
nature of the criticisms circulating among development professionals
in Chiang Mai. Through off-the-record gossip, informal conversation
and rumour, the development community debated how truly participatory the program was. Through these discussions certain parameters

122

were laid out for judging who was and who was not a properly participatory, pro-local professional. It seemed to me that what I was hearing was an informal policing of the boundaries of a participatory orthodoxy. Through gossip and rumour, the professional community was defining an ideal of professional practice and judging those who did not seem to be living up to it.

The Uplands Program was a multi-disciplinary, German-funded research program investigating a range of highland development issues in northern Thailand and northern Vietnam. The Thai part of the program was preceded by four years of preparation during which the program manager had built up a relationship with leaders of Mae Sa Mai Hmong village, just north of Chiang Mai, where the project would base much of its early work (Map 3). Meanwhile, researchers had worked to obtain support from universities and funding agencies in both Thailand and Germany. The multi-disciplinary, participatory approach was central to the project as a whole. As stated in its Conceptual Framework and Summary, the objective of the research program was to "contribute to better management of natural resources and to the improvement of rural livelihoods in the mountainous regions of Northern Thailand" (Uplands Program, 2000). The summary goes on to state:

> This can only be achieved if the research activities in these areas take into account the priorities of stakeholders involved in the management of natural resources and in development processes (Uplands Program, 2000: 1).

To contribute to better management, the program sought to integrate the priorities of all stakeholders, from the Royal Forest Department to highland farmers. The entire program was therefore conducted under the umbrella of a sub-project entitled "Participatory Research Approaches and Interdisciplinarity in an Intercultural Context".

I made contact with the Uplands Program very soon after arriving in Chiang Mai in late 2000. It was immediately apparent that I could collaborate with several program researchers to obtain basic data about the range of organisations working in the highlands. With two of the program's Masters students, I began a shared survey of NGOs working in highland communities. Through this I negotiated with the program manager, Andreas Neef, for permission to observe the progress of program work and interview researchers working under his leadership. I also developed close friendships with several of these young researchers and learned more about their work through casual conversations and evenings out than in the course of formal interviews or field visits.

Some of the stories that I draw upon later in this chapter are taken from discussions with the Masters and PhD students who came to Chiang Mai to conduct their fieldwork in the first phase of the program. For young researchers, especially those doing international fieldwork for the first time, the expectations of what their research might achieve and how it should be conducted are shaped by often untested expectations and the uncertainty and angst that usually accompany a postgraduate student's initial forays. This was certainly the case for me and, even though I had worked in the highlands before and knew how complex the local situation could be, I shared many of the hopes of the Uplands Program students. We all arrived to do our research with varying knowledge and preconceptions about participatory practice. All of us came with a vision of what our roles as professionals should be, expectations of the contributions we could make, and the ethical standards we should maintain. With varying degrees of cynicism, we identified our roles through a familiar discourse of transformation and empowerment and a vision of a professional who works to do good for the people.

Our idealistic vision was shared by many established professionals in Chiang Mai. Much of the criticism from these young researchers as well as from more senior colleagues focused on the ways in which the ideals were not being met. Both inexperienced and experienced commentators had difficulty in matching the ideal to the messy particularities of the context in which the Uplands Program was executed. As discussed in Chapter Five, the highlands themselves remained the object of much debate. The Uplands Program was also constrained by an established agenda and the expectations of sponsoring institutions in Europe and Thailand. This context shaped what the program could do and how it should go about it, yet the ideal of a pro-local professional remained unmodified. In this chapter I explore the gossip and complaints that circulated around the Uplands Program and discuss how these professionals continued to desire an ideal while being constantly confronted with the impossibility of bringing it into being.

The Participatory Professional in Contemporary Discourse

The present vision of the ideal development professional has evolved from the professional envisioned in the early participation literature of the 1970s and 1980s. Contemporary participation literature continues to make many of the same arguments, critiquing top-down development approaches and arguing that the professional must act for local interests, facilitating a process through which local communities develop according to their own priorities and principles. One important shift, however, is that this view is no longer in the minority. Manuals and 'tool kits' for participatory approaches such as Participatory Action Research (PAR) or Participatory Rural Appraisal (PRA) abound and many funders now require all their projects to include a participatory planning component. Indeed, participation is now so widely recognised as a dominant discourse that by the early 2000s participation was being referred to as a "new orthodoxy" (Henkel and Stirrat, 2001), while the expression of doubts about its merit was regarded as being "almost heresy" (Manikutty, 1997: 115).

At the same time, there is a much more extensive discussion of the practicalities of achieving good participation — not simply introducing some participatory approaches but adopting the whole approach and philosophy properly. As Jonathan Rigg noted in the early 1990s, a polarised perspective on participation has emerged: either you have it or you don't (Rigg, 1991: 208). To help developers get it right, manuals for participatory practice share ideas and analyse the successes and failures of participatory methods.[1] The 'lessons learned' almost always specify that, in order to succeed, the professional should learn from local people, "striving to appreciate their knowledge instead of teaching them or imposing your knowledge or ideas ... letting the local people do the investigation, analysis and presentation themselves" (de Negri *et al.*, 1998a: 29).

As is recognised in the manuals and the wider literature, however, the process of letting the community lead is not unproblematic. There is now ample recognition of the difficulties and complexities of putting the ideals of participation into practice and extensive debates about the value of participation. The ever-present possibility of conflict within communities is recognised in manuals that provide practical guidelines for negotiating through conflict while trying to facilitate a consensus-based decision-making process. Elsewhere

---

[1] See Attfield *et al.*, 2004; Case, 1990; de Negri *et al.*, 1998a, 1998b; Goldman and Abbot, 2004; Hope and Timmel, 1995; Jones, 1996; Pretty *et al.*, 1995.

critics have explored whether participation is inevitably tyrannical and whether it lends itself to illegitimate and/or unjust use of power (Cooke and Kothari, 2001). It has been argued that participation fails because of the misuse of tools such as PRA or reliance on processes inappropriate to a participatory approach such as benchmarking (Snell and Prasad, 1999) or use of indigenous knowledge (Briggs and Sharp, 2004). Participation is seen to maintain uneven power relations within local communities and between the 'participants' and outside professionals (Agarwal, 1997, 2001, 2007; Akerkar, 2001; Chhotray, 2004; Cornwall, 2003; Resurreccion *et al.*, 2004). Rigg has argued that participation has gone so far as a remedy for top-down approaches that expert knowledge now counts for nothing and "ideology, consciousness raising and empowerment" have become more important than "the achievement of development" (Rigg, 1991: 208). Included in this body of critical literature is discussion of a spectrum of 'participations' ranging from 'genuine' participation at one end to mere rhetoric at the other (Botchway, 2001; Cornwall and Brock, 2005; Leeuwis, 2000; Parfitt, 2004; Raju, 2005). Overwhelmingly, participatory approaches are still seen to be of value only if the many barriers to genuine participation can be addressed (Michener, 1998; Mosse, 2003, 2004). Participation may be problematic but there is a strong reaffirmation that it must nonetheless be striven for: grassroots development "is a cause which should not be allowed to be lost" (Hewison, 1993: 1706).

Similar considerations apply to debates about participation in research. Here as well there are barriers to meaningful participation that need to be overcome but additional concerns are knowledge production and the question of where 'good' knowledge is to be found (Pain and Francis, 2003; Campbell, 2001; Krimerman, 2000; Martin and Sherington, 1997; Stoecker, 1999). The local continues to be perceived as both a field of intervention and the site of truth (Mohan and Stokke, 2000; Triantafillou and Nielson, 2001). This is evident, for example, in the assertion that "the most valid information" is that "generated by, and for, the communities themselves" and the hope that participatory methods can overcome the limitations of conventional research methods (Berardi, 2002: 849; Mosse, 1994).

As in the 1970s and 1980s, the ideal professional envisioned in this literature is still a pro-local professional. The professional is still required to battle a top-down system, although these days it is often disguised by a veneer of participatory rhetoric. The authenticity of the professional's participatory commitment is under scrutiny, but both the ideal of participation and the pro-local professional subject remain central. This literature conveys a strong sense that, applied correctly, participatory approaches can achieve positive results in any community, anywhere in the world.

Good participation, and thus good development, remains in this discourse both a universal value and universally achievable. At the root of this universalism, however, is a contradictory appeal to a kind of cultural relativism in which local truths and local knowledges serve as the correct guide for intervention. The ideology that underpins participatory approaches, nevertheless, appeals quite clearly to universalist values. Take, for example, Chambers' discussion of the responsibility of the professional (Chambers, 1992, 1997). His discourse of participatory practice establishes a vision of the ideal professional working with an approach that can and should be implemented regardless of the bureaucratic or local context. He argues that a participatory approach is universally applicable and furthermore, that participation done properly has a universal potential to achieve its goals of empowerment. His publication, *Whose Reality Counts? Putting the Last First* (1997), presents a case for why it is so important that development undergo a "paradigm shift" towards participation and explains how development professionals everywhere could enact it. For Chambers a participatory approach is, with its aims of empowerment and its focus on the local and on putting 'people first', applicable at all levels of development work and in all locations.

Yet, as anyone who has tried to apply a participatory approach would recognise, the universal and the particular are necessarily irreconcilable. As soon as the universal is translated into the particular, it takes on the hues and colours of that context and is no longer universal (Laclau, 1996). Chambers assumes that the democratic ideology of participation and the tools of 'bottom-up' development are equally relevant in every community, that all individuals everywhere desire an equal voice in consensual decision-making as they strive for an egalitarian future. He writes as if it were possible to realise these universal ideals in every situation. As the prolific debate on participation discussed above demonstrates, however, discursive practices of participation continually confront the fact that these ideals are seldom realised. Attempts to do participatory development always encounter a gap between the ideal and implementation, between the universal and the particular.

Participation in the Uplands Program

The Uplands Program was no exception to this. During the year I followed its progress, it dealt simultaneously with the expectation that good participation ought to be possible and the impossibility of achieving that ideal. The program was accused of failing to meet the mark in many of the ways identified in the literature: of focusing on knowledge over adhering to participatory ideals; of treating participation as a 'box to be ticked' in order to fulfil bureaucratic requirements; and of perpetuating dynamics of dominance and control that were present within local communities and within the hierarchies of institutional decision-making. In the literature, all these are identified as factors that prevent true participation. It was not at all clear that the Uplands Program indeed 'failed' on these counts and it is not my purpose to assess whether it did.[2] What is relevant is how the accusations emerged.

1. Funding Realities

The expectation that the Uplands Program could somehow embody a true participatory approach emerged most clearly during the conference on Participatory Technology Development hosted by the program in mid-2001. The conference brought together a broad cross-section of professionals working with participatory approaches throughout rural Southeast Asia, including many who had worked in northern Thailand in the 1970s and 1980s. Most attendees were either academics or development professionals. They presented papers and discussed issues concerning the use of participatory processes to develop new technologies for improved land management, crop production and improved livelihoods in rural areas of Southeast Asia.

At the conference the manager of the Uplands Program, Andreas Neef, gave a presentation that focused on the process of participatory planning through which the Uplands Program was designed. Neef and his colleagues had submitted their first research proposal based on participatory research using Participatory Rural Appraisal (PRA) tools to try and identify "farmers' priorities for research in the field of agriculture and natural resource management" (Neef, 2001: 4).

---

[2] An insightful and reflective piece on the program's difficulties in the early phases is Neef Friederichsen and Neubert (2008).

The initial research in Mae Sa Mai revealed "a high variability of priorities depending on socio-economic status, ethnic origin, age and gender of the respondent" so that it was difficult for the researchers to identify a clear set of priorities (Neef, 2001: 5). In response, the researchers revised their methodology to focus on a more homogenous group made up only of farmers, without necessarily including representatives of all groups within the village. Beyond the challenge of trying to distil clear priorities from the heterogeneous views of the community, Neef went on to discuss the challenges that followed as community priorities had to pass the scrutiny of academic reviewers and funding agencies:

> To develop a research concept that would at the same time satisfy local academic partners, cooperating stakeholders in research areas, and scientific reviewers has proven extremely difficult. Reviewers of the donor agency expect a comprehensive conceptual framework and not just a kaleidoscope of local stakeholders' priority topics. They would base their judgement on the innovative character of the research proposal, the expertise of the scientists in the proposed field of research and the number of relevant publications in international journals. One subproject that was designed mainly on the basis of priorities given by farmers but whose scientific approach was not considered innovative enough by the reviewers was therefore not approved for funding (Neef, 2001: 11).

Although a pro-local discourse of participation would require that the farmers' priorities should have driven the research, that proved to be impossible in this case:

> It can be concluded that priority setting in agricultural research will always be based on a multitude of factors — donors' preferences, government policies, consumers' needs, researchers' perspectives and farmers' priorities (Neef, 2001: 14).

Neef recognised that participatory research programs cannot ignore the concerns and priorities of academic and funding institutions. The need to address the priorities of funders is familiar to anyone used to applying for grants, but is also a direct challenge to a pro-local discourse in which local priorities are meant to guide interventions.

Neef's argument that a range of interests had to be considered in setting priorities drew some criticism. A member of the audience accused Neef of "still" using a "traditional" format to set a research agenda focused on negotiating around a set amount of money, a set time frame and the pre-established priorities of the university (field notes, June 2001). Neef's response was that part of the problem lay with funding agencies and reviewers, who were not convinced of the validity of research priorities set by local communities. These reviewers were looking for innovative approaches and researchers with expertise and previous publications: "this is the reality, for an international program, this is how it works" (Neef, conference presentation, June 2001). In order to get funding, the professional is obliged to conform to the funders' desire to have a professional who can demonstrate expertise. The professional is obliged to perform as an 'expert' professional subject. For Neef, the requirements of funding institutions compounded the problem created by the lack of clear local priorities, making it difficult to work to a research agenda decided entirely within the community.

To obtain funding, the project manager therefore had to strike a compromise with the project's participatory goals. For example, during preliminary studies three years before the program's commencement in 2000, a Masters student working under Neef's supervision had identified that narcotics were a central concern for a majority of respondents in Mae Sa Mai village:

> Asking the villagers about the main problem of this village almost everybody mentioned drugs. This includes drug addicts and related crimes such as stealing and trafficking activities that cause insecurity in the village. Already school children are addicted to heroin (Schiller, 1999: 27).

Despite the identification of narcotics as a priority issue for the people of Mae Sa Mai and despite the program's focus on participatory development, drug-related research was not included in the central aims and objectives of the program. When I asked Neef why this was so, he responded that it was simply because the narcotics issue was not a priority that could be fitted within the broad priorities defined by the funding agencies, Deutsche Forchungsgemeinschaft (DFG) and the National Research Council of Thailand (NRCT). Nor could the host institutions, which were agricultural departments within universities known for agricultural science, provide appropriate expertise. The purpose of the program as a whole was to develop environmental information systems that would be useful for local people, specifically "decision support systems that are useful for farmers"

(Neef, pers. comm., Sept. 2001). While narcotics may have been a community priority, it was not an institutional priority and, in order to obtain institutional support, Neef needed to be pragmatic. For the professionals who struggled to find a place for local voices to be heard in the 1970s and 1980s, these organisations — DFG, NRCT and the universities that were hosting the research — would probably represent 'the system'. The ideal professional subject that their discursive practices invoked would be obliged to struggle against these institutions on behalf of local people. For Neef, however, the professional achieves results through compromise, both between ideals of empowerment and effective development of new agricultural technolologies, and between the intention of helping farmers and the necessity of pleasing funding agencies.

Neef's position of compromise was criticised in many of the informal discussions that I was party to during the conference. Both senior researchers and development consultants, as well as younger professionals, were sceptical. Neef himself had a very different understanding of the overall feedback from the conference and the comments he received were much more positive. But the consensus in many of the informal conversations to which I was party was that the program was not really working in a participatory mode. The absence of representatives from the study village of Mae Sa Mai was taken as one indicator of this. Casual comment found a public voice during question time on the last day of the Uplands Program conference:

> Many of the people present here have been surprised that the majority of us taking part in this workshop are foreigners. Why are there not so many Asian faces here? Why are there no local representatives when we're taking all this time talking about participation? (field notes, June 2001).

The absence of local representatives was seen by critics to indicate an inadequate commitment to pro-localism and a participatory approach. Whether the locals would have wanted to attend the conference, and whether their attendance was within the Uplands Program's control was not discussed. The program had in fact invited the headman of the project village and the head of the Highland NGO to participate in the workshop, but they could not attend. Those professionals who criticised the absence of local people assumed that the conference should have been planned around and centred on local participation.

Overall the Uplands Program was criticised by members of the Chiang Mai development community as a project that merely paid lip service to participation. Neef advocated compromise as indispensable for establishing the research program and for gaining institutional support. In the public forum of the Uplands Program participatory research conference, Neef's plea that a program must always balance a "multitude of factors" was not necessarily well received (Neef, 2001: 14). For many who adhere to a strict sense of what true participation ought to mean, the Upland Program's practice of compromise and negotiation seemed to have failed to put the people first.

2. *The Difficulties of Working in 'the Community'*

In the past, participatory approaches have tended to assume the presence of a homogeneous community that can participate in research and development and is able to make decisions and set priorities by consensus. In the literature this assumption has been critiqued. The difficulties of achieving consensus and accounting for heterogeneous communities with often conflicting perspectives is well recognised (Case, 1990; de Negri *et al.*, 1998a, 1998b; Goldman and Abbot, 2004; Manikutty, 1997). The failure to consider such heterogeneity and conflict is discussed as a potential barrier to achieving true participation. Interventions may fail to emancipate and empower all sections of the community through inclusive and egalitarian processes, shoring up instead existing hierarchies (Chambers, 1997; Cooke and Kothari, 2001).

These debates about the difficulties and dangers of working with communities also became relevant to the work of the Uplands Program as it struggled to negotiate relationships with the community of Mae Sa Mai, the first study site for its researchers. In this case it was the young researchers in the program who began to feel that the relationship between the program and the village was problematic, beginning with their first introduction to the community. In my interviews, many of them expressed surprise at the way their access to Mae Sa Mai had been negotiated. Most of the students had expected to be introduced to the village en masse, assuming that the headman and other village leaders already had a detailed understanding of the planned research. In fact, their introduction to the village was quite different. It had been proposed that the new researchers be introduced to the village leadership and the community as a whole in a large meeting in which each of them would briefly present a poster summarising their research project. However, the population of Mae Sa Mai is over 1,000 people so Neef asked the village headman to arrange a meeting with just the village committee because "to invite the whole village would be too big" (Neef, pers. comm., Aug. 2001).

For the students, it seemed apparent at that first meeting and during subsequent interactions that many villagers actually had very little idea of what research had been planned in their community. This, they believed, was the result of inadequate consultation. While they had envisioned themselves participating in lengthy discussion with villagers, the truncated introduction seemed to have compromised between the logistics of introducing a handful of researchers to a very large village population and an ethical concern for inflating village expectations. Neef did encourage one student to work on producing posters that would provide information on the research program and introduce the students. The idea was that these would be posted at a central point in the village so that many people would have the opportunity to find out what was going on and whom to approach with concerns or questions. The student assigned the job, however, thought that such widespread consultation and information sharing should have come before any researchers arrived in the village, so she decided not to go ahead.

Neef was aware that some of the students had been disappointed by their first introduction to the village and he felt himself that it had not been "a successful meeting" (Neef, pers. comm., Aug. 2001). He explained the decision to introduce the researchers on a small scale as a way to avoid raising expectations within the community, that it was better to "start small and enlarge if appropriate" (Neef, pers. comm., Aug. 2001). For him, this one introduction was building upon a long relationship with Mae Sa Mai village since four years had already been spent laying the groundwork for the research to take place in this community. The conflicting perspectives between Neef and the young researchers seemed to boil down to different expectations about how much of a pro-local participatory ethic was possible. What the students saw as being inadequate, Neef saw as a sensible compromise.

The challenges of working in a partnership with the Mae Sa Mai community deepened as increasing internal tensions emerged around the issue of drug trafficking. Mae Sa Mai had been drawn into trafficking networks ferrying *yaa baa* (methamphetamines) to consumers in Chiang Mai from production sites in the mountains or over the border in Myanmar. In early 2001 the village headman, with whom Neef had negotiated access for researchers, resigned from his post as he came under increasing pressure from the Thai authorities to act against traffickers. With his resignation, it became apparent that the drug problem in the village could affect the safety of researchers. The new headman, Khun Win, who was already working as translator and research assistant to Maren Tomforde, a PhD student loosely affiliated with the Uplands Program (see Tomforde, 2006), soon took steps to keep drugs out of the community. Along with some other members of the community, he underwent weapons training with the Thai military and carried arms to protect the village against drug traffickers, erecting a barricade across the road to prevent the access of outsiders coming to the village to purchase *yaa baa*. In the meantime, villagers who made a living in the drug trade carried on as best they could, although their clients were forced to creep across the fields in the dark to make their purchases.

Khun Win began to receive death threats and had to carry a rifle with him at all times. Tomforde's personal connection placed her in particular danger, but even those conducting their research in the lychee fields adjacent to the village and who had little to do with the people living in Mae Sa Mai were touched by the drug trafficking. One student, for example, sometimes had to stay overnight in the fields in order to conduct experiments. He would come across groups of young men making their way to or from the village seeking *yaa baa*, or having already purchased and consumed it.

These circumstances challenged many assumptions of the participatory approach. It seems all too simple to assume that there is a cohesive local community, or that all members of that community are equally free to negotiate with professionals and represent themselves and their interests honestly. In addition, the assumption that professionals can somehow empower the community seems equally ridiculous. In the context of potentially life-threatening power struggles in the village, the professionals in the Upland Program were powerless and indeed quite vulnerable. The negotiations between drug traffickers, village leaders and state authorities brought into play local power hierarchies whose complexities were beyond the understanding or control of most outsiders. While professionals might stick closely to a participatory approach and value its emancipatory aims, local power dynamics can present non-negotiable limits to what they can do. Tomforde, for example, believed strongly in a participatory approach and in her own research emphasised the importance of taking time to come to the village and operate in a way that was "humble and showed respect" (Tomforde, pers. comm., Aug. 2001). Nevertheless, her experience of being caught in the midst of community conflict caused by drug trafficking showed the extent to which community politics often make it impossible for any outsider, albeit informed by ideals of emancipation and empowerment, to hold any kind of power in the local context, even the power of a facilitator who can help people to find a better way forward.

3. Conflicts Between Participation and 'Good Science'

The third issue confronted by the Uplands Program during its first year was the question of how to balance good scientific research with participatory research. This issue had a big impact on personal relationships and work practices within the Uplands Program. Some of the program supervisors argued that the relationship between good research and participation was a fairly distant one. While participatory tools could be used in research practices, the processes of empowerment, which are such an important component of a participatory ethic, were not seen as central to the research aims. Dieter Neubert, for example, a sociology professor at one of the program's university partners in Europe, explored the idea of participation in his address to delegates at the Participatory Technology Development conference:

> The objectives of participatory research still vary between empowerment and political action (Fals Borda and Rahman, 1991) at the one hand of the extreme, and much more restricted approaches of inclusion of farmers into the process of technology development at the other.... (Neubert, 2001: 2).

Neubert (2001: 4) recognised a tension between a sense of participation as a tool for transformation and participation as a means of "achieving better user orientation and a method of developing and testing solutions under real life conditions". He did not place the Uplands Program explicitly along this spectrum of approaches, but he did say that the program was subject to competing demands and expectations that pulled it both ways, towards a mission of empowerment on the one hand and towards an effective, but inclusive, process of technology development on the other. During discussion, Neubert also commented on the tension between the imperatives of doing "good participation", in terms of producing outcomes around an agenda of empowerment, and doing "good research", which would produce "quality science" (Neubert, public comment, field notes, June 2001):

> Only the most radical participatory projects blur the difference between research and development projects and focus on direct change. Besides, participatory research is aimed at the production of knowledge. The quality of participatory research is, therefore, measured by its ability to produce knowledge (Neubert, 2001: 4).

"Quality science" and the production of knowledge are here constructed as being quite separate from the transformative and emancipatory goals of intervention. Yet within much of the literature on participation, an ethic of working for the people means privileging local priorities, local demands and local needs. The vision of participatory research espoused by the Uplands Program management and the vision of participation as part of a moral obligation towards local communities were clearly in conflict.

Conflicting views of how to define participation and how it ought to shape research are typified by one example that dominated conversations at social gatherings for months. A disagreement had emerged between Neef and one of the Program students over how best to manage relationships with local farmers. One evening on my verandah, the student told me his side of the story at length. My household was hosting a party to which we had invited all the Uplands Program students and other friends. We sat outside in the cool evening, drinking Heineken beer and chatting. The student worked in lychee orchards belonging to two different families in the same village that was the main field site for most program researchers. He had negotiated access to their land in order to set up insect traps to gather data on the insect species present in the orchards. The participatory aspect of this work was that, instead of gathering data at a pristine test site, the work took place in fields that were in use and under the management of the local Hmong farmer. This meant that regular communications with farmers were necessary to maintain good relations and ensure that that both farmers and researcher knew what the other was doing. For the student, this meant being informed when farmers were planning to spray, apply fertiliser or harvest.

One day, a farmer with whom the student worked saw him and walked over from the neighbouring field to take him to see some trees that had become infested with a particular insect. Such an infestation was very common and could damage the crop. The student did not know how to deal with the problem but assured the farmer that he would investigate and get back to him. Despite his promise, he did not go back to the farmer with this information. According to the student, Neef had advised him not to tell the farmer how to deal with the problem because it would change the field site in ways that would make any subsequent research programs less scientifically sound. The student felt that, by doing as instructed, he would be neglecting a responsibility to share information with the farmer. He argued that he had access to specific knowledge that the farmers had not yet learned because this crop was still quite new to the area. Farmers had not yet built up a repertoire of knowledge about how to deal with the pests that had come along with the crop. The student argued that it was his responsibility as a researcher to give help where he could and this was one situation in which he could contribute to the people who were cooperating with his research.

The program students seemed at large to agree with this student's perspective, so I made a point of bringing up the issue when I interviewed Andreas Neef. The project manager's version of why the student should not have stepped in with advice was rather different. He told me he believed that no researcher was in the position to give advice at this stage of research:

> At this stage we are just involved in knowledge generation. We can ask about what knowledge farmers have on the insect when they appear, what management techniques seem to work, and bring greater knowledge together with the farmers (Neef, pers. comm., Aug. 2001).

While the research should generate benefits for farmers — even if those benefits are not necessarily direct or concrete — it was too early for the student to be able to give reliable practical advice and solutions. Neef emphasised that there was an important distinction between the program's research work and any practical future outcomes or positive change that the program could bring to the village. The Uplands Program was primarily about research and knowledge generation. Only after several years in the field could practical results feed into something useful for the community (Neef, pers. comm.,

Aug. 2001). In order to reach a point of being able to offer practical help and to undertake work to bring about change, it was important to first complete a stage of careful research and knowledge generation.

The student's frustration, and the focus of sympathetic comment from his colleagues, revolved around his inability to enact a specific ethic of participation or to bring into being an ethical, participatory, professional subject, by failing to lend what help he could, even though his knowledge might still be limited. Neef's ideal, however, was a subject producing good science in stages that would lead to practical intervention only when the researcher could be confident in the quality of the information offered. For Neef the desire to offer immediate practical intervention was inappropriate. Though both program manager and student had in mind the best outcome for the farmer, their reference points for ideal practices were far apart.

For some of the students debating the issue, Neef's position was evidence of a less ethical approach, a failure to give back to villagers who were sharing their knowledge and allowing researchers access to their field and their homes. Within this small group of student researchers, it mattered greatly whether or not the program was being properly participatory. They could not reconcile the two competing visions of what their professional identities should be: a professional researcher engaged in creating knowledge or a pro-local participatory professional helping to transform local communities for the better. Their frustrations came through in many conversations at parties and over dinner. I can now recognise to an extent that many of these frustrations were part of the typical discomfort of initial fieldwork. First-time fieldworkers often feel out of place, are affected by culture shock, and spend a great deal of time wondering what contribution they can possibly make to the communities they study. However, the angst that emerged amongst these students about the potential conflict between their roles as researchers and their hopes as pro-local professionals was also an indication of something deeper: it was part of a policing of appropriate professional conduct affected by gossip and rumour across the professional community in Chiang Mai.

Participatory Policing

Discussion of the conflict between the student and the program manager and analysis of the program's relationships with Mae Sa Mai are both examples of how the Uplands Program was being judged against a standard of participatory practice. The informal discussion at the program's conference, as well as comments made during formal question-and-answer sessions, both incorporated a discourse that haunted casual conversations about the Uplands Program. In informal discussions and gossip, as well as in public discussion in open forums, the Uplands Program's commitment to participation was called into question and the actions of program researchers monitored against this ideal standard. In this way, informal discussions and gossip sessions appeared to be a mode through which the professional community, and specifically this small group of early career researchers, regulated itself. If one was not pro-local, if one was not identifying with an inclusive and facilitative professional subject and actively distancing oneself from being merely a 'tokenistic' expert professional subject, then the informal discussion condemned the professional as being unethical and ineffective.

Both the criticism that the program had not been participatory enough, and the program manager's recognition that there needed to be compromise, demonstrate how impossible it is to achieve an ideal form of liberal, democratic and egalitarian intervention. Despite ample recognition of the difficulty of participation and the experience shared by many professionals of being constantly thwarted in their efforts, the professional community at large continues to insist that it must be possible. Professionals continue to desire to better the lives of local others via participatory practices, even as they constantly confront the impossibility of that task. In the case of the Uplands Program and the assessments of the program made by both young and senior researchers alike, this impossible desire acted as a policing device. Professionals used it to judge their own and others' behaviour in a way that located participation as an achievable universal ideal without allowing that it was contingent, politically inflected and morally positioned.

Conclusion

Manuals for participatory methods and literature on the politics of field research and community development recognise the multiple constraints and barriers to an ideal form of participatory intervention. Yet there seems to be an equally widespread belief that the ideal is achievable. The international professional community continues to expect that the egalitarian democratic ideal is possible within development and research interventions anywhere. This universalising ideal still shapes goals and objectives of professional practice and a sense of professional identity. An ideal of the participatory professional subject continues to represent what is both ethical and effective and the best way of achieving empowerment.

Among professionals in Chiang Mai, however, there was constant angst and debate about how, or if, that ideal was being realised. The Uplands Program, for example, had to negotiate a range of interests: local political and social contexts of the village, community and nation-state; the requirements of the bureaucracies that regulated researchers and their funding in universities, organisations and government agencies; and university demands that the program meet its formula for what constitutes good science. At the same time, the program was subject to informal regulations imposed by the professional community and its assessment of how well a program met the moral criteria of participation. The power of informal critique should not be underestimated because it is often through informal networks and casual conversations that a program's reputation is made. The Uplands Program, and researchers working within it, had to balance these institutional demands along with the demands of villagers. For the students in the program, most of whom were just starting to form their own professional identities and who were in many cases new to fieldwork, the necessary compromises did not come easily. Their frustration arose from a sense that the program was failing to be participatory, either in practising participation itself, or in supporting them to become the ideal participatory professionals that they wished to be. For the student who argued with the progam manager, the inability to put into practice his vision of what he ought to be doing could be read as a failure to materialise a participatory professional subject and put into practice a particular discourse of ethical and effective methods. However, given the contradictory demands of the various stakeholders — the villagers, funding agency, university, the Thai government authorities with which the program was cooperating — it was impossible to achieve the ideal within the constraints imposed by the need to meet these dispersed interests. Yet it remained vital to appear to be trying, to gain the respect of the local professional community by performing the ideal subject, by materialising the normative discourse of the ethical and effective practitioner.

It is impossible to realise such a set of universalising values and ideal practice in any single actual place or person. Yet that impossible desire has become a means through which the professional community regulates and polices itself. The discourse of the ideal pro-local participatory professional subject creates strict standards that must be adhered to and provides a means of ranking professionals on an informal scale of success or failure. The new orthodoxy of participation has become a means through which the professional development community sets and polices boundaries of professional morality.

7

Engaging with the
Politics of Development

When outsiders go up to the village and ask the Akha people if they would like to have a big Akha Chief or a King, the answer is: "No, we don't want any chiefs or kings. That is against our egalitarian system. What we need", they say, "is good Akha lawyers" (Deuleu Choopoh in Deuleu and Næss, 1997: 202).

Indigenous NGOs are often assumed to be 'insiders' who are able to represent local interests and are thereby in high demand as local partners in development programs. While such NGOs may seem to be free of the moral dilemmas faced by 'outsiders' regarding what they have the right to do, the reality is not so simple. Professionals who work for the highland communities of their origins have to negotiate tensions and possibilities very different from those faced by 'outsider' professionals. If anything, highlander professionals are even more deeply embedded in the politics of the highlands. For them the implications of development are direct and personal. Instead of the angst of doing participation 'properly' that governs the professional identities of non-highlander professionals, the close and enduring nature of relationships between highlander professionals and their village partners seem both to necessitate and to legitimise a more politically aware and pragmatic approach.

The NGO movement is increasingly relied upon worldwide by the development industry to respond more effectively to local needs and to represent more accurately grassroots concerns than inter-national development agencies (Fisher, 1997). It is often assumed that close connections with 'the local' enable NGOs to better achieve

142

contemporary development objectives of participation and empowerment. However, the participatory work conducted by NGOs does not necessarily adhere to a pro-local agenda. In some cases it may instead function as a mechanism of government, training participants to become the types of citizens desired by the state: self-sufficient, active, productive and responsible (Cruikshank, 1999: 69; see also Triantafillou and Nielson, 2001). Fisher (1997) notes that expectations that NGOs are able to 'empower' are often misplaced. Jonathan Rigg's (1991) analysis of NGOs in Thailand showed that they are not necessarily any better equipped to implement a grassroots approach. Bryant (2002: 286) has argued that while NGOs contribute to social change and may confront "political or economic oppressors", unintentionally they may also be a means for the state to consolidate its power over local communities.

In this chapter I show how the Highland NGO (introduced in Chapter Four) may be susceptible to all of these shortcomings of the non-government sector and the governing effects of practices of participation and empowerment. I discuss how the Highland NGO contrasts with the Uplands Program, and the sense of thwarted effort and regulatory ideals of participation that accompanied it. While a participatory approach is important to the Highland NGO, in many ways it is an overtly political organisation with a vision of its work as politically embedded and politically relevant.

In some ways the Highland NGO embodies the kind of political awareness called for by Li (2007) in her analysis of development programs in Indonesia. Li details how programs based on aims of empowerment and participatory development constitute regimes of government that are as much about controlling and managing local populations as emancipating them. Although the intentions stem from a desire to make things better, or what Li calls the "will to improve", this desire must negotiate complex political realities. The failure of development programs to improve life in target communities can be remedied, according to Li, with a better understanding of the "messy actualities" through critical ethnographic research that is more attentive to the politics of development and its links with governing rationalities (Li, 2007: 281). Better knowledge of the "messy actualities" is certainly important to the work of the Highland NGO but for a different reason. Whereas Li seems to assume that better knowledge will lead ultimately to better kinds of development, for the Highland NGO such knowledge is needed as a background to the central task of entering and shaping the flow of political discourses, acting through an understanding of the ways in which development is innately political.

I introduce the political engagement of the Highland NGO with a discussion of how the organisation has engaged with the so-called 'Karen consensus' and what it hopes to achieve for highland communities by promoting this discourse of Karen as caretakers of the forest. I discuss how, despite its admirable aims and participatory structure, the Highland NGO's strategies can work to extend state rule or introduce outside agendas in ways that may work against the interests of local communities. In part this is because strategies are never, in the terms of Fisher (1997: 458), "value neutral" and are guided not by strict adherence to a participatory orthodoxy but by a pragmatic political engagement. Like NGO groups in the Chimalapas, Mexico, the Highland NGO uses participatory development as a tool for political engagement (Walker *et al.*, 2007). Through a discussion of the organisation's efforts to obtain citizenship for highlanders, I demonstrate how this very lack of neutrality and the willingness to engage with the politics of development is what allows the Highland NGO to negotiate successfully for real benefits.

The Karen Consensus: Identity Politics and Discursive Strategies

The Highland NGO's political engagement is demonstrated in its contributions to contemporary debates on who belongs in the mountains and who does not, who can be trusted to care for the watershed and who cannot. On the issue of watershed management, a contingent of pro-highland professionals continues to represent highlanders as 'guardians of the forest', most notably in regard to the environmental management practices of the Karen. Australian anthropologist Andrew Walker has termed this representation of the Karen as natural conservationists and caretakers of the forest as the "Karen consensus" (Walker, 2001, 2004). It has come under criticism both for its inaccuracies and for working against the interests of the pro-highland cause. Walker (2001: 155) states that the Karen consensus "makes a strong case for the legitimate presence of Karen communities in upland catchments". He argues, however, that it also idealises rural life, delegitimises cash cropping (on which many Karen rely) and portrays Karen as 'good' hill tribe subjects in contrast with other highland groups, such as the Hmong, who have become characterised as 'bad' hill tribe subjects. Such divisions are based on unsubstantiated assumptions about the environmental impacts of traditional land use: in the past the Karen tended to establish more permanent communities and practise rotational swiddening, whereas the Hmong were pioneer swiddeners and moved regularly to clear new parts of the forest for farming and to establish new communities (see discussion in Chapters One and Three). The belief persists in some quarters that the pioneer swiddening method damaged the forest and that Hmong culture has never incorporated a sense of caring for the land. Rather than reviving these old prejudices and placing Karen in opposition to Hmong, Walker prefers a vision of Karen identity that celebrates the broad diversity of contemporary Karen experience, including urban-based or entrepreneurial livelihoods, as part of legitimate Karen identity.

Nevertheless, the Karen consensus has been a surprisingly effective strategy for disrupting dominant political discourses that had previously denied highlanders of any tribal group a legitimate place "within contested northern Thai landscapes" (Walker 2001: 155). This vision of Karen identity is perhaps too narrow but it also helps the Karen to find a positive identity within the political discourses of watershed management. As argued by anthropologist Yos Santhasombat of Chiang Mai University, it may also form the means to:

> reproduce and advocate, on a national scale, the desire and ability of forest-dwelling farmers to preserve and manage local forest resources in a sustainable manner, to demand official recognition of community forest management, and to present an image of local people — Karen in particular — as guardians of the forest (Yos, 2004: 119).

The Highland NGO is one of the organisations that have worked to popularise such a positive Karen identity. Early in my acquaintance with the Highland NGO, it became apparent that much of its work was intended to contest and displace popular perceptions of highlanders as problematic and dangerous subjects. One of my first meetings with the Highland NGO staff took place in conjunction with researchers from the Uplands Program. The two organisations formed a stark contrast. Where the Uplands Program's manager, Andreas Neef, was concerned with the scientific robustness and ncutrality of the knowledge produced by the Uplands Program researchers, his counterpart, then deputy director of the Highland NGO, Khun Sunan,[1] seemed more concerned with knowledge as political strategy.

My first visit to the Highland NGO took place in January 2001 and was one of many interviews that I conducted in collaboration with two of the young Uplands Program researchers. At the time I was working with the Uplands Program to create a database on NGOs working in the highlands, including information on what kind of work they did, what methods they used and the composition of the organisations themselves. Because of the prominence of the Highland NGO, the Uplands Program's manager, Andreas Neef, joined us for the meeting. I contributed very little to the discussion but sat at the table listening and recording the conversation in shorthand in my notebook. Over the following months I would arrange to spend more time at the offices of the Highland NGO and accompanied the organisation's staff into the field. As I got to know the organisation better, I started to see how that first conversation was characteristic of the approaches used by the Highland NGO. The exchange between Upland Program staff and the NGO illustrated the benefits and risks of engaging the Karen consensus as part of a deliberate strategy.

During this first meeting Khun Sunan (who was subsequently elected director of the Highland NGO in 2001) explained that the organisation was working to establish recognition of highlanders' capacity for good environmental management. Thus a large part of its approach had been to encourage more positive representations of highland people and their practices in the public arena. This included promoting representations of the Karen as being natural conservationists whose ability to care for and manage Thailand's forest resources was to be trusted and encouraged (field notes, Jan. 2001). Sunan made the point that this reconceptualisation of Karen practices had been very successful and now was the time to build on this success and begin to combat the negative view of the practices of other highland groups such as the Hmong. For Sunan, positive representations of the Karen formed a starting point for creating a broader popular discourse of a positive highlander identity.

---

[1] Khun Sunan is a pseudonym, as are the names of all the Highland NGO staff discussed in this chapter.

Sunan explained that the Highland NGO had decided to focus on traditional agricultural practices in part because the planting cycle and the associated ceremonies incorporated a broad range of village life. Thus within the scope of resource management it was possible to reinvigorate a wide range of cultural practices. One aim of the work was to promote self-esteem among highland farmers by encouraging them to value their traditional knowledge and approaches. Sunan explained that the Highland NGO was also looking to traditional practices as a way of addressing the ability of communities to take care of themselves:

> Some people try to follow a modern pattern of cash cropping. But in many areas they are turning back to traditional knowledge. In this way they can farm the area for a long time successfully. We hope that in an area without so many development projects it will be easier to understand and encourage people to turn back to the traditional ways, to adapt them for use in a contemporary circumstance. Some development projects were good, but some projects seemed to make highland people more weak and more dependent on social welfare — always waiting for agency assistance.[2] So we try to work from their own knowledge and understanding to make the community stronger, build leadership and networks between villages (field notes, Jan. 2001).[3]

In response, Neef argued that this strategy would disadvantage highland groups for whom cash cropping was not a part of their traditional practices:

> If Karen stick to their environmentally friendly way of agriculture, the result is that they are relatively poor compared with the Hmong, who adopt cash crops on a large scale. You can tell the Karen 'OK live in harmony' and it's good, but the Hmong have a much higher income and can earn a good wage … in the end cash croppers are the most successful in terms of income. Is it difficult to negotiate these issues? (field notes, Jan. 2001).

---

[2] The term 'social welfare' was being used loosely here because Thailand does not have a welfare system in the manner of Australia or the USA.

[3] Khun Sunan spoke in English. While he spoke eloquently and clearly, his syntax and expression were not always correct. In this transcription I have reinterpreted his language into more 'correct' English while trying to keep as true to his words as possible.

Here, Neef was falling back on the discourse of Karen as rotational subsistence farmers and Hmong as cash croppers, which Walker insists is erroneous. Sunan also sought to point out the inaccuracy of this assumption:

> Certainly some development projects think in this way. But it is not just the Hmong who can do this. In some places the Karen lead the Hmong in terms of cash cropping (field notes, Jan. 2001).

Sunan went on to point out that the intention of the Highland NGO was not to discourage cash cropping but to utilise traditional knowledge and cultural practices within a new agricultural system:

> I don't mean the cash cropping isn't good — it's fine for making an income but you need to think about how to make it more sustainable. This is a problem in the highlands because of the use of chemicals. You also have a situation where some highlanders can grow cash crops but can't access outside markets.... Also, if you want to survive then you have to compete within your own group.... This means that relationships change and the culture changes. The Highland NGO looks at the old ways that can bridge this gap. It's not that we want people to turn to the old way, but to find out how the old way of life and the new technologies can blend and coexist. We also want to work within the law and try to explain to the government the scientific value of traditional knowledge systems (field notes, Jan. 2001).

By emphasising the 'scientific' value of traditional knowledge and encouraging a process through which traditional practices are incorporated into new agricultural modes of production, the Highland NGO was attempting to establish a sense of the value of the "old way of life".

In contrast to Walker's concerns for accurate representations of contemporary Karen identities, Sunan portrayed the Highland NGO as an organisation that readily engaged any available opening through which to reconfigure discourses of the highlands. This included finding ways for highlanders to identify themselves proudly as highlanders. In doing so, the organisation emphasised traditional knowledge and practices as the foundation for highland identities. Representing Karen as guardians of the forest was not intended to reflect precise contemporary realities. Rather it was being utilised as a political strategy that was effective in a contemporary context.

Thus representation itself, rather than questions of accuracy or truth, was central to this new politics of the highlands. Nevertheless there were dangers in this political strategy. As the exchange between Neef and Sunan shows, a rhetoric of tradition sat uncomfortably with discussions of cash cropping and led to simplistic categorisations of Karen and Hmong for both of the Uplands Program researchers taking part. Broad generalisations about farming practices on the basis of ethnic group do not hold true and invoking them may work against the aim of promoting the value of traditional knowledge and land-use practices across all highland groups. Accurate or not, however, Neef's questions about traditional practices were questions about reality, aimed at gaining knowledge and an understanding of the world as it is. Sunan's perspective was very different. He spoke of strategies to create new realities, a strategy of building on existing discourses of positive identity (the Karen as guardians of the forest) in order to break down negative stereotypes of other highland groups and ensure that a new generation of highlanders gain a sense of pride and positive identification with their highland origins. In this work the Highland NGO was interested in knowledge not so much in terms of gathering facts about the world but as a political tool.

Extending State Rule? Local Advocacy and Governance

In applying knowledge as a political tool and engaging in a game of identity politics, the Highland NGO worked to bring into being a "particular vision of society" in the terms of Fisher (1997). While the NGO's main aim was to benefit highlanders, at times the strategies did not seem to be entirely pro-local. In keeping with the origins of the organisation, the Highland NGO played a dual role in supporting and promoting traditional cultural practice while assisting highlanders to access a better quality of life in modern Thailand. The organisation's approach remained true to the ethic of respect for local communities and indigenous knowledge that marks contemporary pro-highland discourse as well as a participatory ethic. Yet, at the same time, the Highland NGO's practices could be understood as facilitating an extension of state rule by creating the kinds of citizens desired by the state. In the rest of this chapter I will suggest that the pro-local approach and cooperation with the state are not necessarily incompatible.

In the months after the meeting between representatives of the Uplands Program and the Highland NGO, I had the opportunity to work more closely with the staff at the Highland NGO. I offered my services as a volunteer in exchange for the opportunity to observe the daily work of the organisation and to participate in its activities for several months. During this time I was able to interview most senior staff members, some several times, and to participate in conversations and meetings for projects where I was involved as translator and writer. I was also invited to accompany teams working on citizenship issues as they made their field visits to highland communities around the provinces of Chiang Mai and Chiang Rai.

The Highland NGO's work from year to year was based ostensibly on a consultative process with representatives from all of its member villages gathering to discuss the needs and concerns of their communities. These concerns formed the basis for the Highland NGO's annual work plan. The system followed a participatory planning framework very closely. Yet translating priorities from felt needs to representative statements, then to annual work plans was still problematic. Like the Uplands Program, the Highland NGO relied on funding from several different international organisations, whose priorities more often than not shaped the work of the Highland NGO. The management committee developed a work plan based on the priorities set by community representatives, but could only undertake work for which there was financial support. The final decisions were made in small meetings of the Highland NGO staff. This decision-making model was repeated constantly through the year on a smaller scale when Highland NGO staff met with village partners for specific projects.

The criticism that could be levelled at this planning process is that it was not achieving empowerment or emancipation as such but rather training highlanders to be good citizens (Cruikshank, 1999). Teaching a select group of village representatives involved in the Highland NGO planning meeting about the workings of a democratic political system could be seen as education in how to participate in political life. Discussing issues, voting on resolutions, making speeches, gathering wider support and seeking to influence the management committee that would make the final decision are mechanisms through which democratic political engagement takes place. While the Highland NGO was run by highlanders and represented highlanders, it could have been accused of 'training citizens' and, albeit unintentionally, assisting in the extension of governmental practices.

Many of the priorities identified by those who spoke at the 2001 annual meeting of the Highland NGO members could only be addressed by engaging in a mainstream political process. For example, the issue of land title was a main concern for the members of the association but little could be done to alter the situation without lobbying the Thai administration, as the Highland NGO recognised. A senior staff member, Khun Rungsarith, told me how staff at the Highland NGO had gradually come to realise that a number of key issues affecting highlanders "could only be solved at the policy level" (pers. comm., Sept. 2001). The organisation therefore had to look at "how to lobby the government and get policy changed" (pers. comm., Sept. 2001). This had led to the adoption of a strategy of political engagement in almost every area of the organisation's work.

While member villages were a vital part of both decision-making and implementation, the long-term functioning of the Highland NGO and its programs also relied on a very different set of partners, that is, large international NGOs and bilateral donors. The work funded by outside donors could not always focus on the priorities set by community representatives because these agencies have their own list of priority work areas. Part of the reason for working with international organisations was the pragmatic necessity to secure an income for the organisation. However,

> there is also a hidden agenda, which is to work through international organisations in order to get our voice heard at the policy level in the Thai government. These institutions have the respect of the Thai government and get listened to. The Highland NGO's voice can be heard much more through the interventions of these organisations than it would be otherwise (Rungsarith, pers. comm., June 2001).

Large international organisations have the potential to influence policy makers and, by working with them, the Highland NGO might be able to capitalise on that influence.

One example of such cooperation was the Sentinel Surveillance Program that UNICEF was in the process of establishing in northern Thailand. The program was an initiative to combat child trafficking and would be an extension of similar programs in Burma and Laos. It involved recruiting individuals from border communities, training them in research and social surveying, then sending them back to their home villages to carry out research in the community on HIV/AIDS, migration patterns and so forth. This information would be fed back to the United Nations, which would compile regional information and alert the appropriate national agencies, such as the Thai Health Department, of problems arising in particular locations. I found the idea of such surveillance a little sinister and asked Rungsarith if he was not also concerned. He agreed that the program was a bit like Big Brother, but emphasised that it would be a useful way to bring the problems of highland communities to the attention of the Thai government.

Rungsarith did not see any conflict between the Highland NGO's efforts to act in the best interests of local communities and interventions which would extend the state's governing practices, such as the close monitoring of communities and the regulation of health. Through cooperation with the United Nations, the Highland NGO hoped to promote a better understanding of the highlands among Thai government officials who, Rungsarith and others at the Highland NGO insisted, continued to adhere to an outdated vision of the 'hill tribe problem'. This strategy also meant that the Highland NGO was involved in a process through which border villages would become more closely monitored, albeit by a UN agency. This would in turn facilitate closer regulation of villages by the state. The kind of regulation Rungsarith anticipated, such as the intervention of the Health Department, involved an extension of government into these peripheral areas. Closer attention to the health of the population and the treatment of disease was unlikely to be unwelcome, but would constitute the extension of the hand of the state into border villages. For communities still struggling to have their basic rights to citizenship and land title recognised, the increased presence of state authorities could also be a concern and certainly was not high on the list of priorities put forward to the Highland NGO. Where communities are marginalised and mistreated by government authorities, the NGO's cooperation with a program that would essentially strengthen government presence in the hills was problematic. However, from the NGO's perspective the benefits of cooperation outweighed the risks. By cooperating with the UN, the Highland NGO would be able to use the Sentinel program and its connection with a high-profile international NGO to have its concerns brought more effectively to the attention of sections of the Thai government.

Introducing 'Outside' Agendas: Gender Equity

The Highland NGO's reliance on international NGOs also made it difficult to maintain its focus on locally appropriate interventions and respect for traditional cultural practices. Under the orthodoxy of participatory practice, all members of a community should be involved in development, including those usually excluded from decision-making: the 'poorest of the poor', members of lower castes, women, and so on. This democratic process, however, can challenge traditional cultural practices. In the course of its work the Highland NGO had to balance the values and perspectives of the highlanders with whom they worked with those of the international NGOs providing their funding.

The introduction of a gender program in the mid-1990s provided one example of the challenges of trying to meet funders' requirements while adhering to cultural norms. I interviewed the head of this program, Khun Arunya, during my residency with the Highland NGO. I asked Arunya to tell me the story of how she became involved in NGO work. She spoke to me at length about the history of her involvement and the work she was doing in the NGO's women's program. She said that the program was initiated partly in response to the requirement from their funding partners for Gender Aware Development approaches. However, it also stemmed from recognition by the Highland NGO that working with the people meant working with women. In Arunya's words, "it could not be avoided" (Arunya, pers. comm., June 2001).

Arunya told me that she felt she had to constantly justify the program, both in the villages where she worked and to other male staff members. Often she was asked, "Isn't this just trying to impose a Western standard?" In the context of an organisation that promoted and encouraged tradition, this focus on gender was taken by some as a threat to their culture. Even among NGO staff, she said, questions were raised as to why the gender working group was trying to change culture, that this went against efforts to revive old cultures and the laws that were given by the divine to allow humans to live together peacefully.

A gender-aware approach seeks to ensure that the concerns of men and women are valued equally in a participatory planning process.[4] Given that technological change in rural communities often

---

[4] See, for example, Chambers (1983, 1997) and Young (1997).

results in increased workloads for women, the gender-aware approach is one attempt to ameliorate this possibility. Arunya's detractors argued that the gender-aware approach had emerged from 'the West' and was thus a non-indigenous approach that could harm an indigenous way of life. Such objections highlighted the possibility that the gender approach conflicted with the value accorded to local priorities and perspectives by a participatory ethic. While the value of gender equity is a core part of the ideals that inform contemporary participatory methods, a strict definition of participation also insists on utmost respect for the local, which often involves the strong defence of traditional practices. In this case, the focus on women introduced exogenous values that would, the critics feared, potentially undermine the strength of local values and social norms.

Although ideas of gender equity are not part of most traditional highland cultures, the introduction of gender work did not necessarily violate the pro-local ethic of the Highland NGO. The decision to introduce a gender program can be seen as part of the same political rationale that led the organisation to utilise a positive discourse of Karen as guardians of the forest and to make the most of opportunities to be heard by the Thai government through cooperation with UNICEF. The gender program was certainly trying to change social norms in highland villages, thereby seeming to go against the wishes of a sector of the community. This was also part of a political and moral agenda introduced from 'outside'. Yet Arunya believed the program was justifiable because she felt that adopting the ideals of gender equity were a crucial part of highland communities' adapting to modern circumstances. She told me that the main task of the gender program was to recover discarded practices and adapt them to new circumstances. She gave the example of the project in Hmong communities:

> In Hmong society people think that the men are very aggressive to women. But in the tradition there is a very, very strong clan system. In that system you have to respect each other. The interconnections between clans are very strong, they are systems of connection and control to protect women. Now the clan system is weaker and protections within the system are weaker. The old system is valuable as a way of trying to show how the systems were different in the past in terms of respect for women. We try and show how it has changed, how the system has collapsed. We work to recover it and use it as a way to try to think about how

> gender relations have changed, and think about how to improve
> the systems in practice (Arunya, pers. comm., June 2001).

Arunya's approach to introducing gender equity programs shows the fine balance that the Highland NGO had to maintain. On the one hand, these professionals depended on the support and cooperation of international donor agencies and espoused many of the values of a new development approach, including a strong advocacy of participatory approaches and a gender-aware approach. On the other hand, they attempted to keep 'traditional' culture alive by using culture as a ground upon which to create new and better futures for highland villagers.

Pragmatic Political Engagement

Keeping a balance between competing stakeholders and potentially contradictory ideologies required that the organisation approach its moral and ideological foundations with a certain flexibility. A participatory ideal drove the work of Arunya and others at the Highland NGO and provided a reference point in the pursuit of particular political outcomes. Where the young researchers at the Uplands Program found themselves frustrated by the sense of not being able to act in keeping with their ideals, staff members at the Highland NGO, while adhering to those same ideals, did not engage with them as an absolute moral imperative.

Because the political nature of the organisation's work was at the forefront, the Highland NGO had a mandate for practices that would otherwise be seen to contradict the participatory ideal. For the Uplands Program's young researchers and a senior generation of development professionals, such pragmatic and flexible adherence to a participatory code could well constitute 'failure'. For the Highland NGO, it did not. This may have been in part because, as highlanders themselves, the Highland NGO staff saw themselves, and were seen by others, to *innately* represent the best interests of other highlanders. Whether or not this was so, I suggest that the Highland NGO's mandate emerged from what Laclau speaks of as a "game of decisions taken in an undecideable terrain" (Laclau, 1996: 34). On such a terrain, no absolute right or wrong can ever exist. Participation, pro-localism and gender equity are not founded upon a fixed moral ground. The ideals of equality, freedom and empowerment upon which they are based cannot be seen as innately, uncontestably good.

Rather, they are ideals that one makes a *political decision* to believe in, to defend and enact (Laclau, 1996).

By engaging overtly in a political struggle, the Highland NGO was not constrained by the sense of moral imperative that affected others in the development community. While the concept of the political decision was not itself part of the Highland NGO's philosophy, this was the way the organisation approached its work. Participation was important but it was not seen as a moral imperative. What was imperative were the political outcomes of their work — the opportunities that the staff could create with a pragmatic and strategic approach.

Political decisions are not, however, made in a vacuum. The political structures of the nation-state, the concepts of national identity, the extent of social or political reform acceptable to the state delimit the possible interventions that the Highland NGO could enact. These constraints may also be slowly altered and remade:

> Power is not stable or static, but is remade at various junctures within everyday life ... social transformation occurs not merely by rallying mass numbers in favour of a cause, but precisely through the ways in which daily social relations are rearticulated, and new conceptual horizons opened up by anomalous or subversive practices (Butler, 2000: 13–14).

Opening up new ways by which a highlander identity could be (re)articulated was precisely the Highland NGO's aim — generating broad social change by bringing their concerns and priorities to the attention of the public and the state. The Highland NGO's interventions exploited the openings that became possible in contemporary struggles of power involving highland professionals, development professionals, researchers, government representatives and villagers.

The Citizenship Movement

The Highland NGO's use of the Karen consensus and their collaboration with the UN in the Sentinel Surveillance Program were both examples of the organisation exploiting available openings in the dominant discourse in order to achieve its goals. The NGO's contributions to the citizenship movement was the best example of how this approach could succeed in achieving significant shifts in government policy. As Laclau (1996, 2000) argues, it is possible for social transformation to occur because, no matter how apparently dominant and immoveable, any hegemonic entity is flawed and incomplete. In the case of the Highland NGO's negotiations with state powers over citizenship, it was the incompleteness of the discourse of Thai national identity that created the possibility for change. By finding and exploiting the flaws in established national identities, the Highland NGO was able to pursue its overarching political project to obtain equal status for highlanders.

The citizenship program has in fact been working to achieve part of the original highland development agenda established in the 1960s, that is, to bring highlanders within the embrace of the Thai state (Torpey, 2000). The Highland NGO worked alongside other community organisations in a broad movement to grant citizenship to eligible highlanders, a project which was also aimed at bringing highlanders within the state. As a campaign for citizenship, it fits clearly with Cruikshank's analysis of how some non-government organisations seek to "[constitute] citizens out of subjects and [maximise] their political participation" (Cruikshank, 1999: 67). Whereas in the 1960s the motivation was to secure highlander loyalties in the face of communist insurgency, now the aim was to get the Thai state to recognise the legitimacy of highlanders as part of the Thai nation and for the government to accept their rights and responsibilities towards these would-be citizens.

Although many highlanders have lived within the borders of Thailand since those modern borders were first drawn (see Chapter Three), by the early 2000s the majority had not been granted citizenship. Thai citizenship was formalised in legislation passed in 1956 to register citizens through a nationwide Household Registration. This was the first legislation to formally distinguish between Thai and non-Thai and to determine citizenship by place of birth (Suppachai, 1999). In 1972 fears of a massive influx of refugees fleeing from the conflict in Vietnam led to the introduction of stricter citizenship laws that no longer gave automatic citizenship to those born on Thai soil (Suppachai, 1999; Wanat, 1989). Thereafter citizenship became possible only if one parent had also been born in Thailand.

Not having been registered under the 1956 Act, highland people were then unable to register themselves as Thai citizens under the new legislation. According to a statement from the Ministry of the Interior, highlanders were not given citizenship due to technical legal details:

> The hill tribe people are Thai but because the officers cannot
> grant Household Registration and legal Thai status to them, this
> in effect means that in the eyes of the law their status is that of
> non-Thai (Ministry of the Interior, 1974, quoted in Suppachai,
> 1999: 3).

Khun Wandii, who led the Highland NGO's citizenship campaign, explained to me that in place of citizenship the government had issued a proportion of highland people with Temporary Household Registration and special hill tribe identification cards. These cards severely restricted movement within the Thai state. Highlanders could not travel between provinces without special letters of permission and could not obtain a passport and were therefore unable to travel legally outside the country.

Issued with temporary registration papers and cards identifying them as non-Thai, highland people were constantly under threat of expulsion (Chupinit, 1987). In 1987, for example, the Thai military conducted raids on 13 Akha villages in Chiang Rai Province (Kammerer, 1989). The villagers were herded onto trucks and driven through the night to the Burmese border, where they were dumped. To the dismay of government officials, photos of the burned villages appeared in the *Bangkok Post* the next day along with comments from a Thai official about the raid. He justified the actions of the military by saying that no-one's homes had been burned down, just some "huts" that had belonged to "illegal immigrants" (*Bangkok Post*, 15 Oct. 1987 cited by McKinnon, 1989: 307–08). While the Ministry of Interior had implicitly recognised hill tribes as Thai back in 1974, without the appropriate papers there was little highlanders could do to contest their classification as illegal immigrants. The threat of expulsion remained even for highlanders who had obtained citizenship. Under citizenship laws introduced in the late 1990s, the Interior Minister has the authority to revoke the citizenship of any naturalised Thai who commits an offence considered a threat to national security.

In 1999 the government decided to designate all highlanders without citizenship papers as aliens. Although a proportion of high-landers had succeeded in obtaining citizenship papers over the years, it was estimated that around 60 per cent remained without. The alien declaration would therefore affect many with a legitimate claim to citizenship. In response, activists and Thai academics, along with the powerful people's organisation, The Assembly of the Poor, organised a Rally for Rights, which took place from April to May of 1999. Thousands gathered in the northern provincial capital of Chiang Mai to call for a delay in the process of conferring alien status and to "ask the government to register hill tribe people as Thai citizens and therefore to grant nationality" (Chainarong and Suppachai, 1999). The campaign of 1999 emphasised the right to citizenship based on the status of many highlanders as "second and third generation Thai" and their recognition in the past as *de facto* citizens (Chainarong and Suppachai, 1999). The movement took pains to distinguish between "native hill tribe and highland peoples and immigrant or refugee hill tribe groups" (Suppachai, 1999: 6). Eventually the Rally was successful in delaying the declaration of non-citizens as illegal aliens. Highlanders were given one year to submit applications for citizenship.

The Highland NGO soon took action to support those who were eligible to apply for citizenship. Many mountain communities had not been informed of this new opportunity to apply for citizenship. Khun Wandii began to visit as many remote communities as possible to spread the word. One recurring problem was that the application form had to be completed in Thai, even though many potential applicants were illiterate. Activists successfully campaigned to make it legal for someone other than the applicant to fill out the necessary paperwork. This enabled the Highland NGO to partner with the District Government (*Amphoe*), responsible for processing the majority of applications, to hold citizenship application field days. Amphoe officials would carry their registration records into a central location in the hills, set up in a school hall or under tarpaulins and, with the help of the Highland NGO team acting as scribes and advisors, slowly evaluate and process the applications of the hundreds of highlanders who showed up.

In April 2001 I went with a team to a Lahu village to the north of Chiang Mai close to the Burmese border. The team set up in the assembly area of a school, essentially an area with just a concrete floor and corrugated-iron roof with no walls. The school grounds were bare dirt and when the wind picked up over the next few days the dust would find its way into everything. Most of the volunteers and government officials resorted to wearing scarves and face masks to avoid breathing in dust. Around the perimeter of the rectangular concrete floor we placed the school desks to face outwards. One of

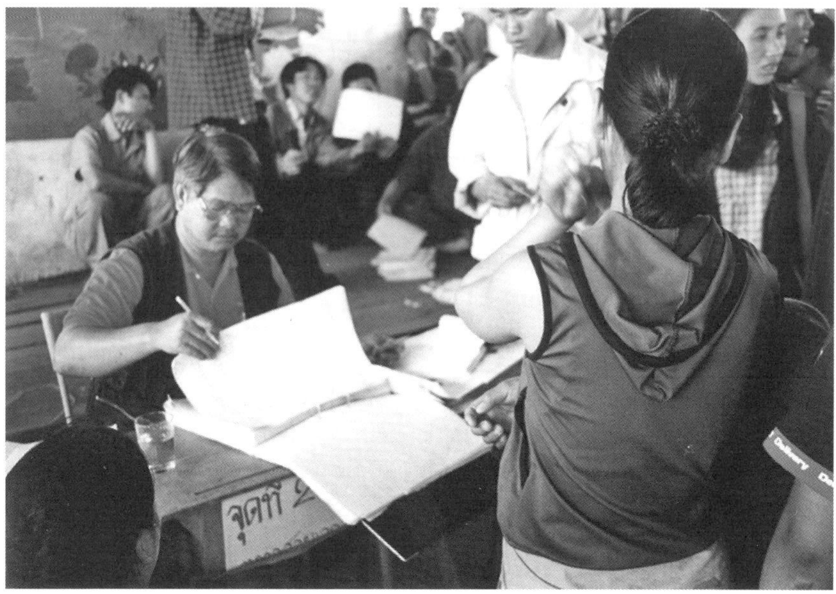

Plate 7   Step one in the citizenship application process: initial assessment of applicants' eligibility for citizenship by Amphoe staff (Lahu village, 2001)

the young men on the team started tying tape around the perimeter of the building to create a narrow entranceway and corridors that applicants would have to follow as they moved through the application process. I remember thinking that this attempt at crowd management was a little extreme. It was not until late in the morning when more and more people began to show up that I realised how necessary it was. Individuals or family groups would be ushered through the entranceway to speak first to the senior *Amphoe* official, who would inform them whether they were eligible to apply (see Plate 7).

Applicants who were eligible moved on to a desk where the volunteers asked them questions and filled out their application forms on their behalf (see Plate 8). This could take hours or even days of confirming birthdays, matching the right individuals to the right paperwork and locating birth certificates. The volunteers were given strict instructions: they had to ensure that applicants and their parents were really born in Thailand. Khun Wandii's instructions were that they must ask: "Is this the truth? You're not lying are you? You know you can't lie. Is the name you give a real name? How exactly is it spelled? If you get a single letter out of place the Amphoe

Plate 8   Step two: filling out the form with the help of volunteers (Lahu village, 2001)

will send it back" (field notes, April 2001). The applicants came clutching old documents that many had stored in their houses for decades, yellowing household registration forms with a photograph of each member of the household, their name and date of birth. After the forms were deemed in order, each applicant was fingerprinted and photographed (see Plates 9 and 10). Then the headman of the village confirmed each person's identity and sanctioned his/her application by putting his thumbprint on each one.

Altogether the team stayed in this village for four days, barely a fraction of applicants had completed the process by the time we left. We had arrived on Sunday and yet by Wednesday there were still so many familiar faces of those who had been waiting there since Monday. Groups gathered to wait in any spot of shade they could find against the school walls, under trees, and loitering by the stands that had been set up selling iced soft drinks, cold Chang beer and sugary snacks.

On one of the days the team received a visit from the Chief District Officer (*Nai Amphoe*). Wearing dark glasses and the stiff public servant's uniform, he made his way through the crowd with a beer in hand. Observing proceedings, he turned to Wandii and

Plate 9   Step three: taking the photo ID (Phrao, 2001)

Plate 10   Step four: fingerprinting the applicants (Phrao, 2001)

asked her, in an accusing tone, "Why is it that NGOs are always getting involved in these things?" (field notes, April 2001). Wandii pointed out that there were many other people present besides the NGOs. The Nai Amphoe replied:

> Ah, so everyone is a good person. Then tell me why is it that when we arrest people the NGOs complain? And why is it that when they practise slash and burn and we arrest them for it, the NGOs speak about rights? What rights do they have to cut the forest? If we didn't arrest them, they would go and do more. Look. Look, over there, it's slash-and-burn farming. What about the environment?

He turned to a villager who happened to be standing nearby and, grasping him by the elbow, asked, "Have you cut enough? Have you cut enough? Yes, you have. That's good. Enough already. You don't need to cut anymore." He moved on through the crowd and later cornered a young mother with a baby on her hip. He asked her, "How many children have you had already?" When he did not get a response he repeated the question and, still getting none, exclaimed in mock horror to Wandii, "What's this? They can't speak Thai! They're getting citizenship but they can't speak Thai!"

Not much more than an hour after the Nai Amphoe and his entourage departed, two Border Patrol Police personnel arrived. Ignoring the presence of Amphoe officials, they went immediately to Wandii and pulled her aside. Wandii later related what they told her, "You can't possibly give these people citizenship. They are drug dealers and they cut down the forest" (field notes, 24 April 2001). The Border Patrol Police later rang the Amphoe office to confirm Wandii's story and did not reappear again in the following days.

To some extent the consternation of the Border Patrol Police and the comments made by the Nai Amphoe were understandable. Previous laws had stated that anyone with drug-related convictions or anyone who had practised swidden farming was ineligible for citizenship. However, these laws had been overturned. Previous citizenship laws had also required that applicants be fluent in spoken and written Thai, but that too was no longer a requirement. The lack of awareness of both the Nai Amphoe and the Border Patrol Police regarding such changes to citizenship legislation testified to the lack of training and to the persistence of negative stereotypes about the hill tribes. The fact that such stereotypes continue to inform the views of parties as powerful as the Nai Amphoe and the Border Patrol Police was significant. Of all the representatives of government, the Border Patrol Police continue to have the most widespread and comprehensive presence in the mountains. And although the Nai Amphoe are located in lowland towns and cities, it was they who held primary responsibility for approving or declining highlanders' applications to become Thai citizens. On that April day in the mountains, these powerful voices served to remind the hopeful applicants of the undesirability of their hill tribe identity, thereby reinforcing the morally charged distinctions between hill tribe and Thai.

While these incidents provided an example of the abiding power of ethnic stereotypes, overall the citizenship field days spoke also of the success of the strategies used by activists to recast hill tribes as Thai. In their reference to 'de facto citizens' activists had constructed a highlander identity that was legitimately Thai, renaming highlanders Thai-hill tribe to clearly distinguish them from outsiders and refugees. As Wandii stated, the whole effort of the citizenship movement was about

> working between government and NGOs and villagers to try and get the maximum applications through and find the best system for getting citizenship to those eligible, to true Thai citizens who were born here.... (Wandii, pers. comm., Feb. 2001).

Dividing hill tribe subjects into those who were 'true Thai citizens' and those who were ineligible for citizenship was therefore an effective campaign. It was effective in part because, rather than challenging the state's discourse of nationhood and belonging, it worked within established definitions of who had a right to be Thai. Instead of contesting the national discourses that had excluded highlanders, the campaign sought to alter how a legitimate national subject was defined. The effect, of course, was that there were still clearly demarcated categories of the legitimate insider (the Thai citizen) and the illegitimate alien. The use of an ethnic category within a discourse of nationhood was itself not questioned. What was questioned was the content of that category.

Within the citizenship campaign, the Highland NGO worked by playing upon the incompleteness of ethnic and national identifications. The campaign deliberately blurred the boundaries between highlander and Thai in an effort to recast the highlander as legitimately Thai. To achieve this, the Highland NGO promoted a new understanding of the closeness of highlanders and Thai by emphasising their shared differences and distance from the non-Thai hill tribe, that is, the refugee or illegal immigrant. This was not a challenge to the foundations of Thai identity but an attempt to shift it just enough to make room for highlanders within the nation. A new sense of what it meant to be Thai now included those highlanders who had been allocated a position at the margins since Thai nationalism took shape in the first part of the twentieth century.

Conclusion

The Highland NGO represents a new way of working in the highlands and one that contrasts greatly with the approaches of the Uplands Program or earlier bilateral highland development programs. Both organisations adhere to a similar participatory ethic and work towards an ultimate goal of 'improvement'. Both are subject to the constraints and agendas of outside funding agencies and have to work within a political terrain shaped by competing interests at the level of state governments, academic institutions and the village. These myriad political interests do not always agree with the participatory approaches they seek to implement. One example of this was the Highland NGO's gender program, which was initiated in large part due to external funding agencies insisting on a Gender Aware Development approach, even though some highlanders felt that this did unacceptable violence to traditional cultural values.

Because of the Highland NGO's overt engagement with national politics and its emphasis on discursive intervention, however, the organisation appears to be able to work well within such outside interests and constraints. The organisation is based on configurations of the highlander development professional and engages very differently with the highlands as a space of development, producing very different insights into modes of 'legitimate' intervention in the highlands. The ability to act differently stems in part from the organisation's willingness to work for the interests of the state when it is advantageous to highland communities. The Highland NGO's annual planning process shows how the organisation may be seen, in Cruikshank's (1999) terms, to be "training citizens". The organisation's involvement in such initiatives as UNICEF's Sentinel Surveillance program and its efforts to obtain citizenship papers for highlanders also demonstrates the degree to which the NGO is complicit with processes through which highland communities will become more closely regulated by the disciplinary mechanisms of the state.

My informants at the Highland NGO presented all of these programs as an integral part of a broad strategy through which the organisation could achieve the central goal of gaining legitimacy and respect for highlanders within the Thai nation-state. In contrast to the discomfort felt by those criticising the Uplands Program, staff members at the Highland NGO did not feel they were violating precepts of ultimate loyalty to and respect for local communities. These highlander professionals felt they were part of the local and were working in 'their own' communities and villages. However, their lack of discomfort is also an indication of the pragmatic and politically aware approach being taken across the organisation.

The politically engaged approach of the Highland NGO focused upon a strategic use of discourse. The organisation's use of the Karen consensus adopted popular understandings of 'good' Karen and 'bad' Hmong and began to reshape popular conceptions of highlanders' abilities to conserve the forest. Likewise, the way the organisation managed its relationships with international NGOs demonstrated how orthodox ideals of 'participation' and 'empowerment' were being used as flexible and open signifiers, to be used tacitly within the play of politics rather than as absolutes to which one must strictly adhere. Finally, the citizenship campaign demonstrated how the organisation and its campaign partners carefully exploited the openings within a dominant discourse of Thai nationhood and national belonging.

Although the Highland NGO was certainly not immune to criticism, the approaches it has taken open up new possibilities for post-development practices. The organisation was founded on a participatory ethic but managed to find a way to operate that did not need to appeal to universalising discourses of absolute moral good. Its approach was instead to take an openly political mode of engagement and pursue interventions that took advantage of the pliability of discourse. Knowledge and representation were used as part of a political strategy in which discourses around ethnicity, development methods and so on, were political tools intended to shape clearly defined outcomes. As a result of its overt political engagement, I suggest that the Highland NGO was able to evade the impossible ideals that plague others. Here participation was not a moral absolute but a guiding philosophy that must sometimes be subordinated to more pressing political goals.

8

Conclusion:
Imagining Post-development

Challenge: Don't let developers get away with their authoritarian and dogmatic ways…. Pester them about moral commitment.
Demonstrate: Show others that the common poor folk are quite capable of making their own decisions, good ones….
Advocate: Speak for the People, but only saying what they have asked you to say (Somsak, 2005: 309).

What we need is a channel to national policy formulation (Hmong NGO worker, 2007).

Every development professional knows that there is an inevitable mismatch between the ideals that underpin their practice and the reality of what they are able to achieve. This book has charted some of the real world conditions that cause this failure in northern Thailand. I have examined the intricacies of Thai nationalism and the accompanying marginalisation of highland peoples, and have discussed how development agendas are co-opted by political agendas and how the hopes and aspirations of professionals are constantly challenged. Experienced professionals expect these obstacles to appear and persevere in the hope that a way will be found to do development better. In the meantime they must be content with achieving small successes and incremental gains. Is there a better way to practise development? Are there different ways to construct a professional identity or are professionals condemned to this unending cycle of hope, disappointment and compromise?

I began this book with the example of the president of the Office of Retired Developers, who typifies the combination of cynicism and hope that characterises professionals with whom I worked in northern Thailand. The president's cynicism is a result of his extensive experience, backed up by a perceptive critique of the development industry. Yet he continues to work and the development industry continues to thrive. Development professionals from Europe still carry out research in poor communities in northern Thailand; Australian development consultants still work with highland farmers on resource management; and educated urban Thai still head to the hills to work on community development projects. The president, along with other professionals discussed in this book, persists in his task because he remains hopeful that he can do good and make a difference, and in some small way make the world a fairer place. More often than not, they believe that this difference can come about if they allow themselves, and the programs they work on, to be guided by the needs and desires of the people with whom they work.

What sustains these professionals is also what shapes their identities and what underlies their cynicism and critiques of the development industry: the desire to help people in disadvantaged or marginalised communities and the belief that it is possible to do so. The accusation that development is a means of domination and control is itself based on a belief that development really should be able to make the world a fairer place, that it should allow the poor to be empowered and bring about the kind of aid that local communities genuinely need. Ultimately, most critiques of development do not reject the aims of development per se; what they criticise is how the development industry has failed to achieve them. This failure is attributed to the fact that the work of development professionals simply cannot be separated from relationships of power and the machinations of regional and global politics. All agree that a fairer, more equitable world is desirable and possible. However, while the desire is ubiquitous, it is seldom achievable, mostly because of the intrusion of politics.

Learning from the case of northern Thailand, I argue that the way forward is not to reject but to embrace the politics of development. Given that power struggles, geopolitics and ideological contests are inevitable, how can development professionals engage with them more effectively, while still trying to achieve their idealistic goals?

In this final chapter I review the overall findings of the book and explore some ideas for a different approach, one that acknowledges that hope and idealism are the necessary starting points for development professionals but eventually it is politics that must shape practice.

Learning from the Highland Development Programs

In northern Thailand there are as many reasons to be hopeful as to be critical of development. From the 1960s onwards, highland development programs have been embedded in the messy power struggles over the highlands and the racialised debates over the rights of the hill tribes to live and farm there. There is no neutral starting point of seeking just to improve the quality of life amongst highland peoples. At the same time, there are dedicated professionals who, with their village counterparts, have had an impact and have made some progress towards equity. An important factor in these modest successes is the discourse of participatory development that has shaped professional identities, together with expectations of their own responsibilities. This discourse emerged from the combination of debates about the ethics of Third World research, analyses of post-colonial power relations, and the search for better development approaches. Within each of these debates it became accepted that the professional has a responsibility to assist and empower the disadvantaged and poor communities of the Third World. That ideal continues to hold fast.

In northern Thailand, as elsewhere, the ideal has also been profoundly challenged by the development industry being called upon to assist in incorporating the highlands into the nation-state. This process has redefined the geopolitical space of the highlands. It has been changed from an expansive non-state space to one bounded and contained within a politically defined sovereign territory. Highland subjects have been redefined as racial 'others', not as a part of the nation but an ambiguous presence within the geobody of the Thai state. As a result, the highlands and highlanders became problematic. Highlander peoples were reconstituted as problematic subjects in need of remedies applied by professional 'experts' from the urban lowlands and from abroad. Development was called upon not to assist and empower the highlanders but to address the problems they were seen to pose to the state. Thus from the 1960s onwards, the northern borderlands became a space that required the transformative power of development interventions and problem-solving research. The highlands thereby became the focus of the Thai state's nation-building efforts, precipitating a discourse of a 'hill tribe problem' that eventually meshed with international concerns about drug trafficking and communism. Both social science research and community development were co-opted by these broad geopolitical concerns. They were called upon to address the international community's preoccupation with a communist threat and heroin trafficking while assisting the Thai government in bringing highland territory under the control and regulation of the state.

Though the professionals who went into the hills in the 1960s and 1970s were not themselves motivated by these political concerns, their work was inevitably bound up with them. Those who hoped to conduct harmless anthropological research, and to adhere to a vision of the researcher as a beneficial presence in highland communities were forced to reconsider their position following the Thailand Controversy. The controversy forced all professionals in the hills to acknowledge that they had access to sensitive information that could potentially be used to harm their highland collaborators. This presented a significant challenge to their vision of benign and beneficial professionalism. The response of the professional community, however, was not to abandon this ideal but to restate more explicitly a professional ethics that emphasised a commitment to local communities. An example is the Code of Ethics put forward by the American Anthropological Association following the Thailand Controversy (see Chapter Two).

Despite the intermingling of politics and intervention, the professionals I worked with in northern Thailand continued to hope that they could serve a greater good beyond politics. Realising that development was being driven by external geopolitical interests, professionals responded by finding ways to work within the system. Throughout the 1980s they pushed for participatory approaches and sought to advocate on behalf of highlanders and support efforts to create indigenous highlander organisations. Their ideal was thus a pro-local professional whose primary role was to act for the communities with which they worked.

This pro-local approach has since risen to a position of orthodoxy. A rhetoric of 'the local' along with participatory methods such as Participatory Rural Appraisal are now intrinsic to the discursive practices of both 'pro-local' professionals and their conservative opponents. Through the work of professionals in the 1970s and 1980s, the pro-local ethic has helped to transform the political landscape of the highlands. The work of these professionals supported and facilitated the rise of new highland subjects that have now come into their own. This is visible in the rise of a new generation of highland professionals and the emergence of outspoken highlander leaders and activists who are neither professionals nor part of an urban Thai society, but are nevertheless able to add their voice to contemporary debates. With the rise of these new subjects, professionals have been repositioned as facilitators instead of experts. Those who are not highlanders have begun to be sidelined as legitimate and knowledgeable advocates for highlanders.

Meanwhile, the region has been transformed. The ideological power struggles that characterised the Cold War have long since dissipated and international attention has shifted to other trouble spots. As the Thai economy has grown, international aid agencies have relocated programs to the poorer nations of Cambodia and Laos. Opium eradication efforts moved to Afghanistan as it became the centre of global opium production and one of the flashpoints for the geopolitics of terror that has filled the gap left by the Cold War. Reforms in China, Laos and Vietnam have opened the Greater Mekhong region for increasing levels of economic cooperation and trade. Cross-border tensions in northern Thailand have diminished. There is no longer any fear of armed insurrection in the highlands and the disbanding of the Tribal Research Centre is to an extent a reflection of the diminishing importance of the highlands to central government policy-makers. The northern border region is now mainly of concern due to the lesser problem of the continuing flow of people escaping the hardships of life in Myanmar. Many of these refugees are highland minority groups and their presence in Thailand as illegal immigrants has complicated negotiations to grant Thai highlanders citizenship rights. The new generation of highland professionals thus has an important role to play in negotiating between highland peoples and successive Thai governments that remain hostile to this population within the Thai border.

In this contemporary context, the belief that development can be politically neutral and that professionals can work according to a pro-local ideal still abides. This was demonstrated in the debates that surrounded the first phase of work in the Uplands Program (see Chapter Six). Notwithstanding ample literature detailing the difficulties of implementing a participatory approach, these debates showed how young researchers and experienced practitioners alike continued to represent the ideal of the participatory professional subject as achievable and participatory methods as a moral imperative. For various reasons, these young researchers expressed a sense of failure in their attempts to realise this ideal and worried that participation was not being done properly within the Uplands Program. The sentiment was shared by many senior professionals from the wider community who considered that the program was not properly following a participatory approach.

The concern that participation was not being undertaken properly failed to recognise that it will always be impossible to achieve the ideal. While the values that shape participatory approaches are meant to be universal, applicable anywhere and everywhere, in reality, there is nowhere they can be put into practice without encountering the messy politics of institutions, communities and nations. The ideal cannot be brought into being. Yet the insistence that it ought to be possible led, in this case, to the participatory ideal becoming a way for the professional community to regulate itself, measuring success or failure against an overarching moral imperative.

Regardless of the constant international, national, local and institutional politics, the ideal of a pro-local professional continues to shape professional identities. The hope that development will succeed in bringing genuine assistance and empowerment continues to be the basis of how professionals find meaningful identities for themselves and locate a sense of purpose in their work. The insistence upon an overarching aim of emancipation nevertheless sits uneasily with the necessary politics of development. As a result, professionals engage in constant rounds of critiquing established practice, finding fault, proposing new methods and approaches, and when these solutions fail, starting all over again. The ideals in which these successive solutions are grounded do not change and as they are reiterated in each new solution, they become more and more of a strict moral imperative. Since it is an imperative that no professional can live up to, development becomes doomed to constant failure.

There are alternatives to this hopeless cycle. One possibility lies in the pragmatism of professionals like Andreas Neef, who subscribed to a participatory ideal but knew he could not manage the Uplands Program without making compromises. The need for funding, the realities of gaining and keeping the necessary institutional support, and the challenges of partnership with large and complex communities meant that strict adherence to a participatory ideal was not always possible. Although such difficulties are not uncommon, the failure to adhere to participatory principles drew criticism from the professional community.

Another possibility lies in the approach of the Highland NGO which explicitly acknowledged the politics of development. In contrast to the angst of those judging the Upland Program, the highlander professionals in the Highland NGO did not configure their professional identities around an overarching moral imperative and the desire to do good as if they could be free from any politics. The work of the Highland NGO was instead overtly political. Unlike the Upland Program's attempted neutrality, and in contrast to the pro-local discourse in which the Highland NGO had at its origins, the organisation engaged deliberately with the state, intervened on political issues and nurtured strategic links through community development programs that sought to advance a particular political agenda. The Highland NGO seemed capable of disengaging from participatory orthodoxy as a moral imperative, while continuing to work in accordance with an ethic of participation that was explicitly 'for the people'. The organisation could do this in part because of its position as 'local' within a participatory discourse. More importantly, however, the Highland NGO positioned itself as a leading player in political struggles over the highlands. Although the authority of the state seemed to be absolute and highlanders were continually marginalised, the Highland NGO recognised the openings and opportunities in these dominant discourses and was skilful in exploiting them. Implicit in its operations was the view that it must play the political game in order to obtain a better quality of life for all highlanders.

Learning from the practices of the Highland NGO, I suggest it is possible to find new ways of doing development that avoid unrealistic ideals and the inexorable sense of failure that ensues. By moving away from universalising discourses of development, it becomes possible to place the necessary politics of development at the forefront of professional identity and practice. The central role of the moral imperative can be replaced with a conscious decision to identify with a particular set of ideals and desired outcomes. Such a shift would enable professionals to abandon their laments of failure and focus instead on a more pragmatic approach of political strategy.

New Perspectives

Appealing to the ideals of empowerment, participation and emancipation as an absolute moral good drives the constant search for better, more effective development methods. The notion that emancipation and empowerment are achievable leads practitioners to search for an approach that will succeed, which leads inevitably to a sense of failure when the desired results do not materialise. Faced constantly with the question of why development interventions are not succeeding, professionals from the 1960s onwards have blamed top-down development approaches and the lack of adequate participation. If only development could extricate itself from external agendas and impositions then, maybe, a truly emancipatory process could occur.

The appeal to an achievable universal ideal, and the sense that the problems of development stem from the failure to achieve this ideal, provides some sense of certainty to professionals: although projects have their setbacks, there is an objective reason for these problems. It is more comforting to think that a project failed because it was not participatory enough than to think that development itself is always going to fail. Assigning blame in this way also allows hope — the hope that by finding better ways to intervene, professionals will be able to overcome the faults of the past and achieve their aims of empowerment, finding new ways to make a difference where their predecessors had failed. This may be reassuring, but it is also self-defeating. The impulse to define good practice as an orthodoxy of participation, then to hold professionals up against this standard, may become a barrier to achieving the objectives of participatory intervention.

There is another way of analysing stories of failure. By placing them in the context of political struggle, it becomes possible to see how discourses of participation are flawed. Participation cannot be the answer. No single approach can be. Participation is simply one idea, arising from a particular cultural, historical and ideological context, that yet claims to be a universal solution to development's ills. Discourses of participation can be likened to discourses of Marxism that, according to Laclau (1996), claimed to have identified the *real* causes of society's ills (class conflict) and proposed a solution to them. This constituted a claim to absolute truth and thus a claim to the universalism of Marxist politics. Laclau, however, argues that the history of Marxist politics demonstrates that "the chasm between the universal and the particular is unbridgeable" (Laclau, 1996: 26). Thus Marxist politics is a particular political perspective, arising from a particular space and time, masquerading as universalism.

The struggle to achieve participatory development, like Marxism, is a political struggle. It involves a claim to have identified the real reasons why development fails and to propose a solution. This solution rests on values that are assumed to be universal: freedom of speech, the right for a people to participate in decision-making that affects them, and to have a voice in representations of themselves. As with Marxism, however, these values are the product of a particular ideology, tied to a particular set of political goals. In Laclau's language, they are particularisms masquerading as universalism.

Understanding development efforts in this way does not make participatory goals any more achievable. What it reveals is that a pro-local participatory agenda will always be impossible to achieve. It is simply impossible to reconcile any universal ideal with messy reality: the values that pro-localism heroically assume to be universal are, in fact, particularisms. Therefore attempts to realise these 'universal' values in the local contexts are better understood as efforts to impose a particular political agenda. This critique of a participatory approach — that participatory development processes impose a particular system of values and conduct that do not necessarily mesh well with any given community — is not new.

The impossibility of realising the ideal may be seen as fairly self-evident but the implications for how we think about development practice and professional identities are not well appreciated. First, at a conceptual level there is a basic flaw in the logic of a pro-local approach that dooms it to constant failure. Participatory discourses are based on a rejection of any kind of politics of domination and are supposed to enable an emancipatory development process to take place. Yet, whenever there is an effort to impose a particular ideology, what results is inevitably authoritarianism. This is just what we see when professionals act as if participation were a moral imperative and are uncompromising in its execution. Putting participation into practice then becomes itself an act of domination. The development professional who strives to realise the ideal and be truly participatory will always fail. It is not just a matter of doing participation better and more effectively. The shortcomings of participatory approaches are bound up with the impossibility of the concept of participatory development itself. Whether the fault lies in unachievable ideals or underlying aims of participation that are flawed to begin with, professionals are still almost certain to fall short of their targets.

Failure is inevitable but not necessarily a problem. One response to the conundrum might be that if universalism is so deeply flawed, it would be best to rely instead solely on localised and particular aims and goals. Indeed participation, with its focus on the local, could be seen as inclined towards radical particularism and a rejection of universality. The stories from northern Thailand, however, show how important the reference to universalist values can be. Although many professionals were disappointed by the record of their achievements over the years, their dogged idealistic persistence did have an impact. Without that idealism and the hope that injustices could be addressed, highlanders could be empowered and the quality of life for mountain villagers could be improved, how would their efforts have been maintained?

Most importantly, a political perspective shows that it may not even be desirable to achieve the ideal — the failures and flaws are themselves vital. The effort towards emancipatory goals, the work of attempting to achieve social change, can be understood as the core of the emancipatory politics in which development professionals are engaged. Put simply, the act of *trying* is the most important thing.

Again, Laclau suggests a way to continue the struggle while embracing the impossibility of realising its goals. For Laclau, the impossibility of reconciling the universal and the particular is central to processes of political struggle. All that we might think of as universally true or universally of value — ideas such as empowerment, justice and equality — are impossible to pin down. "The universal ... does not have a concrete content of its own" (Laclau, 1996: 34). As soon as a universal value such as empowerment is seen to mean something in particular, such as the ability to vote, then it is no longer universal. Instead it becomes part of a historical moment, a particular place and time. Thus "universality is incommensurable with any particularity but cannot ... exist apart from the particular". Laclau argues that this paradox cannot be solved, but neither do we want to solve it: "its non-solution is the very precondition of democracy" (Laclau, 1996: 35).

> If democracy is possible, it is because the universal has no necessary body and no necessary content; different groups, instead,

compete between themselves to temporarily give to their particularisms a function of universal representation (Laclau, 1996: 34–5).

In their appeal to the universality of human rights, individualism, freedom and empowerment, participatory approaches are therefore part of a process of democracy in which competing ideologies attempt to achieve universality — and inevitably fail. This failure, while unavoidable, is also necessary. Laclau insists that democratic politics exists *because* universality is unachievable. While constantly seeking to appeal to a universal value, no one group is ever able to lay claim to any final truth. There is no point at which the answer is found and the process of contesting power is complete. In fact "incompletion and provisionality belong to the essence of democracy" (Laclau, 1996: 15–16).

Laclau's discussion of democracy and its ever-present incompletion and contingency has significant implications for how we think about development practice and the work of development professionals. Development, and particularly participatory development, is essentially part of the same democratic politics to which Laclau refers. The ethical foundations of development efforts are based on a vision of a fairer world, where there are no longer sharp disparities of wealth between a First World and Third World. This is a vision of a world where all have an equal voice and an equal opportunity and the accident of birth does not determine power or opportunity. Participatory development holds even closer to this vision by proposing that, in order to achieve such a world, the process of change must also be inclusive and empowering so that everyone has an equal voice and an equal ability to determine their future. According to Laclau's analysis, as well as to stories of development efforts in northern Thailand, Lesotho (Ferguson, 1994) or India (Mosse, 2005), this vision is unachievable. There are achievements, but the outcomes are never quite what was expected, and are always partial and incomplete. As we have seen, no mode of intervention can be a neutral formula for success, no single method can work unfailingly in every context.

Is there a way forward? I argue that development professionals should abandon their habit of dwelling on failure and their constant search for ways to achieve better intervention and truer, more genuine participation. Instead, they might focus on the inherent particularities of any discourse of intervention, its politicisation and its political goals in the context of social struggle. Far from being beholden to any universal moral imperatives, a pro-local participatory intervention must be understood as a political decision. It is a decision to follow a certain set of ideals, to attempt to apply a particular set of values and engage in an effort that will be inevitably partial and contingent.

By recognising the impossibility of achieving a universal ideal, and the inevitable partiality of any attempt, it becomes possible to reframe intervention and its egalitarian, emancipatory goals. The emancipation that professionals seek to achieve, and the democratic methods through which they hope to work, can thus be recast, not as moral imperative or absolute good but as something that they have chosen. Emancipation becomes something to work towards while recognising that compromise, partiality and negotiation are an inevitable part of the process. This means being cognisant that development interventions are not in service of an absolute or universal good but a contingent and politically embedded sense of 'goodness' that is bound up in regional politics and a particular moment in time.

Because development is inherently political, professionals can only begin to achieve the change they hope for by becoming conscious political actors. The discursive practices of the Highland NGO outlined in Chapter Seven point towards this approach as a legitimate form of development intervention. Here, perhaps, is an indication of what a post-development practice might look like: the political nature of development interventions and research are explicitly acknowledged, doing away with the unreal assumption of the purity and political neutrality of knowledge, or the universal good of improvement. In place of an essentialist, universalising moral imperative, a post-development practice could be acknowledged as part of a broader struggle through which professionals strive to bring into being particular democratic principles of an egalitarian society. Through these kinds of practices a post-development subject might emerge: a subject formed through an awareness of the mythical nature of development's moral aspirations, and one that acknowledges itself as a political creature and is able to formulate strategies based on an alert engagement with the politics of development.

Dialogues

In the following section three of the professionals discussed in this book offer their commentary and reflections on their own professional lives. Such dialogues seem an appropriate way to conclude a book about discourses of development professionalism. It is an opportunity for the professionals whose discursive practices I have analysed to have the final word and respond to my text. In doing so they provide a counterpoint to the arguments I present in this book and a corrective to the inevitable gaps and biases of my authorial voice.

These three contributors are not representative of the group of professionals I worked with in Chiang Mai. Unfortunately some key people could no longer be contacted at their old addresses; others were not able to deliver their pieces due to family and work commitments. It is particularly unfortunate that there is no highlander view represented here as those who had previously agreed to write were occupied with the unfolding political crisis in Thailand following Red Shirt demonstrations in early 2010.

The pieces that follow do, however, offer the insights of three professionals who have been prominently featured in this book. Andreas Neef was the manager of the Uplands Program discussed extensively in Chapter Six, and is now Professor in Resource Governance and Participatory Development at the Graduate School of Global Environmental Studies, Kyoto University. David Thomas is featured in Chapter Four as an example of the professionals of the 1980s and 1990s who worked to battle against 'the system', against mainstream ideas of top-down development and the vagaries of aid bureaucracies. He is recently retired from his position with Chiang Mai-based ICRAF. Finally, Ken Kampe, whose cynical yet hopeful views I borrowed in the opening of Chapter One, has been a development professional based in Chiang Mai since the 1970s and is President of the Office of Retired Developers. These three pieces have been written in dialogue with my book and will, I hope, also provide an opening for further reflection and debate.

A Personal Reflection on the Past and Future of Participatory Research for Rural Development

I first came across the issue of participatory research when I conducted field research for my PhD thesis on customary resource tenure systems in West Africa in the early 1990s. Throughout nearly two years of interviewing farmers and pastoralists in villages in Benin and Niger, I was confronted with the questions: "What is the benefit of your work for us?" and "When do you start the 'real' [development] project?" I always tried to adhere to the 'do no harm principle' and to avoid raising any false expectations. Sometimes I tried to explain the purpose of my research using a simple tree analogy: "Research is like planting a tree — it may take several years to get the first harvest and in some cases, the tree may never yield any fruits." Yet, I constantly felt the need to return at least something to my research subjects for their information and heart-warming hospitality. Small gifts, joint meals, video sessions and short excursions to agricultural research stations were among the favours I could return to them. I also gave them access to development workers who could provide them with direct help such as providing assistance to establish a women's processing group in one of the villages, although this did not lead to long-term support.

At the time, I was affiliated with a long-term collaborative research program known as Adapted Farming in West Africa, working in a larger, multi-disciplinary context and was just another junior researcher in a long line of young scientists from various disciplines. In my study area in Benin, most villagers had seen several researchers come and go without leaving anything behind but photos. When my time in this fascinating country drew to an end, I could pass the baton to a dedicated and experienced female scientist who spoke the local language and planned to engage 'my farmers' in agronomic, participatory on-farm experiments to improve soil fertility and raise crop productivity to enhance these people's livelihoods. She also hired the local research assistants who had worked with me for several months. I was glad to hear from her after a few months that she could make good use of my data and previous intensive contact with the farmers and that her work could provide them with substantial benefits.

In Niger, where I headed next, I was less fortunate in finding such a promising successor. When the time came to return to my university in Germany to write my thesis, I was well aware that this dissertation would ultimately not make any significant difference to the lives of rural people in the study areas because policy-makers would generally not read such academic work. Yet I left with the certainty that I had, at least, not harmed my research subjects and that I would be able to go back to these villages and enjoy the same level of trust and hospitability as before.

Before completing my PhD thesis, I was offered the chance to conceptualise and prepare another large-scale and long-term collaborative research program in Southeast Asia. Reluctantly I accepted the offer, participated in various preparatory missions to Thailand and Vietnam and organised a number of interdisciplinary study projects in the two countries to help identify relevant research topics. Since I had been dissatisfied with the lack of impact on people's lives of my PhD dissertation, I suggested to the program director — my former PhD advisor — that we jointly formulate a sub-project proposal with a participatory component to complement the academic sub-projects that were directly supported by the German Research Foundation (Deutsche Forschungsgemeinschaft).

Initially we designed the sub-project to look at the "Potential and constraints of participatory research approaches", one of more than 15 sub-projects in the program. To our surprise, as part of the program's review process in February 1999, a group of professors from various German universities and research institutions recommended that this sub-project be elevated to a super-ordinate role in the research program, ensuring that participatory approaches would be researched as a cross-cutting issue across the program. This role was later confirmed during the final evaluation in December 1999. Some reviewers were concerned that conflict might arise between our roles in giving advice to researchers employing participatory approaches and evaluating the potential and limitations of participatory approaches. However, the reviewers also regarded the systematic evaluation of the effectiveness of participatory research in different disciplines and in different phases of the research program as one of the most innovative features of the Uplands Program.

The reviewers' views were certainly not shared by all our fellow sub-project leaders in the program. Many of these branded participatory research as 'populist' and 'pseudo-scientific'. Some argued that research beyond the fences of research stations could not create *ceteris paribus* conditions because undesired farmer interventions or the micro-variability of agro-ecological conditions of farmers' fields, for example, would prevent control of the results. Others who had practised participatory approaches in previous research projects raised doubts about our competence to properly conduct participatory research, questioning the legitimacy of our role in this program. Nonetheless, even the critics eventually recognised the importance of the 'participation sub-project' in this program.

The German junior researchers were PhD students who, with only two exceptions, had not been involved in the preparatory, design and review phases of the project proposal and did not understand the debates surrounding participatory approaches. None of them was familiar with the critical discourse on participatory approaches to agricultural research and rural development. Only one had applied participatory tools in previous field research for her Master's thesis. Scientists from our Thai partner universities tended to equate participatory approaches simply with the use of Participatory Rural Appraisal (PRA), a set of tools that international and national development agencies had previously employed in various parts of the northern Thai highlands. The appeal of PRA for Thai scientists from the natural science disciplines seemed to be its potential to "generate quick results", as one of our counterparts put it. Only the Thai social scientists, who were counterparts in our sub-project, appeared to differentiate between the increasingly extractive and instrumental use of PRA tools and the ethical and political dimensions of participatory approaches.

I was confronted with this program's internal socio-political and institutional set-up when I moved to Chiang Mai in mid-2000. It dominated the inception phase of the Uplands Program in Thailand from August 2000 to December 2001, which Katharine describes so aptly in Chapter Five, employing the nuanced and critical perspective of a direct — and sometimes participant — observer. However, given her limited access to the higher levels of the German Uplands Program and the short time frame of her study, I welcome the opportunity to mention a few additional points that may help complete the picture.

Firstly, our stance from the beginning was to regard 'participatory approaches to agricultural research' as both an objective and a research question in itself. In other words, we wanted to find out which forms and degrees of stakeholder participation were possible and appropriate for different stages and topics of the research. It was this critical look at the potential and constraints of participatory approaches — instead of a naïve view that 'the more participation the better' — that turned out to be most appealing to our program's reviewers. It also promised to generate new insights into the challenges that participatory research faces in the diverse socio-political and institutional settings in Thailand, Vietnam and Germany. Hence, we never aimed at maximising participation in our research program, but rather at optimising the use of participatory methods in their respective research contexts.

Secondly, my role as program manager or, more precisely, as Scientific Coordinator, appears somewhat overstated in Katharine's account. In the Uplands Program's first phase in Thailand, none of the junior researchers was under my direct supervision. All of them obtained advice or received 'orders' by e-mail or occasional phone calls from the sub-project leaders in Germany. Since participation was rarely among the leaders' top priorities, the junior researchers were encouraged to complete technical tasks such as getting their data-loggers calibrated and their scientific equipment set up in the field rather than engaging with farmers and evaluating the potential social impact that their fieldwork was having on the local community. Thus, the sentiment expressed among some young scientists in the inception phase of our program that it was "failing to be participatory", as described by Katharine, was certainly more the exception than the rule. More often I was accused by junior researchers in Thailand and Vietnam that I (or another member of the 'participation sub-project') was pressing them to be more 'stakeholder-responsive', which they felt was an additional burden to deal with among the onerous challenges of working in an interdisciplinary program in a new cultural environment. Many of them developed various and often quite creative mechanisms to escape from this 'participatory imperative' in our program (see Neef *et al.*, 2008).

Thirdly, the 'snapshot' character of Katharine's analysis has to be put in the perspective of the program's lifespan of 12 years. As I write these few lines, the program is in its tenth year after a fourth funding phase was approved in May 2009. Most of the turmoil, conflicts and misunderstandings of the inception phase that Katharine witnessed and for which I bear a great deal of responsibility have given way to a well-oiled research routine with many participatory elements, mostly conducted as add-on activities to the cutting-edge science work that our reviewers demand and value in their periodic assessments. In the program's current and final phase, participatory approaches are neither severely contested nor completely institutionalised among the participating scientific institutions. By collaborating with a few strategic allies among the German and Thai senior scientists in our program who share our concern for at least partly addressing farmers' and other local stakeholders' priorities through our research, our sub-project team has managed to initiate various so-called Knowledge and Innovation Partnerships (KIPs) in some of the communities in our study areas in Thailand (and in Vietnam), which we believe can contribute both to expanding the research frontier in sustainability science and innovation studies and to improving rural people's livelihoods. One such multi-stakeholder partnership, a lychee-processing and marketing cooperative comprising five ethnic minority villages, was a 2008 finalist in the global SEED competition, an initiative of the United Nations' Commission for Sustainable Development that supports local, multi-stakeholder initiatives to encourage sustainable development. Most of the research and development activities are now conducted by Thai research assistants and senior scientists as well as villagers themselves, to ensure sustainability beyond the Uplands Program's funding period.

During the nearly nine years that I worked with the Uplands Program, initially also in Vietnam, then only in Thailand, I came to believe that participatory agricultural research should not be regarded as an alternative paradigm but as an approach that can be applied to and integrated with any conventional research in the agricultural sciences, that is, qualitative inquiries, agronomic experiments, agro-ecological studies and even quantitative surveys. This is a view that is gaining currency among many proponents of participatory approaches.

In my view, the major challenge remains to find the right balance between formal research and stakeholder participation in its respective research context. In the approval notification for the fourth and final phase of the Uplands Program, our funding agency, the German Research Foundation, acknowledged that "through its participatory approach the Uplands Program has achieved a sustainable impact in the study regions.... The extremely difficult balancing act between basic research and development assistance has been very successfully performed." Even the rather conservative German Science Council, which evaluated the University of Hohenheim's agricultural faculty in 2006, was impressed by the activities of the Uplands Program and concluded that participatory approaches should be further promoted in future development-oriented agricultural research projects. However, these rather enthusiastic testimonies in favour of participatory research cannot gloss over the deep scepticism that most agricultural scientists continue to have towards involving farmers and other non-scientific actors in their research — beyond a brief feedback workshop for local stakeholders when the project draws to an end. Aside from strong reservations about the chances of participatory research being published in high-impact journals, one of the probable reasons is that participatory research has been promoted for too long as a counter-concept to conventional research, thus raising fears among natural scientists and economists that they would need to give up a certain degree of scientific validity and rigour in their research work when engaging with actors external to science.

My assessment of the future of participatory research in the agricultural sciences — even in the compromised form as described above and in parts of Katharine's exciting work — is therefore somewhat gloomy. The pressure for 'scientific excellence' and 'research at the frontier' appears to be at odds with the down-to-earth participatory approaches that call for engaging farmers and other local stakeholders at various levels of decision-making and implementation of research programs. Since April 2009 I have worked in a new institutional and cultural environment, first as a visiting research scholar at Kyoto University's Center for Southeast Asian Studies and then as an adjunct full professor in Knowledge and Innovation Management at Kyushu University, Fukuoka. Here in Japan, where boundaries between agricultural sub-disciplines remain extremely strong and difficult to permeate, where most of the agricultural research is laboratory-based and where multidisciplinarity is a rare phenomenon, most scientists have never even heard of the term 'participatory research'.

In November 2009 I completed a scientific advisory report for the German Parliament on the "Potential of participatory agricultural research to contribute to solving the global food security problem". After reviewing the relevant literature and current trends among the agricultural sciences in Germany, other European countries and in international research centres under the Consultative Group of International Agricultural Research (CGIAR), I concluded that participatory research is likely to remain a niche activity within the agricultural sciences. This is despite more than three decades of advocacy and attempts to institutionalise participatory approaches in international agricultural research through the success of participatory research in many developing countries. In fact, the social sciences — with the exception of agricultural and resource economics — are becoming more and more sidelined within the agricultural science domain. This trend can be observed in the CGIAR centres, where social scientists are assigned a merely supportive role, and, most notably, in Germany's agricultural faculties, where professorships in the field of rural sociology and agricultural extension have become virtually extinct within the last decade. Unless a U-turn is brought about by a change of donor priorities and/or civil society demands, future participatory research activities may be conducted only as a sideline by a minority of agricultural scientists. They also risk being stripped of their empowerment claims and reduced to a purely functional role in terms of raising the effectiveness of agricultural research.

Andreas Neef
Fukuoka, 2010

Development by Accident: Serendipity and a Sense of Humour

In the past we drank unboiled creek water. Now we drink unboiled well water.

'Developed' highland villager

Self-determination should precede all development. It is closely linked to free and prior informed consent.

Indigenous workshop participants

Ignorance, War and Finding Oneself on the Far Side

Once upon a time I was unenlightened, ignorant so to speak. But I had a sense of humour. That was comforting. More than once upon a time the US government was ignorant, engulfed in political darkness and, having learned no lessons from previous experience, got into yet another war, this time in Vietnam and two nearby countries. Having learned few lessons myself and with US military conscription hovering, I became part of that war — but only at a distance — and in the process accidentally learned where Southeast Asia was. I found myself in the aerial forces of an aggressive military and based on a small radar site in the not-yet-province of Mukdahan along the Mekong River in the northeast of Thailand. Lacking any militant skills, I found work in two local Thai schools, one primary and one secondary. I pretended to teach English, a subject requiring no demonstrable skills when you're from the United States. This was the beginning of a more worldly education cum understanding of what happens around us globally. The US government — though not its people — was at war with an allegedly nasty bunch of communists controlling the upper half of Vietnam. Mr Nixon and Mr Kissinger stated categorically that we were not at war with either Cambodia or Laos and repeatedly proclaimed, "We are not bombing in Laos." I heard this frequently on Armed Forces Radio. But I was aware of something different, heard it clearly from my off-base rented house perched on solid stilts, which would shake with every passing B-52 dropping its load onto the fields and folks just to the east and across the muddy Mekong. Due to good fortune and a lack of wartime talent, I was never involved in any fighting — other than the make-shift hockey games on the floor of the officers' club fueled by beer and spirits. The time and events were ripe for reflection and a bit of research. I began to question and, most importantly, to question authority.

Having duly served my government — but not necessarily my country — in the Southeast Asian Theatre (of the Abused and Absurd?), I was allowed to choose a new country of minor American occupation. Spain it was. I became an administrative ('paperwork') commander of several hundred troops, including lowly single-stripe airmen up through the ranks of captains and colonels and one lofty general. There, through papers and persons, I learned the value of the lesser beings and the machinations of the officer corps. I felt an affinity for the enlisted and a need to further question the authorities. The military force was a militant farce and that over repeated generations. A comedy of eras.

Formal Education, Institutions and the Institutionalised

Running short on funds and tolerance of a rote and rural educational system, I applied for a Master's program in Educational Psychology at the College of Education in Bangkok. I was accepted, perhaps as the token white man. Thus, armed with low-level funding from the GI Bill, I could learn of life in the big city and gain academic credentials. It was not long before I realised that I had escaped the boring field of rural schooling for the boring academia of education in the university. As my professor, Dr. Ravipan, noted, "Schooling is a business, not necessarily related to education." Two years and a higher degree later, I could not refute this.

Having no other prospects and no other sources of income, I applied for yet another higher-level degree program and completed the course in less than the allotted time to become a graduate of Srinakharinwirote University. An institutional name that was a mouthful. I had a head full of rigid academic answers to complex human behaviours. It was a pretty good educational experience at a very low price. Yes, I had done my studies and my research and conformed to standards set by those with their heads in the clouds and with feet occasionally on the ground. Henceforth I was formally qualified by persons in institutions and persons who should have been institutionalised to make decisions on behalf of others, the so-called 'uneducated'. I laughed at the system while accepting the paper credentials. I was ready.

The Ministry of Education: Ad/ministering Education to Others

Having no other options, by default or by accident, I was hired, right back in the field of education. Boring education. In the Division of Adult Education, soon to become, through a massive World Bank loan, the Department of Non-formal Education. Was this karmic retribution for past transgressions? Actually, I was in luck, for in this division-soon-to-be-department there lived a whole bunch of forward-thinking folk who found no discrete distinction between 'education' and 'development'. I was on the road to increased reality.

In the beginning, I was still in the formal stages of institutionalised education. I thought I had the answers from the textbooks when I didn't even get the questions right. For example, on a survey in the Northeast, I asked an old and poor man, "Uncle, how do you see your life five years from now?" A quizzical/blank stare. "What?" I repeated the question. "How can I tell you about five years when I don't even know if I'll have enough food to eat tomorrow!" Uh oh. Academia had met reality. Back to Bangkok and the safety of a large cement building.

Fortunately, I was in the vicinity and care of better minds than my own, that is, Ministry of Education officials and consultants such as Chanida and Lou and Kowit and Ekavidya and Cherdsak who had eschewed their own higher academia for common sense, for education only as it relates to development ... of the mind, of capacities and opportunities, of ethics, and so on. However, I wasn't getting paid much, so I moonlighted. Actually, I daylighted. Working in the very early morning to attempt to summarise into English wordy Thai research documents from Dr. Sippanondha's Office of the National Education Council. It was hard work. It was frustrating work. It was enlightening work. How could such simple concepts and results be transformed into such convoluted and confusing expositions requiring 100 pages when 20 would had sufficed? It was amusing, with many a good laugh amidst the tears of labour. I began to question academic research.

Rising to Higher Levels: About 800 metres and more above Sea Level

In 1980, I met with a very advantageous accident. USAID had $1.6 million unspent near the end of its fiscal year. Not spending or even not allocating such a sum means you are a bad planner, a poor administrator. Your record will reflect this. A recipient was needed immediately, a recipient who could do something sexy with the money. Something like… well… non-formal education… maybe with tribal peoples. Lo and behold, there was the new Department of Non-formal Education and there was a red-blooded foreigner in the Department who could serve as the required Yankee advisor. Me. So, after some negotiations, the Hill Areas Education Project or HAE (misheard by one USAID official as 'hilarious education') came into being. So I began the move to higher levels in the development of a whole new system of primary education for ethnic groups in the highlands of the north. Yes, there I was in the midst and margins of 1) education, 2) development, 3) a modicum of research and 4) indigenous peoples.

It was all coming together and hilarity was evident at many turns. One example was our sincere and often bumbling efforts to create an educational system for the people, though not by the people. Of course, the people already had an educational system, albeit one that we hardly recognised. Certainly we did not build much upon it, nor seriously include them in the process. This was overcome, or at least overshadowed, by the youth and spirit and good sense of the Thai educators/developers/activists responsible. More hilarity — actually, a kind of black humour — was evident in the machinations of the Thai Department of Technical and Economic Cooperation

(DTEC) and the US Agency for International Development (USAID), both euphemisms for 'politics and control'. This was a severe learning experience, mitigated by the Ministry of Education people mentioned above and two others: Prachuap Kumbunratana, Inspector General of the Ministry of Education showed how one could actually communicate and reason with the Third Army and the Office of the National Security Council, and David Delgado of USAID continued to stand up for the people as the authorities edged him closer to the margins of management.

This generally uplifting experience at 800-1,000 meters above sea level was followed by another 'development in the hills' episode, the Mae Chaem Watershed Development Project. There I was plugged into the empty advisor hole (all USAID-funded projects require one) and further exposed to ministerial machinations in the name of developing other 'undeveloped' people, as well as a small and hard core of sincere developers and educators. Like the other large-scale Australian, German, Norwegian, Swedish and UN projects in the highland development heydays of the 1980s to mid-1990s, the aim was to push the blame for western drug addiction onto eastern opium-producing peoples. These western-conceived and -driven efforts were resourced with sacks of money, planeloads of western 'experts' (like myself), 'scientific research', bureaucratic mechanisms, limited timeframes and virtually no input from or acknowledgement of the local wisdom of the developees. I was being educated in the soil and muck of international aid, as opposed to the theoretical cleanliness of the university.

Then I Got Really Educated and Better Understood the Politics of 'Development'

This, in 1989, was the end of my inadvertent full-time development ride at taxpayers' expense, and the instant and non-accidental establishment of the Office of Retired Developers, a conscious but half-hearted attempt to wash away the crust of my 'development crimes'. I had accumulated sufficient financial profit from allegedly helping the poor and voiceless over the past ten years to do this. I had also accrued a wealth of suspicion, and even cynicism, perpetrated by the whole of us, as well said by Leonard Frank:

> Development, as in Third World Development, is a debauched
> word, a whore of a word. Its users can't look you in the eye.

> Among biologists, the word means progress, the realization of
> an innate potential. The word is good. Incontestable, a cause
> for celebration. In the mouths of economists, politicians, and
> development experts like myself, it claims the same approval but
> means nothing … it is an empty word which can be filled by any
> user to conceal any hidden intention, a Trojan horse of a word
> (GRANTA Issue 20, 1986)

Yet, the intention of 'development' was not fundamentally bad. What has gone wrong is the concept and practice, fired first by politics and second by the vested interests of governments, so-called development institutions, and too many of the persons responsible. Development was and is conceived and directed externally of the targeted communities — targets being what the military and 'sportsmen' shoot at. Early on, I was told by Lao 'developers' that there was no local word for 'development' — the term had asserted itself through Thai and western expatriates in an effort to export their own models. No, development was not bad to the core but it was highly undemocratic and unethical in practice, the intended beneficiaries having almost no say whatsoever. It was simply done wrongly and was in need of intense reform. With this poor attitude, I was branded with a scarlet letter: 'C', for cynic.

Bolstered by my still intact sense of humour and residual hope that the People would be allowed to take more control of their own future, I began to slide (backslide?) into the development industry through part-time consulting. Expanding my territory to cover Southeast Asia and points west, I was on the road again and being paid to visit exotic places and intervene in local lives. This is when I really began to learn. This time from the real masters of development and research: the People. The people who were often no longer the masters of their own lives when external development projects were set loose. I was educated by example, by Mae Pranee of the Assembly of the Poor in northeast Thailand and Jonni Odochao of the Mae Wang watershed in the north, the Ati People of the Philippines (who threw out their village chief), the farmer with leprosy in Cambodia, recovering drug addicts in Afghanistan … and the children of Bangladesh and China and Nepal and Vietnam. People with a formal fourth-grade education but PhDs in Life. And there was the Centre for Integrated Agricultural Development in Beijing, the only government agency I have found in 29 years that officially believed in the capacities of the People to carry out their own development and research. Yes, I was learning indigenous knowledge. Learning from the developees of our externally imposed 'development'.

And what did I learn from these developers and researchers lacking any formal recognition due to their lack of formal research and academic papers? Well ... I guess I did not really learn in the traditional sense. I just sort of accumulated real life experiences and on-the-ground realities. These realities were demonstrated over and over by the local people, the indigenous philosophers, leaders, participants and followers, who were the real developers and researchers. These were realities that we on the outside have great difficulty in understanding or relating to and therefore incorporating into our conceptualisation, planning and implementation of the thing we call 'development'. So, should we non-local folks dealing with development see ourselves as developers or students? Should we: 1) lead, 2) guide, 3) provide information and support or 4) get out of the way?

What Has All This Got To Do with Katharine McKinnon's Book?

From my own point of view and myriad experiences, gained through a concatenation of several accidents and a few choices, she's got it right. Not just basically right, but right on. 'Development' is guided and misguided, used and abused. It is a complicated, convoluted and confusing thing, this industry, this offence against the People, this passionate undertaking, this good idea that we have termed 'development', capable of both good and bad. But, like Chambers' 'Participatory Learning & Action', it must not be boxed in, it should not be defined. For therein lies the death of its heart and soul, as well as the opportunity of its misuse. Every case is indeed a special case. There are no answers, no templates, no guaranteed approaches. Yet there are certainly vested interests — after all, this is an industry and a launching pad for politics. The so-called 'developers' themselves are all special cases, some of whom should be lauded and some of whom should be locked up. Each and every 'development instance' must be planned with regard to its own circumstances and judged on its own merits. But don't try to analyse it all too deeply. You'll go crazy if you do. In fact, you are probably already crazy if you do try to analyse it.

Yes, Katharine got it right, but she did not get everything because in a book you are supposed to focus. Focus. Unlike the development thing, which should relate to life and be holistic and inclusive. What she was not able to include was discussion of the developees as developers themselves — the very ones who have conducted their own research and implemented their own processes of improvement for hundreds of years to ensure their own survival. The fact is that 'development' is not the sole province of human foreign and domestic developers (who tend to be so male) and their organisations.

The Twilight Years: A Few Conclusions from a Retired and Retreaded Developer

- Advice does not work. Support does. Advice about development is cheap, although the advisors are not. Without political or financial backing ... well, forget it. Support of the indigenous and other people does work, albeit slowly. They must be the decision-makers — right and sometimes wrong — because it is their lives we are meddling in.

- There is research, and then there is Research. It is not the universities and academics and big business and international organisations alone that do research, although this is the claim. The local people — the allegedly uneducated and undeveloped — have done this all their lives, over generations, but without publication and without journals. How else have farmers selected the seed, soil and agricultural methods they use to survive without doing their own research? Yet we on the outside, with our own motives, claim otherwise. We prefer to denigrate their research and their science and maintain our control.

- Much the same can be said for 'development'. There is development and then there is Development. Nearly all the development discourse focuses on *our* development of *them*. Because they supposedly have little clue how to develop themselves. Thus we rush to define 'the problem', making it a negative. Whereas the developees first consider their own local intellectual, social and physical resources before deciding what interrelated problems they will deal with in developing their community. Our unspoken rationale is self-development.

- Above all, there are people. People, good people, are the key. It is not projects or programs or plans and schemes or budgets or curricula or meetings that make development work. It is the people. I have proposed this idea to a couple of international development organisations — supporting selected people rather than projects. Their response: Yes, we agree … but we cannot do that. So there you have it. My role over the past ten years has been to support people … and accumulate warm fuzzy feelings. In the words of J.P. Donleavy:

> *It is the*
> *Random*
> *Accumulation*
> *Of triumphs*
> *Which is*
> *So nice.*

Ken Kampe
President-for-Life
Office of Retired Developers
Sometime in 2010

Becoming a Developer: A Personal History

My father is a descendant of a 'half-breed' clan of 'hillbillies' from the Ozark Mountains, a product of generations of 'outlaws, outcasts and renegades' who escaped into the mountain forests from the outrageous human rights tragedy of the Cherokee Nation's 'Trail of Tears', as well as from various other perceived injustices inflicted by power elites of earlier times. He was the first in our extended family to graduate from secondary school, after which he left through the network being established by the young generation to seek factory work in industrializing urban centres. He settled in a Midwestern city and met my mother, a secondary school drop-out and daughter of a German-British union that never quite accepted the racial 'impurity' of my father, but at least finally admitted that he was sincere and a hard worker.

Since my parents were struggling financially, I went to school in the city but spent summers and all school holidays with my grandparents at their Ozark Mountain farm. There more time was spent on fishing, hunting and gathering than on agriculture, but we did sell canned tomatoes and bird-hunting dogs trained by my grandfather for cash. It was a big deal when electricity arrived in the 1950s. It was there that I learned the ways of the half-breed mountain clans and their relationships with nature, each other and the outside world. Although I did not think too much about it at the time, this constant shuffling between two very different worlds affected how I saw things during the 1950s and early 1960s, with its urban racial tensions, class discrimination and disdain for 'backward' rural people. In a response somewhat similar to that of many of the Cherokee and other native peoples who had been subjected to systematic cultural genocide, the lower classes in both urban and rural settings sought survival and a better life by trying to fit in with the vision of the ruling elites. Thus, an important component of my parents' dream was for at least one of their sons to graduate from college and become truly 'respectable'. Since my older brother took up full-time work after secondary school, the burden of my parents' dream then fell on me.

Having done fairly well in secondary school, I managed to get accepted to study at the University of Missouri. But without anyone to help me interpret the way things worked — none of my close friends went to college — I failed to pre-register and thus was only able to get into classes that were still open, which meant the least popular classes. Thus, I found myself studying philosophy, French, honors composition and a seemingly bizarre but fascinating anthropology course called 'Comparative Studies of Human and Non-Human Societies'. And at the same time, my dormitory room-mate introduced me to the music of a young Bob Dylan, as well as some poets and other radical thinkers of the time. The overall impact of what seemed like a tsunami of new ideas and information was too much for me to digest and incorporate into the semi-thought-out directions I had been heading. Thus I dropped out of the university after just one semester and hit the road with my brother, following what had become, in the traditions of the Santa Fe Trail and Route 66, the 'yellow brick road' to (southern) California.

In the Greater Los Angeles Megapolis, I found work in a small machine shop and discovered the community college system. Soon I had laid a foundation that would allow me to be an apprentice tool-and-die maker and pursue a college degree at the same time. I also began a fascinating dialogue with an aunt who had migrated before me about Cherokee lore and the history of our 'half-breed' Ozark clan (of which she was very proud), which gave me a new level of insight and identity. But I had to work very hard to eliminate my Missouri accent so that young people in California would even talk to me. The future seemed bright . Then darkness fell swiftly. I received a telegram signed by then President Lyndon Johnson that I was conscripted into military service. Since everyone was just starting to talk about Vietnam, I went to the library to find out where it was.

Thus in October 1966 I became one of more than 60,000 young men to be inducted into the US Army in what I was told was the largest monthly call of military conscripts in the US since World War II. After training in California and Louisiana, I was assigned to be a light weapons infantryman and shipped out to Vietnam just after my twentieth birthday. We were given a few weeks' leave, during which we basically told our families goodbye.

Rather than dwell on what happened during the Vietnam War, I mention just a few points that turned out to be strong influences on my subsequent ideas and behaviour:

- I was sent to a British Jungle Warfare School in Malaysia for several months of secret training by special British, New Zealand and Gurkha military units that worked with tracker dogs. This gave me an opportunity to learn about life within quite pristine tropical rainforest (now all gone in that area), with all its critters and hazards, while trying to keep up with skilled jungle fighters.
- Once in Vietnam, our Ninth Infantry Division base camp was shared with the newly arriving Queen's Cobra Regiment from Thailand, which was my first encounter with people and things Thai.
- During some of the lulls between periods of violence, our small unit would try to assess who we were and what we were doing there. One observation was that almost all of us conscripted into the infantry, as opposed to units like clerks or engineering, came from urban minorities or 'backward' rural areas, or were college drop-outs – more 'respectable' middle and upper classes were most noticeable by their absence. We found ourselves asking if this was social triage?
- Up till the last few weeks of our assignments in Vietnam, we believed that we would not return home alive or, even worse, that we would be so badly maimed that it would not be an existence worth living. This taught us a lot about transcending fear and living every day as it comes.
- Just after the 1968 Tet Offensive, which for us began on the morning of my twenty-first birthday such that I was of official voting age, I took a friend into Saigon at the end of his tour. Although he had earlier been seriously wounded and still carried shrapnel lodged in his throat, he commented that, "If I were Vietnamese and had any self-respect, I would be fighting with the Viet Cong." We nodded in agreement and never forgot this reflection.

I returned to the US during 1968, the year of the long hot summer of urban riots across America, the assassinations of Martin Luther King and Robert Kennedy, and the now infamous events associated with the Democratic National Convention in Chicago. I was assigned to an infantry unit with the dual duties of helping guard Cheyenne Mountain in Colorado, home of the North American Air Defense Command, and being on standby to be airlifted with two hours' notice to control urban riots anywhere in the continental United States. Almost everyone in this unit had, like me, just returned from combat duty in Vietnam. The irony was not lost on us. Feelings of bitterness grew intense. I was lucky to obtain a release to begin a new term at my community college in California. Otherwise I would have been one of the 7,500 army troops in Chicago (or joined those refusing to go).

Returning to college campus in late 1968 as a Vietnam combat veteran was just the opposite of receiving a hero's welcome. Friendships were few, but very strong where they could be found. One even included a member of the Black Panthers, who proudly showed me their operations base a few months before it became the target of a massive attack by the new Los Angeles SWAT team linked with the FBI's national counter-intelligence operation. After a four-hour firefight, all inside were jailed. Being older with a head full of demons and distractions, I threw myself into very intensive study and simultaneous full-time work to pay for it. I found myself driven in directions that might help me understand more about how and why all the things I had been going through happened in the first place. Before I had a chance to step back and think much about what I was doing, I had an AA in social science and a bachelor's degree in political science with a 4.0 grade point average — I had never come close to doing that well in school before. Although I had learned a lot and had come to grips with some of my demons, the question that then hit me was, "Where should I go from here?"

The conventional wisdom of those times was that the only options for someone with a degree in political science were to (a) become a politician, (b) study more and become a professor, (c) go to law school, or (d) work for a big company as a junior administrator. Given those choices, and not ready yet to defy conventional wisdom, I applied to law school. Much to my amazement, I was accepted at three places considered to be very good schools. But still feeling I needed to better fulfil my parents' dreams, I accepted the one that I thought would make them happiest — Harvard Law School, which required serious loans.

My time at Harvard turned out to be brief, just one semester, but very important to me. While life experiences had already helped me overcome most elements of fear, I still remained intimidated by upper-class social elites, who I had always been taught were superior. This gave me a chance to live among them, where I learned that their access to money and influence was all that distinguished them from those in lower social strata. And once I found out how 'hotshot' lawyers lived their life and what they were like as people, I decided that was clearly not what I should spend the rest of my life pursuing. While I was withdrawing from study, the Vice-Dean (later long-time Dean) spent nearly half a day trying to talk me out of it, reasoning that this was a once-in-a-lifetime opportunity for "people like me". He seemed to not realise that type of reasoning would only strengthen my resolve. Although my parents were perplexed and other relatives believed I was insane, they could understand my logic and encouraged me to go where I needed to go.

At this point, it seemed that all I had learned was an increasingly long list of things that I did not want to do. The challenge now was to find something that I did want to do. For some reason, I began to seek escape by developing an interest in science and renewed relations with nature. Through a strange set of relationships and decisions, I found myself at the University of California, Berkeley, applying to re-boot my education with a second bachelor's degree in natural sciences. Although they were not sure about my mental state, my academic record was by then good enough that I was allowed to pursue my fantasy which, they chuckled, would mean my taking the entire regime of basic science courses taken by the frenzied pre-med student crowd. And in order to pay for it, I needed to work nights and weekends conducting laboratory analyses for their research projects. Perhaps underestimating my will to transform myself, they were somewhat surprised when I emerged from all that with a degree in Soil Science and Plant Nutrition that included Phi Beta Kappa honors (a rather unusual combination). During the process, one of the professors that impressed me most was Paul Zinke, whose lectures included extensive coverage of research he was still conducting in collaboration with Pete Kunstadter and others on forest fallow shifting cultivation systems used by Lawa communities in the mountains of northern Thailand.

My next decision was to return to spend some time with my aging grandparents in the Ozark Mountains. Although this coincided with some of the 'back to the land' movement in the US, and fit well with my renewed interest in nature, I was really interested in getting to know my grandparents and learning more about the past and potential future of life in the Ozarks. I found a job as field operations foreman of the Missouri State Fruit Experiment Station located next to the town nearest my grandparents' remote home. During my two years there I gained a new level of understanding from my grandparents, who many years ago had opened my eyes to so many things as a child. I also witnessed the continuing effects of 'development' on the Ozark region by increasingly powerful town elites and their distant backers, destroying remnants of what had been to me for so long a grand and wondrous place. As a clan blood relative and a Vietnam Vet, I was allowed into remaining social circles of those who were still trying to maintain some of the traditions and spirit of earlier times. But since the Internet and alternative channels for access to the outside world did not yet exist, the grip of the local elites was extremely strong. With warm sincerity, my friends encouraged me to seek my opportunities elsewhere. We all wished things might have been different. The day I left the Ozarks was the last time I ever saw my grandparents.

I then returned to graduate school at Berkeley and began exploring other options. While in the Ozarks I had also done a lot of reading about science, and my new assault on academia took me to new levels of biochemistry and ecology. It also brought me back to Paul Zinke, and to auditing classes on the side, which exposed me to writings of people like Paulo Freire and others. Somehow my experience in the Ozarks and in Southeast Asia began to merge, leading me to take my studies in science into more applied directions. Thus, I transferred to a masters program in pomology at the Davis campus of the University of California, where I was lucky to work with one of the grand masters of plant propagation while I studied production horticulture, as well as economic and agricultural development, which included field studies in Mexico. Very few Americans were enrolled in these programs. It was there that Southeast Asia returned to my consciousness, and upon graduation I applied for a foreign service position in the US Agency for International Development (USAID). I first worked for a year or so in Washington DC, where I also studied the 'party line' of Advanced Southeast Asian Studies at the Foreign Service Institute. Then finally I was assigned to Thailand, where PM General Kriangsak had just asked the US to expand its development assistance programs.

After arriving in the USAID office in Bangkok, in early 1979, I was assigned to work with Terry Grandstaff, who was leading the design of the first big new project initiative of this new era, the Mae Chaem Watershed Development Project. Terry had just completed his PhD in anthropology, focused on people and their agro-ecosystems in the mountains of northern Thailand. He was a West Point graduate and Vietnam Vet. We hit it off well, especially after he found out that I had studied under Paul Zinke, and I learned a great deal from him about the many ideas, people and places he had explored during his research. Terry sought design assistance from many of the best-known people of the time and eventually was able to recruit consultants like Pete Kunstadter, Paul Zinke and Grahame Keen, as well as Thais like Chai-anan Samudavanija and others. My main duties were to work with Paul and the foresters and 'aggies' on the 'techie' side of things, but we tried to brainstorm together on the big picture as we helicoptered and trekked in the mountains beyond the roads. We listened to the views of Wanat Bhruksasri, Sanga Sabhasri, Prince Bhisadej, Dick Mann and many others; the work of Peter Hinton and the views of John McKinnon were also frequently mentioned. And of course, there was frequent interaction with Thai and US drug control and national security agencies, whose agendas were behind the emergence of the project in the first place. In any event, Terry led a noble effort to make the project design as good as possible and to ensure maximum benefit for people in the mountains. As I recall, Ken Kampe began working with the Hill Area Education Project during this period.

For the next two years, I was project officer in charge of collaborative development of the Northeast Rainfed Agricultural Development Project, based at the Northeast Regional Office of Agriculture in Tha Phra, Khon Kaen. Together with Utai Pisone and colleagues, and with backing from Deputy Permanent Secretary Kangwan Devahastin, we tried to design a pilot project that could address the real needs of rural communities with no access to irrigation service areas, while using processes that built on local initiative at household, village and *tambon* levels — then still quite a radical notion. Project sites were chosen to represent the basic range of conditions found in such areas. This work included travelling to almost every district in every province of Isan with teams that included research and development officials from all agencies in the Ministry of Agriculture and Cooperatives. We also interacted with the NESDB team led by Kosit

Panpiemras, who was using many new ideas in designing the fifth Five Year Plan. Kosit's vision for the future development of Thailand was inspiring. As I was the only USAID foreign service officer based outside Bangkok, additional duties included relations with Khon Kaen University and with other projects on village woodlots, land settlements and medium- and large-scale irrigation areas, as well as military-led tours along the Cambodian border, in the Phu Phan mountains, and helicopter trips that extended into mountains of Nan province. While work in the mountains of the North began stimulating notions about parallels with both the Ozark Mountains and some aspects of Vietnam, it was here in Isan where my language capability began to be good enough to really begin seeing parallels with Ozark conditions, mindsets and attitudes, as well as how locals were viewed by outside ruling elites. It is also where I met my wife, a new M.Sc. graduate of AIT from Maha Sarakham, and became a son-in-law of Isan. We also met the McKinnon family in Udon — John promoted sanity and perspective at a time when there was little outside access for us.

By mid-1981 it was becoming clear that this type of development project work, all the associated bureaucracy, and being caught between agencies on both the US and Thai side that still viewed rural people basically as objects, was not as satisfying or productive as we had hoped. Thus, with encouragement from Terry Grandstaff and others, my wife and I decided to return again to graduate school and pursue doctoral degrees. We first returned to Berkeley, where I began a program in Wildland Resource Science under a committee that included Jeff Romm, Paul Zinke and professors in geography and anthropology with experience in Southeast Asia. My wife worked in Paul Zinke's laboratory, took graduate classes, and began trying to adapt to American language and culture. It took a bit more than two years of very intensive study with paying research and teaching assistantships to complete classwork, pass qualifying exams, develop a proposal and seek funding for it. Almost everything was focused on subjects directly relevant to further study and life in Thailand. Finally, I received a Fulbright research scholarship, which I was told, was the first awarded to anyone studying forestry. We sold our car to buy our first microcomputer and packed up for our return to Thailand.

We returned to Khon Kaen, where we set up shop within Khon Kaen University (KKU), in association with the Farming Systems Group, which was then hosting Terry and Somluckrat Grandstaff (who had also left USAID) under a project to develop 'rapid rural appraisal', the predecessor to PRA. I was also linked through the National Research Council of Thailand with the Faculty of Forestry at Kasetsart University, where I was known mainly as a student of Paul Zinke and Jeff Romm. My research involved intensive year-long household record-keeping studies in collaboration with households in five villages spanning three provinces of the Chi River watershed. This generated a mountain of data that was coded into English, Thai and Lao by a team of student translators led by my wife. Although only a small portion of this data came to be used in my dissertation, exploration of the information in the data was the opportunity of a lifetime for me. Indeed, it articulated in great detail the extensive similarities between the people I had known in the Ozarks and my new friends and teachers in Isan. My dissertation was dedicated to both.

Since my field research ended up taking a bit more than two years to complete, colleagues at Khon Kaen University helped me out by requesting the Ford Foundation to provide me with a small individual grant to allow us to complete the work. Ford did so on condition that I also work on the side with their efforts to develop a new 'social forestry' program in Thailand. So I began working with groups at KKU, Kasetsart University and the Royal Forest Department, many of which I had encountered earlier, as well as with a team of social scientists at Chiang Mai University led by Uraivan Tankimyong, and which at that point also included Ajans Anan and Shaladchai. I also participated in the 1985 International Conference on Rapid Rural Appraisal organised by the Grandstaffs and colleagues, where we first met Robert Chambers, Robert Rhodes and other emerging vocal advocates of such work. While it was all very interesting, I often feel that the guru status assigned to Robert Chambers is a bit overstated, diminishing the contributions of many others.

It was now my wife's turn, and she took the initiative by obtaining a scholarship from the East-West Center for doctoral studies at the University of Hawaii's College of Tropical Agriculture. I followed her there to work on the analysis of my field research data and was fortunate to find part-time employment with Terry Rambo's Human Ecology Project at the Environment and Policy Institute of the East-West Center. That led to further work under a Research Fellowship that had me return to Bangkok as a resident social forestry advisor working with Komon Pragtong, Sittichai Ungphakorn and many other colleagues within the Royal Forest Department, in collaboration with teams at Kasetsart, KKU and Chiang Mai University. This involved another period of extensive travel around Northeast Thailand, this time focused on forest areas occupied by local communities, mostly hill and mountain areas around the edges of Isan, and in the north, where most effort was beginning to focus on the large Mae Taeng sub-basin. The output of this work was several proposals to the Ford Foundation, which were accepted and became a major program for the Foundation's work in Thailand. With this initiative, the Ford Foundation re-established a program officer position in Bangkok after they had all been withdrawn to Jakarta in the early 1980s. I was encouraged to apply and was eventually hired.

For the next seven years I was in charge of the Ford Foundation's tiny sub-office in Bangkok (under the regional office in Jakarta), and programs related to social forestry, agricultural systems, small-scale water resource management and later, AIDS and women's rights. I also worked with Bill Klausner on activities related to international affairs, with Jakarta staff on women's reproductive health, and with Mark Sidel on his work in Vietnam that led to the establishment of the Hanoi office. The overall context of this work and especially activities related to the large 'centrepiece' social forestry program were summarised in a document I wrote for the Ford Foundation in 1996. Since the people promoting development of 'social forestry' programs in various countries (mostly Asia) began leaving the Foundation in the early 1990s, I was somewhat disappointed when their successors seemed to pay little attention to what we were trying to do in Thailand. I then realised, however, that their disinterest was actually a good opportunity for us. Together with a network of very interesting and creative Thai colleagues, we moved ahead with our own visions and interpretations of what supporting innovation was all about. We identified and provided support for motivated, promising groups in government agencies, academic institutions and non-governmental organisations alike. Rather than seek to impose or promote some vision from our outside organisation, we tried our best to promote a range of creative visions and efforts to support and promote local initiatives, and to give voice to those poorly represented in public policy debate and elite-dominated social processes. As opportunities opened we also helped build bridges with like-minded groups in Yunnan, Laos and Vietnam. The work drew upon all the education and experience that I had accumulated but beyond that were steep learning curves. What I would consider our successes and failures were, of course, mixed. Nevertheless, it was a rare opportunity and a dramatic difference from what I consider to be the patronising 'development project' mindsets of governments, bilateral and multi-lateral donors, and even many international NGOs. As I held this position beyond the normal five-year limit, it then became time to move on. It was obvious, however, that this would be a hard act to follow.

And so I took up the position with the World Agroforestry Centre (ICRAF), which is the incarnation in which Katharine and I met and discussed the topics in *Development Professionals in Northern Thailand*. As a senior policy analyst focusing on management of agro-forestry mosaic landscapes in river basins of northern Thailand and Montane Mainland Southeast Asia (MMSEA) for the past 12 years, I believe that I have managed to continue weaving the various threads of my life together and have achieved some internal sense of cohe-rence. We have tried to apply science-based tools in ways that can be used by many types of people to help raise the level of debate and negotiation about issues directly related to the lives and livelihoods of diverse peoples and communities living in mountain areas and their interactions with lowland-dominated, urbanising societies. For me, research systems like the CGIAR should not be about 'develop-ment' in the sense that word has come to mean. Rather, they should be about helping to evolve a global web of peer-to-peer relationships that can provide a mechanism for improving and extending the dis-tributed knowledge base needed to take humanity to a new level of consciousness. Together with many friends and colleagues, I have tried to do my bit to contribute toward this goal. I am not sure how much progress I will see in this lifetime but giving it a try has certainly been better than being a lawyer.

I am now past the 60-year threshold in life, half of which has been spent in Southeast Asia. I am still working a bit with ICRAF as a part-time consultant but have moved into a more reflective mode. In some ways, I feel that in my life here I have been able to do many of the things that I wished I could have done in the Ozark Moun-tains. And I have been able to develop some strong friendships with people I greatly respect in China, Laos, Vietnam and Thailand. I have sat and drank until the wee hours with aging former hard-core com-munist cadres. Now whenever I go to Mae Chaem or meet people from there at outside events, I feel like I am meeting old friends who have partly replaced the Ozark clans in my life. Have I become 'respectable'? No, thankfully, and even my 93-year-old father laughs at that idea now, while my 15-year-old daughter is learning the yin and the yang of 'half-breed' life.

Has my life been embedded within geopolitical agendas? You bet! Has the 'development' construct been used to dominate and impose ways of life on people? Absolutely — and not just in the 'Third World'! Is it possible to lend assistance without also calling into being an imperialist or governmental agenda? Yes, if instead of assistance, it is a peer-to-peer partnership among people with diverse interests, experience and skills, who enjoy learning and living together. Since it is quite human to have different values and opinions, most social processes are inherently 'political'. For me, reduced domination and increased creativity are central issues for all of us. So it is still a good laugh when Ken Kampe asks, "How many people have you developed today?"

David Thomas
Chiang Mai, 2007

Bibliography

AAA (1998). *AAA Code of Ethics*, <http://www.aaanet.org/committees/ethics/ethcode.htm> [accessed 16 April 2010].

Achara, R. (2001). "Forest Fire in the Context of Territorial Rights". In *International Symposium on Watershed Management. Highland and Lowland in the Protected Regime: Towards New Principles and Practices*, convener V. Chayan. Chiang Mai: Northern Development Foundation, RCSD, TERRA, World Rainforest Movement, RECOFTC, IMPECT.

Acharya, A. (2003). "Democratisation and the Prospects for Participatory Regionalism in Southeast Asia". *Third World Quarterly* 24 (2): 375–90.

Adams, R.N. and D.J. Jones (1971). "Responsibilities of the Foreign Scholar to the Local Scholarly Community Author(s)". *Current Anthropology* 12 (3): 335–6.

Agarwal, B. (1997). "Environmental Action, Gender Equity and Women's Participation". *Development and Change* 28: 1–44.

———— (2001). "Participatory exclusions, community forestry, and gender: An analysis for South Asia and a conceptual framework". *World Development* 29 (10): 1623–48.

———— (2007). "Gender inequality, cooperation and environmental sustainability". In *Inequality, Cooperation and Environmental Sustainability*, ed. J. Baland, P. Bardhan and S. Bowles. Princeton, New Jersey: Princeton University Press.

Akerkar, S. (2001). *Gender and Participation*. Sussex: Institute of Development Studies.

Alcoff, L. (1991). "The Problem of Speaking for Others". *Cultural Critique* 20: 5–31.

Anderson, B. (1991). *Imagined Communities: Reflections on the Origin and Spread of Nationalism*. Verso: London and New York.

Asad, T. (1973). *Anthropology and the Colonial Encounter*. London: Ithaca Press.

Attfield, R., J. Hattigh and M. Matshabaphala (2004). "Sustainable Development, Sustainable Livelihoods and Land Reform in South Africa: A Conceptual and Ethical Enquiry". *Third World Quarterly* 25 (2): 405–21.

Attwood, H. and J. Gaventa (1997). *Participatory Research: Ideas on the Use of Participatory Approaches by Post-Graduate Students and Others in Formal*

Learning and Research Institutes. Brighton, Sussex: Institute of Development Studies, University of Sussex.

Barrett, M. and A. Phillips (eds) (1992). *Destabilising Theory: Contemporary Feminist Debates*. Stanford: Stanford University Press.

Baudrillard, J. (1981). *For a Critique of the Political Economy of the Sign*. St Louis: Telos Press.

Bello, W. (2006). "A Siamese Tragedy". *Foreign Policy in Focus*, Transnational Institute, 29 September.

Berardi, G. (2002). "Commentary on the Challenge to Change: Participatory Research and Professional Realities". *Social and Natural Resources* 15: 847–52.

Bhabha, H.K. (1994). *The Location of Culture*. London and New York: Routledge.

Blaikie, P. (2000). "Development, post-, anti-, and populist: A critical review". *Environment and Planning A* 32: 1033–50.

Blofield, J. (1955). "Some hill tribes of north Thailand (Miaos and Yaos)". *Journal of the Siam Society* 43 (1): 1–19.

Botchway, K. (2001). "Paradox of empowerment: Reflections on a case study from Northern Ghana". *World Development* 29 (1): 135–53.

Bowie, K.A. (2000). "Ethnic Heterogeneity and Elephants in Nineteenth-Century Lanna Statecraft". In *Civility and Savagery: Social Identity in Tai States*, ed. Andrew Turton. Richmond, Surrey: Curzon Press, pp. 330–48.

Brandenberg, L. (1982). *Internal Paper 3: Project Concept*. Chiang Mai: Thai-German Highland Development Project.

Briggs, J. and J. Sharp (2004). "Indigenous Knowledges and Development: A Postcolonial Caution". *Third World Quarterly* 25 (4): 661–76.

Bryant, R. (2002). "Non-Governmental Organisations and Governmentality: "Consuming" Biodiversity and Indigenous People in the Philippines". *Political Studies* 50: 268–92.

Buadaeng, K. (2006). "Redefining otherness from northern Thailand. The rise and fall of the Tribal Research Institute (TRI): 'hill tribe' policy and studies in Thailand". *Southeast Asian Studies* 44 (3): 359–84.

Buck, P.S. (1945). *Tell the People: Talks with James Yen About the Mass Education Movement*. New York: The John Day Company.

Bull, T.A. (1993). "Project Overview". In *Proceedings of the TA-HASD Project Completion Seminar*. Chiang Mai: AACM International, pp. 9–17.

Butler, J. (1990). *Gender Trouble: Feminism and the Subversion of Identity*. New York and London: Routledge.

———— (1993a). *Bodies That Matter: On the Discursive Limits of "Sex"*. New York: Routledge.

———— (1993b). "Critically Queer". *GLQ: A Journal of Lesbian and Gay Studies* 1: 17–32.

————— (1997). *Theories of Subjection: The Pyschic Life of Power*. Stanford: Stanford University Press.

————— (2000). "Restaging the Universal: Hegemony and the Limits of Formalism". In *Contingency, Hegemony, Universality*, ed. J. Butler, L. Laclau and S. Zizek. London and New York: Verso, pp. 11–43.

Butler, J., L. Ernesto and Z. Slavoj (2000). *Contingency, Hegemony, Universality: Contemporary Dialogues on the Left*. London: Phronesis.

Cahill, A. (2008). "Power over, power to, power with: shifting perceptions of power for local economic development". *Asia-Pacific Viewpoint* 49 (3): 294–304.

Callahan W.A. (2000). *Pollwatching, Elections and Civil Society in Southeast Asia*. Aldershot: Ashgate.

Campbell, J.R. (2001). "Participatory Rural Appraisal as Qualitative Research: Distinguishing Methodological Issues from Participatory Claims". *Human Organisation* 60 (4): 380–9.

Case, D.A.D. (1990). *The Community's Toolbox: The Idea, Methods and Tools for Participatory Assessment, Monitoring and Evaluation in Community Forestry*. Rome: Food and Agriculture Organisation of the United Nations.

Chainarong, S. and J. Suppachai (1999). "Citizenship, Ethnic Identity and State Policy: Thai or Non-Thai for Hilltribe People?". Paper presented at the 7th International Thai Studies Conference, Special Round Table, Amsterdam.

Chambers, R. (1983). *Rural Development: Putting the Last First*. London and New York: Longman.

————— (1992). *Rural Appraisal: Rapid, Relaxed, Participatory*. Brighton, Sussex: Institute of Development Studies.

————— (1997). *Whose Reality Counts? Putting the First Last*. London: Intermediate Technology Publications.

Chayan, V. (convener) (2001). *International Symposium on Watershed Management Highland and Lowland in the Protected Regime: Towards New Principles and Practices*. Chiang Mai: Northern Development Foundation, RCSD, TERRA, World Rainforest Movement, RECOFTC, IMPECT.

Chhotray, V. (2004). "The Negation of Politics in Participatory Development Projects, Kurnool, Andhra Pradesh". *Development and Change* 35 (2): 327–52.

Chouvy, P. and J. Meissonnier (2004). *Yaa Baa: Production, Traffic and Consumption of Methamphetamine in Mainland Southeast Asia*. Singapore: NUS Press.

Chupinit, K. (1987). *Hilltribe Relocation Policy: Is There a Way Out of the Labyrinth? A Case Study of Kampaeng Phet*. Chiang Mai: Tribal Research Institute.

Chupinit, K. and R. Gebert (1993). *Drug Abuse in Pang Ma Pha Sub-district: Genesis and Current Situation*. Chiang Mai: Thai-German Highland Development Program.

Chusak, W. and P. Dearden (1999). "Decision-Making Arrangements in Community-Based Watershed Management in Northern Thailand". *Society and Natural Resources* 12: 673–91.

Clammer, J. (2003). "Globalisation, Class, Consumption and Civil Society in South-East Asian Cities". *Urban Studies* 40 (2): 403–19.

Clarke, G. (1998). *The Politics of NGOs in South-East Asia: Participation and Protest in the Philippines*. London: Routledge.

Cleaver, F. (2001). "Institutions, Agency and the Limitations of Participatory Approaches to Development". In *Participation: The New Tyranny?*, ed. Bill Cooke and Uma Kothari. London and New York: Zed Books, pp. 36–55.

Connors, M.K. (2002). "Framing the People's Constitution". In *Political Reform in Thailand*, ed. Duncan McCargo. Copenhagen: Nordic Institute of Asian Studies, pp. 37–55.

Conrad, Y. (1989). "Lisu Identity in Northern Thailand: A Problematique for Anthropology". In *Hill Tribes Today: Problems in Change*, ed. John McKinnon and Bernard Vienne. Bangkok: White Lotus-Orstom, pp. 191–222.

Cooke, B. and U. Kothari (eds) (2001). *Participation: The New Tyranny?*. London and New York: Zed Books.

Cooper, R.G. (1979). "The Tribal Minorities of Northern Thailand: Problems and Prospects". In *Southeast Asian Affairs 1979*. Singapore: Institute of Southeast Asian Studies, pp. 323–32.

Corbridge, S. (1998). "Beneath the pavement only soil: the poverty of post-development". *Journal of Development Studies* 34 (6): 138–48.

———— (2007). "The (im)possibility of development studies". *Economy and Society* 36 (2): 179–211.

Cornwall, A. (2003). "Whose voices? Whose choices? Reflections on gender and participatory development". *World Development* 31 (8): 1325–42.

Cornwall, A. and K. Brock (2005). "What do buzzwords do for development policy? A critical look at 'participation', 'empowerment' and 'poverty reduction'". *Third World Quarterly* 26 (7): 1043–60.

Cosgrove, D. and M. Domosh (1993). "Author and Authority: Writing the New Cultural Geography". In *Place/Culture/Representation,* ed. James Duncan and David Ley. London and New York: Routledge, pp. 25–38.

Cowen, M.P. and R.W. Shenton (1996). *Doctrines of Development*. London and New York: Routledge.

Crespo, I., C. Palli and J.L. Lalueza (2002). "Moving Communities: A Process of Negotiation with a Gypsy Minority for Empowerment". *Community, Work and Family* 5 (1): 49–65.

Crewe, E. and E. Harrison (1998). *Whose development? An ethnography of aid*. London and New York: Zed Books.

Crouch, B.R. (1984). *The Problem Census: Farmer Centred Problem Identification*. Food and Agriculture Organisation of the United Nations.

Cruikshank, B. (1999). *The Will to Empower: Democratic Citizens and Other Subjects*. Ithaca, New York: Cornell University Press.

Curnow, J. (2008). "Making a living on Flores, Indonesia: why understanding surplus distribution is crucial to economic development". *Asia-Pacific Viewpoint* 49 (3): 370–80.

D'Amico-Samuels, D. (1991). "Undoing Fieldwork: Personal, Political, Theoretical and Methodological Implications". In *Decolonising Anthropology: Moving Further Towards an Anthropology for Liberation,* ed. F.V. Harrison. Washington DC: Association of Black Anthropologists, American Anthropological Association, pp. 68–87.

Davis-Case, D.A. (1989). *Community Forestry: Participatory Assessment and Evaluation*. Food and Agriculture Organisation of the United Nations.

Department of Public Welfare, Thailand (1964). *A Brief on Hill Tribe Development and Welfare Program in Northern Thailand*. Bangkok: Department of Public Welfare, Ministry of the Interior.

Derrida, J. (1976). *Of Grammatology*. Baltimore: John Hopkins University Press.

Deuleu, C. and M. Næss (1997). "Deuleu: A life history of an Akha woman". In *Development or domestication? Indigenous peoples of Southeast Asia,* ed. Duncan MacCaskil and Ken Kampe. Chiang Mai: Silkworm Books, pp. 183–204.

Di Leonardo, M. (ed.) (1991). *Gender at the Crossroads of Knowledge: Feminist Anthropology in the Postmodern Era*. Berkeley: University of California Press.

Dirksen, H. (1993). *Solving Problems of Opium Production in Thailand: Lessons Learnt from the TGHDP*. Chiang Mai: Thai-German Highland Development Program.

Dixon, D.P. and J.P. Jones III (1996). "For a Supercalifragilisticexpialidocious Scientific Geography". *Annals of the Association of American Geographers* 86 (4): 767–79.

Duncan, J. and L. David (eds) (1993). *Place/Culture/Representation*. London and New York: Routledge.

Eiss, P. and T.C. Wolfe (2004). "Deconstruct to Reconstruct: An Interview with Maurice Godelier", <http://info.interactivist.net/article.pl?sid=04/05/27/1420204> <accessed 11 July 2004>.

Ekachai, S. (1994). *Seeds of Hope, Local Initiatives in Thailand*. Bangkok: The Post Publishing Public Co. Ltd.

England, K.V.L. (1994). "Getting Personal: Reflexivity, Positionality, and Feminist Research". *Professional Geographer* 46 (1): 80–9.

Eriksen, T.H. and F.S. Nielsen (2001). *A History of Anthropology*. London: Pluto Press.

Escobar, A. (1995a). *Encountering Development: The Making and Unmaking of the Third World*. Princeton, New Jersey: Princeton University Press.

———— (1995b). "Imagining a Postdevelopment Era". In *Power of Development*, ed. J. Crush. London: Routledge, pp. 211–27.

———— (2004). "Beyond the Third World: Imperial Globality, Global Coloniality, and Anti-Globalisation Social Movements". *Third World Quarterly* 25 (1): 207–30.

———— (2007). "'Post-development' as concept and social practice". In *Exploring Post-development: Theory and practice, problems and perspectives*, ed. A. Ziai. NY: Routledge, pp. 18–32.

Esteva, G. (1992). "Development". In *The Dictionary of Development*, ed. W. Sachs. London and New Jersey: Zed Books, pp. 6–25.

Esteva, G. and M.S. Prakesh (1998). *Grassroots Post-Modernism: Remaking the Soil of Cultures*. London and New York: Zed Books.

Ferguson, J. (1994). *The Anti-Politics Machine: 'Development', Depoliticization, and Bureacratic Power in Lesotho*. Minneapolis, London: University of Minnesota Press.

Fisher, R. and P. Hirsch (2008). "Poverty and Agrarian-Forest Interactions in Thailand". *Geographical Research* 46 (1): 74–84.

Fisher, W.F. (1997). "Doing Good? The Politics and Antipolitics of NGO Practices". *Annual Review of Anthropology* 26: 439–64.

Fluehr-Lobban, C. (ed.) (1991). *Ethics and the Profession of Anthropology: Dialogue for a New Era*. Philadelphia: University of Pennsylvania Press.

Forsyth, T. (2001). "Watershed and Science: Why the Concern?". In *International Symposium on Watershed Management Highland and Lowland in the Protected Regime: Towards New Principles and Practices*, Chayan, V. (convener). Chiang Mai: Northern Development Foundation, RCSD, TERRA, World Rainforest Movement, RECOFTC, IMPECT.

Forsyth, T. and A. Walker (2008). *Forest Guardians, Forest Destroyers: The Politics of Environmental Knowledge in Northern Thailand*. Chiang Mai: Silkworm Books.

Foucault, M. (1970 [1966]). *The Order of Things: An Archaeology of the Human Sciences*. New York: Pantheon Books.

———— (1977). *Discipline and Punish: The Birth of the Prison*. London: Allen Lane.

———— (1989 [1970]). *The Birth of the Clinic: An Archaeology of Medical Perception*. London: Routledge.

———— (1990). *The History of Sexuality*. New York: Vintage Books.

Fox, J. (2000). "How Blaming 'Slash and Burn' Farmers Is Deforesting Mainland Southeast Asia". *Analysis from the East-West Center* 47: 35–42.

Fox, J., D.M. Truong, A.T. Rambo, N.P. Tuyen, L.T. Cuc and S. Leisz (2001). "Shifting Cultivation: A New Old Paradigm for Managing Tropical Forests". In *International Symposium on Watershed Management Highland and Lowland in the Protected Regime: Towards New Principles and Practices*,

Chayan V. (convener). Chiang Mai: Northern Development Foundation, RCSD, TERRA, World Rainforest Movement, RECOFTC, IMPECT.

Freire, P. (1970). *Pedagogy of the Oppressed*. Harmondsworth: Penguin Books.

Geddes, W.R. (1967). "The Tribal Research Centre, Thailand: An Account of Plans and Activities". In *Southeast Asian Tribes, Minorities and Nations, Vol. 2*, ed. P. Kunstadter. Princeton: Princeton University Press, pp. 553–81.

———— (1976). *Migrants of the Mountains: The Cultural Ecology of the Blue Miao (Hmong Njua) of Thailand*. Oxford: Clarendon Press.

Geddes, W.R., J.F.V. Phillips, F.T. Merrill and A. Messing-Mierzejewski (1967). *Report of the United Nations Survey Team on the Economic and Social Needs of the Opium-Producing Areas of Thailand*. Bangkok: United Nations.

Geusau, L.A. (1992). "The Akha: Ten Years Later". *Pacific Viewpoint* 33 (2): 178–84.

Giambelluca, T., A.D. Ziegler and R.A. Sutherland (2001). "Influence of Shifting Agriculture and Rural Roads on Watershed Processes in Pang Khum, Chiang Mai, Thailand". In *International Symposium on Watershed Management Highland and Lowland in the Protected Regime: Towards New Principles and Practices*, V. Chayan (convener). Chiang Mai: Northern Development Foundation, RCSD, TERRA, World Rainforest Movement, RECOFTC, IMPECT.

Gibson, K. and J. Cameron (2001). *Shifting Focus: Alternative Pathways for Communities and Economies, a Resource Kit*. Melbourne: LaTrobe City and Monash University.

Gibson-Graham, J.K. (1996). *The End of Capitalism (As We Knew It)*. Cambridge, Massachusetts: Blackwell.

———— (2000). "Postructural Interventions". In *A Companion to Economic Geography*, ed. E. Sheppard and T.J. Barnes. Oxford: Blackwell, pp. 95–110.

———— (2005). "Surplus Possibilities: Postdevelopment and Community Economies". *Singapore Journal of Tropical Geography* 26 (1): 4–26.

———— (2006). *A post-capitalist politics*. Minneapolis and London: University of Minnesota Press.

Gillogly, K. (2004). "Developing the 'Hill Tribes' of Northern Thailand". In *Civilizing the Margins: Southeast Asian Government Policies for the Development of Minorities*, ed. C.R. Duncan. Ithaca and London: Cornell University Press, pp. 116–49.

Gladwin, C.H. and J.S. Peterson (2002). "The Quality Assignments in Participatory Research: A Case Study from Eastern Zambia". *World Development* 30 (4): 523–43.

Godelier, M. (1997). "American Anthropology as Seen in France". *Anthropology Today* 13 (1): 3–5.

Goldman, I. and J. Abbot (2004). "Overview: Decentralisation and Participatory Planning". *PLA Notes: participatory learning and action* 49: 5–14.

Goodwin, P. (1998). "'Hired Hands' or 'Local Voice': Understandings and Experience of Local Participation and Conservation". *Transactions of the Institute of British Geographers* 23: 481–99.

Grandstaff, T. (1980). "Shifting Cultivation in Northern Thailand". *United Nations University Resource Systems Theory and Methods Series* (No. 3).

Grandstaff, T.B. and S.W. Grandstaff (1987 [1985]). "A Conceptual Basis for Methodological Development in Rapid Rural Appraisal". In *Proceedings of the 1985 International Conference on Rapid Rural Appraisal.* Khon Kaen: Khon Kaen University Rural Systems Research and Farming Systems Research Projects, pp. 69–87.

Gudeman, S. and A. Rivera (1995). "From Car to House (Del Coche a La Casa)". *American Anthropologist* 97 (2): 242–50.

Hanks, J.R. and L.M. Hanks (2001). *Tribes of the North Thailand Frontier.* New Haven: Yale Southeast Asia Studies.

Harcourt, W. (2003). "Clearing the Path for Collective Compassion". *Development* 46 (4): 3–5.

Hargreaves, S. (1999). *Environmentalism, Development and Inter-Ethnic Relationships in Thailand: Case study — Doi Inthanon National Park.* MA Thesis, Development Studies, University of Auckland, Auckland.

Harrison, E. (2002). "'The Problem with the Locals': Partnership and Participation in Ethiopia". *Development and Change* 33 (4): 587–610.

Henkel, H. and R. Stirrat (2001). "Participation as Spiritual Duty: Empowerment as Secular Subjection". In *Participation: The New Tyranny?*, ed. B. Cooke and U. Kothari. London and New York: Zed Books, pp. 168–84.

Hewison, K. (1993). "Nongovernmental organisations and the cultural development perspective in Thailand: A comment on Rigg (1991)". *World Development* 21 (10): 1699–1708.

Hinton, P. (1967). "Introduction". In *TRC Tribesmen and Peasants in Northern Thailand: Proceedings of the First Symposium of the Tribal Research Centre.* Chiang Mai: Tribal Research Centre, pp. 1–11.

———— (1969). *ABC by Hinton.* Chiang Mai: Tribal Research Centre.

———— (1979). "The Karen, millennialism, and the politics of accommodation to lowland states". In *Ethnic Adaptation and Identity: The Karen on the Thai frontier with Burma*, ed. C. Keyes. Philadelphia: Institute for the Study of Human Issues, pp. 81–94.

———— (1983). "Do the Karen Really Exist?". In *Highlanders of Thailand*, ed. J. McKinnon and W. Bhuksasri. Kuala Lumpur: Oxford University Press, pp. 155–68.

———— (2002). "The 'Thailand Controversy' Revisited". *The Australian Journal of Anthropology* 13 (2): 155–78.

Hirsch, P. (1987). "Deforestation and Development in Thailand". *Singapore Journal of Tropical Geography* 8 (2): 129–38.

———— (1990). "Forests, Forest Reserve, and Forest Land in Thailand". *The Geographical Journal* 156 (2): 166–74.

Hirsch, P. (ed.) (1997). *Seeing forests for trees: environment and environmentalism in Thailand.* Chiang Mai, Thailand: Silkworm.

Hirsch, P. and C. Warren (1998). *The Politics of Environment in Southeast Asia: Resources and Resistance.* Murdoch University Asia Research Centre London: Routledge.

Hoare, P. (1986). *Methodology of Rural Development in Northern Thailand.* MSc Thesis, Department of Agriculture, University of Queensland, Brisbane.

Hoare, Q. and G.N. Smith (1971). *Selections from the Prison Notebooks of Antonio Gramsci.* London: Lawrence and Wishart.

Hooks, B. (1992). *Black Looks: Race and Representation.* Boston: South End Press.

———— (1994). *Outlaw Culture: Resisting Representations.* New York: Routledge.

Hope, A. and S. Timmel (1995). *Training for Transformation: A Handbook for Community Workers.* London: ITDG Publishing.

Horowitz, I. (1967). *The Rise and Fall of Project Camelot.* Cambridge, MA: MIT Press.

Ives, J. and B. Messerli (1989). *The Himalayan Dilemma: Reconciling Development and Conservation.* London: Routledge.

Johnson, C. and T. Forsyth (2002). "In the Eyes of the State: Negotiating a 'Rights-Based Approach' to Forest Conservation in Thailand". *World Development* 30 (9): 1591–1605.

Jones, C. (1996). *PRA Behaviour and Attitudes.* Brighton: Institute of Development Studies, University of Sussex.

Jonsson, H. (1998). "Forest Products and Peoples: Upland Groups, Thai Polities, and Regional Space". *Sojourn* 13 (1): 1–37.

———— (2000a). "Traditional Tribal What? Sports, Culture and the State in the Northern Hills of Thailand". In *Turbulent Times and Enduring Peoples: Mountain Minorities in the Southeast Asian Massif,* ed. J. Michaud. Richmond: Curzon Press, pp. 219–45.

———— (2000b). "Yao Minority Identity and the Location of Difference in the South China Borderlands". *Ethnos* 65 (1): 56–82.

———— (2005). *Mien Relations: Mountain People and State Control in Thailand.* Ithaca and London: Cornell University Press.

Kammerer, C.A. (1988). "Of Labels and Laws: Thailand's Resettlement and Repatriation Policies". *Cultural Studies Quarterly* 12 (4): 7–12.

———— (1989). "Territorial Imperatives: Akha Ethnic Identity and Thailand's National Integration". In *Hill Tribes Today,* ed. J. McKinnon and B. Vienne. Bangkok: White Lotus-Orstom, pp. 259–301.

———— (1990). "Customs and Christian Conversion among Akha Highlanders of Burma and Thailand". *American Ethnologist* 17 (2): 277–91.

Kampe, K. (1992). "Northern Highlands: Development, Bureacracy and Life on the Margins". *Pacific Viewpoint* 33 (2): 159–64.

———— (1995). *Tribal Development NGOs in Thailand, 1995.* Unpublished data, Chiang Mai.

———— (1997a). "The Culture of Development in Developing Indigenous Peoples". In *Development or Domestication? Indigenous Peoples of Southeast Asia*, ed. K. Kampe and D. McCaskill. Chiang Mai: Silkworm Books, pp. 132–82.

———— (1997b). "What Does Foreign Aid for Education Contribute to the Maintenance of Indigenous Knowledge in Laos, Thailand, and Vietnam?". *Asia Pacific Viewpoint* 38 (2): 155–60.

Kampe, K. and D. McCaskill (eds) (1997). *Development or Domestication? Indigenous Peoples of Southeast Asia.* Chiang Mai: Silkworm Books.

Katz, C. (1994). "Playing the Field: Questions of Fieldwork in Geography". *Professional Geographer* 46 (1): 67–72.

Kaufmann, G. (1997). "Watching the Developers: A Partial Ethnography". In *Discourses of Development: Anthropological Perspectives*, ed. R.D. Grillo and R.L. Stirrat. Oxford and New York: Berg, pp. 107–32.

Keen, F.B.G. (1972). *Upland Tenure and Land Use in North Thailand.* Chiang Mai: Tribal Research Centre.

Keyes, C. (1979a). "Introduction". In *Ethnic Adaptation and Identity: The Karen on the Thai frontier with Burma*, ed. C. Keyes. Philadelphia: Institute for the Study of Human Issues, pp. 1–23.

———— (1979b). "The Karen in Thai history and the history of the Karen in Thailand". In *Ethnic Adaptation and Identity: The Karen on the Thai frontier with Burma*, ed. C. Keyes. Philadelphia: Institute for the Study of Human Issues, pp. 25–62.

———— (1993). "Who Are the Lue? Revisited Ethnic Identity in Laos, Thailand and China". In *Conference on the State of Thai Cultural Studies.* Bangkok: Office of the National Commission on Culture.

Kobayashi, A. (1994). "Colouring the Field: Gender, 'Race', and Politics of Fieldwork". *Professional Geographer* 46 (1): 73–80.

Krimerman, L. (2000). "Participatory Action Research: Should Social Inquiry Be Conducted Democratically?". *Philosophy of the Social Sciences* 31 (1): 60–82.

Kunstadter, P. and E.C. Chapman (1978). "Introduction: Problems of Shifting Cultivation and Economic Development in Northern Thailand". In *Farmers in the Forest: Economic Development and Marginal Agriculture in Northern Thailand*, ed. P. Kunstadter, E.C. Chapman and S. Sabhasri. Honolulu: The University Press of Hawaii, pp. 1–23.

Kunstadter, P., E.C. Chapman and S. Sabhasri (eds) (1978). *Farmers in the Forest: Economic Development and Marginal Agriculture in Northern Thailand*. Honolulu: The University Press of Hawaii.

Kunstadter, P. (1979). "Ethnic group, category and identity: Karen in northern Thailand". In *Ethnic Adaptation and Identity: The Karen on the Thai frontier with Burma*, ed. C. Keyes. Philadelphia: Institute for the Study of Human Issues, pp. 119–63.

——— (2000). "Changing patterns of economics among Hmong in Northern Thailand 1960–1990". In *Turbulent Times and Enduring Peoples*, ed. J. Michaud. Richmond, Surrey: Curzon Press, pp. 167–19.

Kwanchewan, B. (2006). "The Rise and Fall of the Tribal Research Institute (TRI): "Hill Tribe" Policy and Studies in Thailand". *Southeast Asian Studies* 44 (3): 359–84.

Kyoko, M. (2003). "Ino Kanori's 'History' of Taiwan: Colonial Ethnology, the Civilising Mission and Struggles for Survival in East Asia". *History and Anthropology* 14 (2): 179–96.

Laclau, E. (1991). *New Reflections on the Revolution of Our Time*. London and New York: Verso.

——— (1996). *Emancipation(s)*. London and New York: Verso.

——— (2000). "Identity and Hegemony". In *Contingency, Hegemony, Universality: Contemporary Dialogues on the Left*, ed. J. Butler, E. Laclau and S. Zizek. London: Phronesis, pp. 44–89.

Laclau, E. and C. Mouffe (1985). *Hegemony and Socialist Strategy: Towards a Radical Democratic Politics*. London: Verso.

Leach, E. (1954). *Political Systems of Highland Burma: A Study of Kachin Social Structure*. London: London School of Economics and Political Science.

Leeuwis, C. (2000). "Reconceptualising Participation for Sustainable Rural Development: Towards a Negotiation Approach". *Development and Change* 31: 931–59.

Levi-Strauss, C. (1966a). "Anthropology: Its Achievement and Future". *Current Anthropology* 7 (2): 124–7.

——— (1966b). "The Scope of Anthropology". *Current Anthropology* 7 (2): 112–23.

Li, T.M. (1999). "Compromising Power: Development, Culture, and Rule in Indonesia". *Cultural Anthropology* 14 (3): 295–322.

——— (2007). *The Will to Improve: Governmentality, development and the practice of politics*. Durham and London: Duke University Press.

Malai, H. (1967). "Foreword". In *Tribesmen and Peasants in Northern Thailand: Proceedings of the First Symposium of the Tribal Research Centre*. Chiang Mai: Tribal Research Centre, p. 11.

Malinowski, B. (1945). *The Dynamics of Culture Change*. New Haven: Yale University Press.

Manikutty, S. (1997). "Community Participation: So What? Evidence from a Comparative Study of Two Rural Water Supply and Sanitation Projects in India". *Development Policy Review* 15: 115–40.

Manndorff, H. (1965). *The Hill Tribe Program of the Public Welfare Department, Ministry for the Interior, Thailand.* Division of Hill Tribe Welfare, Bureau of Self-help Land Settlement, Department of Public Welfare.

———— (1967). "The Hill Tribe Program of the Public Welfare Department, Ministry of the Interior, Thailand: Research and Socio-Economic Development". In *Southeast Asian Tribes, Minorities and Nations,* ed. P. Kunstadter. Princeton: Princeton University Press, pp. 525–52.

Marcus, G.E. and M.M.J. Fischer (1986). *Anthropology as Cultural Critique: An Experimental Moment in the Human Sciences.* Chicago: University Of Chicago Press.

Martin, A. and J. Sherington (1997). "Participatory Research Methods — Implementation, Effectiveness and Institutional Context". *Agricultural Systems* 55 (2): 195–216.

Matthews, M. (2003). "Thailand Today". *Asian Affairs* XXXIV(II): 148–54.

Mayfield, J.B. (1985). *Go to the People: Releasing the Rural Poor through the People's School System.* Connecticut: Kumarian Press.

McCargo, D. (ed.) (2002). *Reforming Thai Politics.* Copenhagen: Nordic Institute of Asian Studies.

———— (2004). "Buddhism, Democracy and Identity in Thailand". *Democratisation* 11 (4): 155–70.

McCoy, A. (1972). *The Politics of Heroin in Southeast Asia.* New York: Harpers and Row.

McKinnon, J. (1976). *Six Years Later: An Interview with Peter Hinton.* Chiang Mai: Tribal Research Centre.

———— (1977). "The Jeremiah Incorporation". Unpublished manuscript. Chiang Mai: Tribal Research Centre.

———— (1983). "Behind and Ahead". In *Highlanders of Thailand* ed. J. McKinnon and B. Wanat. Kuala Lumpur: Oxford University Press, pp. 326–35.

———— (1989). "Structural Assimilation and the Consensus: Clearing Grounds on which to Arrange Our Thoughts". In *Hill Tribes Today*, ed. J. McKinnon and B. Vienne. Bangkok: White Lotus-Orstom, pp. 303–59.

———— (1992). "Marginalisation in Thailand: Disparities, Democracy and Development Intervention". *Pacific Viewpoint* 33 (2): 119–20.

McKinnon, J. and J. McKinnon (2005). *Participatory Learning and Action: Guide for NGO Facilitators.* Wellington: Kinsa Associates.

McKinnon, J. and J. Michaud (2000). "Montagnard domain in the South-east Asian massif". In *Turbulent times and enduring peoples,* ed. J. Michaud. Richmond, Surrey: Curzon Press, pp. 1–25.

McKinnon, J. and B. Vienne (1989). *Hill tribes today*. Bangkok: White Lotus-Orstom.

McKinnon, J. and B. Wanat (eds) (1983). *Highlanders of Thailand*. Kuala Lumpur: Oxford University Press.

McKinnon, K. (2005). "(Im)mobilisation and hegemony: 'Hill tribe' subjects and the 'Thai' state". *Social and Cultural Geography* 6 (1): 31–46.

———— (2006). "An orthodoxy of 'the local': post-colonialism, participation and professionalism in northern Thailand". *The Geographical Journal* 172 (1): 22–34.

Michener, V.J. (1998). "The participatory approach: contradiction and co-option in Burkina Faso". *World Development* 26 (12): 2105–18.

Miles, D. (1967). "Shifting cultivation — threats and prospects". In *Tribesmen and Peasants in Northern Thailand: Proceedings of the First Symposium of the Tribal Research Centre*. Chiang Mai: Tribal Research Centre, pp. 93–9.

Missingham, B. (2002). "The village of the poor confronts the state: A geography of protest in the assembly of the poor". *Urban Studies* 39 (9): 1647–63.

Mohan, G. and K. Stokke (2000). "Participatory development and empowerment: The dangers of localism". *Third World Quarterly* 21 (2): 247–68.

Moss, P. and I. Dyck (1999). "Body, corporeal space, and legitimating chronic illness: women diagnosed with M". *Antipode* 31 (4): 372–97.

Mosse, D. (1994). "Authority, gender and knowledge: theoretical reflections on the practice of participatory rural appraisal". *Development and Change* 25: 497–526.

———— (2003). "The making and marketing of participatory development". In *A moral critique of development,* ed. P.Q. Ufford and A.K. Giri. London: Routledge, pp. 43–74.

———— (2004). "Is good policy unimplementable? Reflections on the ethnography of aid policy and practice". *Development and Change* 35 (4): 639–71.

———— (2005). *Cultivating Development: An Ethnography of Aid Policy and Practice*. London and Ann Arbor, Michigan: Pluto Press.

Nartsupha, C. (1984). "The ideology of 'holy men' revolts in north east Thailand". In *History and peasant consciousness in South East Asia*, ed. A. Turton and S. Tanabe. Osaka: National Museum of Ethnology, pp. 111–34.

Natter, W. and J.P. Jones III (1997). "Identity, space and other uncertainties". In *Space and social theory: Interpreting modernity and postmodernity*, ed. G. Benko and U. Strohmayer. Oxford: Blackwell, pp. 141–61.

Nederveen P.J. (1998). "My paradigm or yours? Alternative development, postdevelopment, reflexive development". *Development and Change* 29 (2): 343–73.

———— (2000). "After postdevelopment". *Third World Quarterly* 21 (2): 175–91.

Neef, A. (2001) "Getting Priorities Right — How to Balance Farmers and Scientists Perspectives in Participatory Agricultural Research?". In *Participatory Technology Development and Local Knowledge for Sustainable Land Use in Southeast Asia*, ed. A. Neef. Chiang Mai: University of Germany.

Neef, A., R. Friederichsen and D. Neubert (2008). "Juggling multiple roles or falling between all stools? Insider action research in a collaborative agricultural research program in Southeast Asia". *Sociologus* 58 (1): 73–98.

de Negri, B., E. Thomas, A. Ilinigumugabo, I. Muvandi and G. Lewis (1998a). *Empowering Communities: Participatory Techniques for Community-Based Program Development, Volume 1 Trainer's Manual*. Centre for African Family Studies.

de Negri, B., E. Thomas, A. Ilinigumugabo, I. Muvandi and G. Lewis (1998b). *Empowering Communities: Participatory Techniques for Community-Based Program Development, Volume 2 Community Manual*. Centre for African Family Studies.

Neubert, D. (2001). "Are the Promises Kept? Towards a Framework for the Evaluation of Participatory Research". In *Participatory Technology Development and Local Knowledge for Sustainable Land Use in Southeast Asia*, ed. A. Neef. Chiang Mai: University of Germany.

Nietzsche, F.W. (1964 [1873]). *Beyond Good and Evil: Prelude to a Philosophy of the Future*. London: Allen and Unwin.

Nightingale, A.J. (2005). ""The Experts Taught Us All We Know"; Professionalism and Knowledge in Nepalese Community Forestry". *Antipode* 37 (3): 581–604.

Osborne, M. (2002). *Exploring Southeast Asia: A Traveller's History of the Region*. Crows Nest, NSW: Allen and Unwin.

Pain, R. and P. Francis (2003). "Reflections on participatory research". *Area* 35 (1): 46–54.

Parfitt, T. (2004). "The Ambiguity of Participation: A Qualified Defence of Participatory Development". *Third World Quarterly* 25 (3): 537–56.

Pasuk, P. and C.J. Baker (2002). *Thailand, Economy and Politics*. Oxford and New York: Oxford University Press.

————— (2004). *Thaksin — The Business of Politics in Thailand*. Chiang Mai: Silkworm Books.

Pathmanand, U. (2001). "Globalization and Democratic Development in Thailand: The New Path of the Military, Private Sector, and Civil Society". *Contemporary Southeast Asia* 23 (1): 24–42.

Patterson, T.C. (2001). *A Social History of Anthropology in the United States*. Oxford: Berg Publishers.

Peet, R. (1999). *Theories of Development*. New York and London: The Guilford Press.

Pendleton, R.L. (1949). "Impressions of Doi Pulanka and the Miao's New Year". *Journal of the Siam Society* 37 (2): 144–8.

Penth, H. (1994). *A Brief History of Lan Na: Civilisations of North Thailand.* Chiang Mai: Silkworm Books.

Pinkaew, L. (2001). *Redefining Nature: Karen Ecological Knowledge and the Challenge to the Modern Conservation Paradigm.* Chennai: Earthworm Books.

Pratt, G. (2000). "Subject formation". In *The Dictionary of Human Geography*, ed. R.J. Johnston, D. Gregory, G. Pratt and M. Watts. Oxford: Blackwell, pp. 802–4.

Pretty, J.N., I. Guijt, J. Thompson and I. Scoones (1995). *A Trainer's Guide for Participatory Learning and Action.* London: Sustainable Agriculture Program, International Institute for Environment and Development.

Rabinow, P. (ed.) (1984). *The Foucault Reader.* New York: Pantheon Books.

Raju, S. (2005). "Limited Options — Rethinking Women's Empowerment 'Projects' in Development Discourses. A Case from Rural India". *Gender, Technology and Development* 9 (2): 253–71.

Ramsay, J.A. (1976). "Modernisation and Centralisation in Northern Thailand, 1875–1911". *Journal of Southeast Asian Studies* VII (1): 16–32.

Renard, R.D. (2000). "The Differential Integration of Hill People into the Thai State". In *Civility and Savagery: Social Identity in Tai States*, ed. A. Turton. Richmond, Surrey: Curzon Press, pp. 63–83.

———— (2001). *Opium Reduction in Thailand 1970–2000.* Chiang Mai: Silkworm Books for UNDCP.

Resurreccion, B., M.J. Real and P. Panadda (2004). "Officialising strategies and gender in Thailand's water resources sector". *Development in Practice* 14 (4): 521–33.

Rigg, J. (1991). 'Grass-Roots Development in Rural Thailand: A Lost Cause?' *World Development* 19 (2/3): 199–211.

———— (2001). *More Than the Soil: Rural Change in Southeast Asia.* Essex: Pearson Education.

———— (2003). *Southeast Asia: The Human Landscape of Modernization and Development.* London and New York: Routledge.

Rigg, J. and N. Sakunee (2001). "Embracing the global in Thailand: Activism and pragmatism in an era of deagrarianization". *World Development* 29 (6): 945–60.

Robinson, K. (2004). "Chandra Jayawardena and the Ethical 'Turn' in Australian Anthropology". *Critique of Anthropology* 24 (4): 379–402.

Royal Project (1996). *The Royal Project Foundation*, <http://www.royalproject thailand.com/general/english/main.html> [accessed 18 January 2010].

Ruxrungtham K and P. Phanuphak (2001). "Update on HIV/AIDS in Thailand". *Journal of the Medical Association of Thailand* Jun 84 (1): 1–17.

Sachs, W. (1992). *The Development Dictionary.* London and New Jersey: Zed Books.

Said, E.W. (1978). *Orientalism*. London: Routledge and Kegan Paul.

————— (1993). *Culture and Imperialism*. London: Vintage.

Saihoo, P. (1963). *The Hill Tribes of Northern Thailand*. Bangkok: Chulalongkorn University.

Satawat, S. and S. Nipatvej (2001). *Desk Reviews: Hill Tribe Situation in Thailand 2001*. Chiang Mai: Tribal Research Institute.

Sattah M.V., S. Supawitkul, T.J. Donderol, P.H. Kilmarx, N.L. Young, T.D. Mastrol, S. Chaikummao, C. Manopaiboon and F. van Griensven (2002). "Prevalence of and risk factors for methamphetamine use in northern Thai youth: results of an audio-computer-assisted self-interviewing survey with urine testing". *Addiction* 97: 801–8.

Schiller, S. (1999). *Natural Resource Use Rights and Management: The Dynamics of Agriculture in Mountainous Areas of Northern Thailand*. Chiang Mai: University of Germany.

Scott, J. (1998). *Seeing like a State: How Certain Schemes to Improve the Human Condition have Failed*. New Haven and London: Yale University Press.

————— (2000). "Hill and Valley in Southeast Asia or Why the State is the Enemy of People Who Move Around or Why Civilizations Can't Climb Hills". Paper presented at the conference "Development and the Nation-State", Washington University.

————— (2010). *The Art of Not Being Governed: An Anarchist History of Upland Southeast Asia*. Singapore: NUS Press.

Sidaway, J. (2007). "Spaces of postdevelopment". *Progress in Human Geography* 31 (3): 345–61.

Simon, D. (1997). "Development reconsidered: new directions in development thinking". *Geografiska Annaler* 79 (B): 183–201.

————— (1998). "Rethinking (post)modernism, postcolonialism and post-traditionalism: South-North perspectives". *Environment and Planning D: Society and Space* 16: 219–45.

————— (2006). "Separated by common ground? Bringing (post)development and (post)colonialism together". *The Geographical Journal* 172 (1): 10–21.

————— (2007). "Beyond antidevelopment: Discourses, convergences, practices". *Singapore Journal of Tropical Geography* 28: 205–18.

Singhanetra-Renard, A. (1997)."Population movement and the AIDS epidemic in Thailand". In *Sexual Cultures and Migration in the era of AIDS: Anthropology and Demography*, ed. Gilbert Herdt. Oxford and New York: Oxford University Press, pp. 70–86.

Smith, L.T. (1999). *Decolonizing Methodologies: Research and Indigenous Peoples*. London and New York: Zed Books.

Snell, D. and S. Prasad (1999). "'Benchmarking' and Participatory Development: The Case of Fiji's Sugar Industry Reforms". *Development and Change* 32: 255–76.

Somsak, J. (2005). *Developing one's brother: good intentions, unnatural practices.* Bloomington, Indiana: Author House.

de Sousa Santos, B. (2004). "The WSF: Toward a Counter-Hegemonic Globalisation". In *World Social Forum: Challenging Empires,* ed. J. Sen, A. Anand, A. Escobar and P. Waterman. New Delhi: The Viveka Foundation, pp. 235–45.

Spivak, G.C. (1985). "The Rani of Sirmur: An Essay in Reading the Archives". *History and Theory* 24 (3): 247–72.

————— (1999). *A Critique of Postcolonial Reason: Toward a History of the Vanishing Present.* Cambridge, Massachusetts: Harvard University Press.

Stoecker, R. (1999). "Are Academics Irrelevant? Roles for Scholars in Participatory Research". *American Behavioural Scientist* 42 (5): 840–54.

Stringer, E., M. Guhathakurta, M. Masaigana and S. Waddell (2008). "Guest editors' commentary: Action research and development". *Action Research* 6 (2): 123–7.

Sturgeon, J. (1997). "Claiming and Naming Resources on the Border of the State: Akha Strategies in China and Thailand". *Asia Pacific Viewpoint* 38 (2): 131–44.

————— (2005). *Border landscapes: The politics of Akha land use in China and Thailand.* Seattle: University of Washington Press.

Suppachai, J. (1999). *Citizenship and State Policy: How We Can Move Beyond the Crisis.* Chiang Mai: Legal Aid for Marginalized People (LAMP) Project.

Tachard, G. (1981 [1688]) *A Relation of the Voyage to Siam Performed by Six Jesuits Sent by the French King, to the Indies and China in the Year 1685.* London (Bangkok): White Orchid Press.

TAHAP (1979). *Program of Work for the Thai Australian Highland Agricultural Project* (TAHAP). Chiang Mai: Department of Agriculture, University of Queensland; Department of Public Welfare; the Faculty of Agriculture, Chiang Mai University; Australian Development Assistance Bureau.

Tambiah, S.J. (1985). *Culture, Thought and Social Action: An Anthropological Perspective.* Cambridge, Massachusetts: Harvard University Press.

————— (2002). *Edmund Leach: An Anthropological Life.* Cambridge: Cambridge University Press.

Tanabe, S. (1984). "Ideological Practice in Peasant Rebellions: Siam at the Turn of the Century". In *History and Peasant Consciousness in South East Asia,* ed. A. Turton and S. Tanabe. Osaka: National Museum of Ethnology, pp. 75–110.

Tapp, N. (1989). *Sovereignty and rebellion. The White Hmong of Northern Thailand.* Oxford, New York and Toronto: Oxford University Press.

————— (2003). *The Hmong of China: Context, Agency, and the Imaginary.* Leiden and Boston: Brill.

Tarling, N. (1998). *Nations and States in Southeast Asia.* Cambridge: Cambridge University Press.

Thongchai, W. (1994). *Siam Mapped: The History of the Geobody of a Nation*. Honolulu: University of Hawaii Press.

——— (2000). "The Others Within: Travel and Ethno-Spatial Differentiation of Siamese Subjects 1885–1910". In *Civility and Savagery: Social Identity in Tai States*, ed. A. Turton. Richmond, Surrey: Curzon Press, pp. 38–62.

Tomforde, M. (2006). *The Hmong Mountains: Cultural spatiality of the Hmong in northern Thailand*. Hamburg: Lit Verlag.

Torfing, J. (1999). *New Theories of Discourse*. Oxford: Blackwell.

Torpey, J. (2000). *The Invention of the Passport: Surveillance, Citizenship and the State*. Cambridge: Cambridge University Press.

Townsend, J.G., G. Porter and E. Mawdsley (2002). "The role of the transnational community of non-government organisations: Governance or poverty reduction?". *Journal of International Development* 14: 829–39.

——— (2003). "Development hegemonies and local outcomes: Women and NGOs in low income countries". In *Globalization: theory and practice* ed. E. Kofman and G. Youngs. London: Continuum, pp. 139–56.

——— (2004). "Creating spaces of resistance: Development NGOs and their clients in Ghana, India and Mexico". *Antipode* 36: 871–9.

Toyota, M. (1998). "Urban Migration and Cross-Border Networks: A Deconstruction of the Akha Identity in Chiang Mai". *Southeast Asian Studies* 35 (4): 803–29.

——— (2003). "Contested Chinese Identities among Ethnic Minorities in the China, Burma and Thai Borderlands". *Ethnic and Racial Studies* 26 (2): 301–20.

Triantafillou, P. and M.R. Nielson (2001). "Policing Empowerment: The Making of Capable Subjects". *History of the Human Sciences* 14 (2): 63–86.

Tribal Research Institute (1992). *Directory of Foreign Researchers on Ethnic Groups in Thailand 1968–1993*. Library, Tribal Research Institute.

Truman, H. (1949). Inaugural address, <http://www.saidnews.org> [accessed 15 July 2011].

Tully, J. (1966). "Towards a Sociological Theory for Extension". *Human Relations* 19 (4): 391–403.

Ungphakorn, P. and D. Millikin (1977). "Violence and the Military Coup in Thailand". In *Bulletin of Concerned Asian Scholars* 9, <http://www.questia. com/googleScholar.qst; jsessionid=MgJTGHFb0GD3yXMLL8bZ06YHF GwLb8kFt71Z1nfv90v26 vrKQB1Z!- 1586998745!547733517?docId=9 7729370> [accessed 22 June 2010].

Uplands Program (2000). *The Uplands Program: Conceptual Framework and Summary of a Thai-Vietnamese-German Collaborative Research Program*. Chiang Mai: University of Hohenheim, Germany.

Usher, A.D. (2009). *Thai Forestry: A Critical History*. Chiang Mai: Silkworm Books.

Vandergeest, P. (2003). "Racialization and citizenship in Thai forest politics". *Society and Natural Resources* 16: 19–37.

Wakin, E. (1992). *Anthropology Goes to War: Professional Ethics and Counter-insurgency in Thailand*. Madison: Center for Southeast Asian Studies, University of Wisconsin-Madison.

Walker, A. (1998). *The Legend of the Golden Boat*. Richmond, Surrey: Curzon Press.

————— (2001). "The 'Karen Consensus', Ethnic Politics and Resource-Use Legitimacy in Northern Thailand". *Asian Ethnicity* 2 (2): 145–62.

————— (2004). "Karen Cultural Capital: Consensus and Contestation". *Asian Ethnicity* 5 (2): 159–265.

————— (2008). "Borders in Motion on the Upper Mekong: Siam and France in the 1890s". In *Nouvelles Recherches sur le Laos,* ed. Y. Goudineau and M. Lorrillard. Collection Etudes Thématiques, Ecole Française d'Extrême-Orient.

————— (2009). "Modern Tai Community". In *Tai Lands and Thailand: Community and State in Southeast Asia.*, ed. A. Walker. Singapore; NUS Press, pp. 1–23.

Walker, A. and M. Scoccimarro (2001). "Agricultural Intensification and Emerging Water Resource Constraints: A Case Study from Northern Thailand". In *International Symposium on Watershed Management. Highland and Lowland in the Protected Area Regime: Towards New Priniciples and Practices,* convener V. Chayan. Chiang Mai: Northern Development Foundation, RCSD, TERRA, World Rainforest Movement, RECOFTC, IMPECT.

Walker, D., J.P. Jones III, S.M. Roberts and O.R. Frohling (2007). "When Participation Meets Empowerment: The WWF and the Politics of Invitation in the Chimalapas, Mexico". *Annals of the Association of American Geographers* 97 (2): 423–44.

Wanat, B. (1989). "Government Policy: Highland Ethnic Minorities". In *Hill Tribes Today*, ed. J. Mckinnon and B. Vienne. Bangkok: White Lotus, pp. 5–31.

Weller, R.P. (2005). *Civil life, globalization, and political change in Asia: Organizing between family and state*. London and New York: Routledge.

Wijeyewardene, G. (1991). "The Frontiers of Thailand". In *National Identity and Its Defenders: Thailand, 1939–1989*, ed. C.J. Reynolds. Chiang Mai: Silkworm Books.

Wilder, G. (2003). "Colonial Ethnology and Political Rationality in French West Africa". *History and Anthropology* 14 (3): 219–52.

Wolf, E.R. and J.G. Jorgensen (1970). "Anthropology on the War Path in Thailand". *The New York Review of Books* 15 (9): 26–35.

———— (1971). "Anthropology on the War Path: An Exchange". *The New York Review of Books* 17 (1): 45–6.

Wood, W.A.R. (1965). *Consul in Paradise: Sixty-Nine Years in Siam*. London: Souvenir Press.

Wright, J.R. (1992). "Thailand's Return to Democracy". *Current History* 91: 418–23.

Wyatt, D. (1984). *Thailand: A Short History*. Chiang Mai: Silkworm Books.

Yapa, L. (2002). "How the Discipline of Geography Exacerbates Poverty in the Third World". *Futures* 34: 33–46.

Yos, S. (2004). "Karen Cultural Economy and the Political Economy of Symbolic Power". *Asian Ethnicity* 5 (1): 105–20.

Young, K. (1997). "Gender and Development". In *The Women, Gender and Development Reader*, ed. N. Visvanathan, L. Duggan, L. Nisonoff and N. Wiegersma. London and New Jersey: Zed Books, pp. 51–4.

Index